Scanners For Dummies
2nd Edition

Recommended Breeds of Scanners

Type	Common Applications	Suitable For
Hand scanner	Portable scanning, barcodes	Laptop owners, businesses
Flatbed scanner	Almost anything	Most computer owners
Sheet-fed scanner	Home office and business	Office users
Photo scanner	Photo prints	Amateur photographers
Negative scanner	Photo slides and negatives	Professional photographers
Business card scanner	Business cards	Office users and laptop owners

Recommended Optical Scanner Resolutions

"Common" DPI	True DPI	Common Applications	Suitable For
600 x 600	600	School projects	Kids
600 x 1200	600	Line art, photographs	Scavengers
1200 x 2400	1200	Almost anything	Most computer owners
2400 x 2400 and higher	2400	Design and graphic art	Photographers, artists, designers

Recommended Scanner Bit Depth

Bit Depth	Common Applications	Suitable For
24, 30, 32, 36 bit	Basic color scanning	Kids, scavengers
42 bit	Almost anything	Most computer owners
48 bit and higher	Design and graphic art	Photographers, artists, designers

For Dummies: Bestselling Book Series for Beginners

Scanners For Dummies,® 2nd Edition

Cheat Sheet

Recommended Scanner Interfaces

Interface	Common Applications	Suitable For
Parallel port	Basic scanning	Scavengers
USB 1.1	Almost anything	Most computer owners
USB 2.0, FireWire, or SCSI	Design and graphic art	Photographers, artists, designers

Image Formats

Format	Compression	Color Depth	Grayscale	Web Friendly
JPEG	Yes	16.7 million (24 bit)	Yes	Yes
GIF	Yes	256 colors (8 bit)	No	Yes
Bitmap	No	16.7 million (24 bit)	Yes	No
TIFF	Yes	16.7 million (24 bit)	Yes	No
PNG	Yes	16.7 million (24 bit)	Yes	Yes

Dispelling Common Copyright Myths

- A work doesn't have to carry a copyright mark to be copyrighted.
- Movement from document to digital does not "cancel" a copyright. Scanning a document does not make it your property.
- The source where you obtained the work is immaterial. Taking an image from a newsgroup or Web site doesn't make it legal. (In some circumstances, such as some information on government Web sites, you may be granted a specific right to reproduce or reuse original material; contact the Web master of the site to determine whether you can freely use an original image.)
- No such thing as "blanket" copyright exists. Permissions must be individually obtained for each work.
- Changing an original doesn't change the copyright.

For Dummies: Bestselling Book Series for Beginners

Scanners
FOR
DUMMIES®
2ND EDITION

by Mark L. Chambers

WILEY

Wiley Publishing, Inc.

Scanners For Dummies, 2nd Edition

Published by
Wiley Publishing, Inc.
111 River Street
Hoboken, NJ 07030-5774

Copyright © 2004 by Wiley Publishing, Inc., Indianapolis, Indiana

Published by Wiley Publishing, Inc., Indianapolis, Indiana

Published simultaneously in Canada

For general information on our other products and services or to obtain technical support, please
contact our Customer Care Department within the U.S. at 800-762-2974, outside the U.S. at 317-572-3993,
or fax 317-572-4002.

Wiley also publishes its books in a variety of electronic formats. Some content that appears in print may
not be available in electronic books.

Library of Congress Control Number: 2004102364

ISBN: 0-7645-6790-X

Manufactured in the United States of America

10 9 8 7 6 5 4 3 2 1

2B/RV/QU/QU/IN

WILEY

About the Author

Mark L. Chambers has been an author, computer consultant, BBS sysop, programmer, and hardware technician for more than 20 years. (He's been pushing computers and their uses far beyond "normal" performance limits for decades now.) His first love affair with a computer peripheral blossomed in 1984 when he bought a lightning-fast 300 BPS modem for his Atari 400. Now he spends entirely too much time on the Internet and drinks far too much caffeine-laden soda.

His favorite pastimes include collecting gargoyles, watching St. Louis Cardinals baseball, playing his three pinball machines and the latest computer games, supercharging computers, and rendering 3-D flights of fancy with TrueSpace — and during all that, he listens to just about every type of music imaginable. (For those of his readers who are keeping track, he's up to 1,200+ audio CDs in his collection.)

With a degree in journalism and creative writing from Louisiana State University, Mark took the logical career choice and started programming computers. After five years as a COBOL programmer for a hospital system, he decided there must be a better way to earn a living, and he became the Documentation Manager for Datastorm Technologies, a well-known communications software developer. Somewhere between organizing and writing software manuals, Mark began writing computer books; his first book, *Running a Perfect BBS*, was published in 1994.

Along with writing several books a year and editing whatever his publishers throw at him, Mark has recently branched out into Web-based education, designing and teaching a number of online classes — called *WebClinics* — for Hewlett-Packard.

Mark's rapidly expanding list of books includes *Building a PC For Dummies, Scanners For Dummies, CD and DVD Recording For Dummies, Mac OS X Panther All-In-One Desk Reference For Dummies, PC All-In-One Desk Reference For Dummies, Microsoft Office v. X Power User's Guide, BURN IT! Creating Your Own Great DVDs and CDs, The Hewlett-Packard Official Printer Handbook, The Hewlett-Packard Official Recordable CD Handbook, The Hewlett-Packard Official Digital Photography Handbook, Computer Gamer's Bible, Recordable CD Bible, Teach Yourself the iMac Visually, Running a Perfect BBS, Official Netscape Guide to Web Animation,* and the *Windows 98 Troubleshooting and Optimizing Little Black Book.*

His books have been translated into 12 languages so far — his favorites are German, Polish, Dutch, and French. Although he can't read them, he enjoys the pictures a great deal.

Mark welcomes all comments and questions about his books — you can reach him at mark@mlcbooks.com, or visit MLC Books Online, his Web site, at www.mlcbooks.com.

Dedication

I'd like to dedicate this book to Tim Kilgore. Tim, for more than ten years now, you've been a fellow hardware technowizard and computer game expert, a door programmer and BBS sysop before modems were cool, and a great friend who has always been there for me. Sometimes I wonder if we're actually twins and don't know it.

Here's to the next ten years!

Author's Acknowledgments

Unlike other types of books an author can tackle, a *For Dummies* book is a very personal project. Writing a book like this one involves distilling everything I know about a subject into words, so just about everyone that I need to appreciate, praise, and applaud works for my favorite publisher — Wiley!

As with all my books, I'd like to first thank my wife, Anne, and my children, Erin, Chelsea, and Rose, for their support and love — and for letting me follow my dream!

I owe a continuing debt of thanks to the Production team, this time led by Project Coordinator Maridee Ennis. You've all done it again! These folks take care of everything from producing new line art to designing the layout and proofreading the text before it heads to the printer, and the quality of this finished book is a tribute to their hard work.

Thanks are also due to my editorial manager, Carol Sheehan, my technical editor, Dennis Cohen, and my editorial assistant, Amanda Foxworth. Each of them reviewed either the grammar or technical accuracy of every page (and even the general coherency from time to time)! It's a demanding job, and I'm always grateful for the extra eyes checking my words.

And no, I will *never* forget the tireless efforts of the two editors who made this very project possible. My heartfelt appreciation goes to the dynamic duo of Bob Woerner, my acquisitions editor, and Susan Pink, my project editor. Without their help, this book would literally not exist — and I wouldn't have been able to work with such a great group of people!

Publisher's Acknowledgments

We're proud of this book; please send us your comments through our online registration form located at www.dummies.com/register/.

Some of the people who helped bring this book to market include the following:

Acquisitions, Editorial, and Media Development

Project Editor: Susan Pink

Acquisitions Editor: Bob Woerner

Technical Editor: Dennis Cohen

Editorial Manager: Carol Sheehan

Permissions Editor: Laura Moss

Media Development Specialist: Kit Malone

Media Development Manager: Laura VanWinkle

Media Development Supervisor: Richard Graves

Editorial Assistant: Amanda Foxworth

Cartoons: Rich Tennant (www.the5thwave.com)

Production

Project Coordinator: Maridee Ennis

Layout and Graphics: Andrea Dahl, Lauren Goddard, Joyce Haughey, Stephanie D. Jumper, Kristin McMullan, Lynsey Osborn, Heather Ryan, Rashell Smith, Melanee Wolven

Proofreaders: Carl W. Pierce, Brian H. Walls, TECHBOOKS Production Services

Indexer: TECHBOOKS Production Services

Publishing and Editorial for Technology Dummies

    Richard Swadley, Vice President and Executive Group Publisher

    Andy Cummings, Vice President and Publisher

    Mary C. Corder, Editorial Director

Publishing for Consumer Dummies

    Diane Graves Steele, Vice President and Publisher

    Joyce Pepple, Acquisitions Director

Composition Services

    Gerry Fahey, Vice President of Production Services

    Debbie Stailey, Director of Composition Services

Contents at a Glance

Table of Contents

Introduction

•••

*W*hen you think of a computer system, what parts automatically come to mind? Of course, you have the box itself, a monitor, a keyboard, and a mouse. What additional pieces do most folks add to their computers? Until three or four years ago, you probably would have considered a printer, a set of speakers, and a joystick. Today, however, more and more prospective computer owners are considering a scanner as a must-have. Scanners are less expensive than ever — you can easily find several models online (or at your local Maze O' Wires computer store) for less than $100 — but I think that's only part of the reason. If you choose a Universal Serial Bus (USB) scanner, it's also among the easiest computer peripherals to install. Again, that counts for something, although I don't think that's the heart of the matter.

The *real* reason that scanners have enjoyed such a surge in popularity is that more computer owners now recognize just how useful a scanner can be! More applications than ever make use of your scanner, and the Internet makes it easy to share the documents and images you scan through e-mail or your Web site. Many computer owners are even turning to their scanners for handicrafts, such as creating custom-printed items!

I wrote this book especially for scanner owners who want to find out all about what that marvelous piece of machinery can do. You can start from the basics and work your way to the tips, tricks, and technology used by scanner experts. As with any other *For Dummies* titles, I use the English language you studied in school, with no jargon and as few ridiculous computer acronyms as I can possibly manage! As you can tell already, I also include a little humor — at least, what my editors *agree* is humorous.

What's Really Required

"Do I need a degree in advanced thakamology to use this thing? Or will I end up spending more on software than I do on food?" Rest easy! Allow me to tell you first what's *not* required for this book:

- ✔ I make no assumptions about your previous knowledge of computers, graphic arts, software, or Italian cooking.
- ✔ Haven't bought your scanner yet? This is the book for you because I introduce you to each of the features you should look for and how to install and configure both your scanning hardware and software.

> ✔ Some unbelievers seem to think that creating great scanned images, editing them just the way you like them, and using them in your projects requires either a lifetime of graphic arts experience or a $1000 program. I'm here to tell you that you can do everything in this book with no previous art training and the software that probably came with your scanner.

So what is required? A scanner, the software it needs to run (which you should have received with the scanner), and a desire to improve your scanning skills. Oh, I almost forgot: A curious nature and an urge to experiment are good when working with special effects, too.

About This Book

Each chapter in this book has been written as a reference on a specific topic relating to your scanner. Note that you can begin anywhere because each chapter is self-contained. Unless you've already had some experience with installing and using a scanner, however, I think that you'll benefit the most from reading from front to back. The book also includes a glossary of computer and scanner terms and an appendix with information about manufacturers of scanning hardware and software.

Conventions Used in This Book

I can decrease the technobabble to a minimum, but, unfortunately, there's no such thing as a computer book that doesn't have at least a few special keys you have to press or menu commands you have to choose.

From time to time, I may ask you to type a command in Windows or Mac OS. That text often appears like this: **Type me**. To execute a command, you press the Enter (or Return) key.

I use the following format for menu commands:

Edit⇨Copy

This shorthand instruction indicates that you should choose the Edit menu and then choose the Copy menu item.

From time to time, I mention messages you should see displayed on-screen by an application or the operating system. Those messages look like this:
`This is a message displayed by an application.`

Few subjects in this book require me to use technical talk — scanners are mild-mannered, cultured creatures — but from time to time, you may be curious about those technical details. Because you don't have to know the techy stuff, it's formatted as a sidebar. Read it only if you want to know what makes things tick.

How This Book Is Organized

After careful thought (read that "flipping a coin"), I've divided this book into six major parts. If additional coverage of an important topic appears elsewhere, it's cross-referenced for your convenience.

Part I: The Scam on Scanners

In Part I, I introduce you to what a scanner does and how it's constructed, discuss the various types of scanners on the market, and establish important concepts, such as color depth and resolution. For those shopping for a scanner, I discuss features, show you how to evaluate your scanning needs, and help you decide whether to buy your new toy online or from a local store.

Part II: Surviving the Installation

You *will* survive your scanner installation unscathed! The chapters in Part II cover the installation of different types of scanners: USB, FireWire, parallel port, and SCSI models. I also provide guidelines for installing your software and testing your new scanner as well as a number of side issues you should consider, such as the addition of a printer, a CD-RW or DVD-RW/+RW drive, and a hard drive to your system.

Part III: Bread-and-Butter Scanning

You can't build without a solid foundation, and the chapters in Part III provide a thorough tutorial in basic scanning techniques. I cover the scanning process, of course, and include tips on scanning different types of materials, procedures for configuring your scanning software, and an introduction to my favorite Windows image editor, Paint Shop Pro.

Part IV: The Lazy Expert's Guide to Advanced Scanning

That's me, all right! In Part IV, you discover the advanced stuff you'll be craving if you read the first three parts first: image formats, Internet and Web tips and tricks, advanced image editing, scanner maintenance and troubleshooting, and even a chapter devoted to projects such as creating a custom T-shirt, creating a slide show CD-ROM of your images, using an OCR program, and sending a fax using a scanned image.

Part V: The Part of Tens

The four chapters that make up the famous "Part of Tens" section are a quick reference of tips and advice on several topics relating to your scanner. Each list has ten tips. I especially recommend Chapter 17, where I introduce you to my top ten favorite special effects. In fact, skim that chapter first so that you get an idea of the magic you can perform on your scanned photographs! A little inspiration never hurts when you're just getting started!

Part VI: Appendixes

The appendixes feature a scanner hardware and software manufacturer list, a glossary of computer terms and (mostly unnecessary) acronyms, and a description of the programs on the companion CD-ROM.

Icons Used in This Book

I like important notes to stand out on the page! To make sure that you see certain paragraphs, they're marked with one of these icons:

Now *there* is a mug of distinction! You'll find this icon parked next to my Mark's Maxims: the "100-percent-practically-without-exception" rules that apply to things (like hardware) and procedures (like wiping your scanner's glass to keep it clean). Commit these Maxims to memory, and you'll thank me later.

If you had a highlighter handy, you would mark this information. The way I see it, a reminder never hurts!

If you're considering buying a used scanner, or if someone has given you one, watch for this icon. It points out information and recommendations for using older hardware.

 This stuff happens behind the curtain. If you used to take apart alarm clocks to see how they worked, you'll like this information. Remember that you can also ignore this stuff with impunity!

 This icon points out information that saves you time and trouble (and perhaps even cash).

 Something could be damaging to your scanner or your software or even both. *Always* read the information for this icon first!

Where to Go from Here

My recommendations?

- ✔ If you're thinking about buying a scanner, the box is still unopened in the trunk of your car, or you're knee deep in the installation, start with Part I.
- ✔ If you need help with operating an existing scanner, start with Part II.
- ✔ For all other concerns, use the index or jump straight to the chapter you need. (You can always return to the beginning of the book later, at your leisure.)

I hope that you find this book valuable. Take your time and remember that your scanner can do *much* more than just reproduce images of documents and photographs!

Part I
The Scam on Scanners

The 5th Wave   By Rich Tennant

"No, it's not a pie chart, it's just a corn chip that got scanned into the document."

In this part . . .

Your journey begins with an introduction to the scanner itself: what it does, what it contains, and what happens during the digitizing process. You find out about resolution and color depth and why they're important to scanner owners. I discuss the features and limitations of each type of scanner, and I help you to evaluate your needs if you're thinking about buying a scanner. I round out this part by weighing the pros and cons of buying online versus buying from a local store.

Chapter 1

Let's Get Digitized!

*I*n medieval times, magicians known as alchemists used to weave tales of a wonderful box. In this box, they said, one could place an ordinary item (an egg, for example), close the lid, and — presto! — the egg would turn to pure gold or a flawless diamond. Many alchemists spent their lives trying to perfect this nifty little household appliance. In fact, some said that they actually did, and these people became the performers we know today as magicians. (A few politicians and used-car salesmen are probably in that group also.) Everyone knows that a machine like that is a fairy tale.

But, wait: What if I told you that such a box really *does* exist — one that can take ordinary paper and turn it into creative magic? Imagine a machine that can bring a smile to the faces of your friends and family or reshape opinions, safeguard your memories, and perhaps even help sell your '79 Pinto?

Computer scanners now can do all that and more, and you don't need a degree in the magical arts (in other words, a computer programming degree) to use one with your PC or Macintosh computer system. The facts get even better, too: The perfect scanner for most home and small business uses costs less than $150, and you can connect it and produce your first scanned image in less than five minutes. After all, the faster you get a picture of that '79 Pinto on your Web site, the better the chance that you can finally unload it!

In this chapter, I introduce you to the computer equivalent of the alchemist's magic box. You discover what you can do with a scanner, what types of scanners are available, what makes them tick (if you want to know), and the importance of resolution and color.

"Okay, I'll Bite — What's a Scanner?"

Although many different types of scanners are available — flatbed, sheet-fed, color, and black-and-white, just to name a few — they all perform the same function. Therefore, it's easy to define exactly what a scanner is:

> **Scanner.** (n) A machine that reproduces an image from a source object, producing an identical digital image for display or processing.

There — that explains everything, at least for technotypes. In plain English, a scanner "reads" the image from an object (typically a piece of paper) and then creates a copy of that image as a picture file on your computer. (If you're curious about what goes on inside, I explain the process later in this chapter.)

Of course, my explanation also has exceptions. It figures, right?

- You don't necessarily have to scan something from a sheet of paper. For example, your source image can be printed on fabric or some other material or can be a photographic negative.

- A scanner doesn't necessarily have to create a picture file on your computer; if you've used a fax machine or a copy machine, you've been using a scanner. After the scanner read the image, it was simply sent somewhere else. The fax machine sent the image as data over the telephone line, and the copy machine sent the image to the built-in printer to create a duplicate.

- You may not be scanning that original to create an image file on your computer. With the right software, scanners can now recognize the printed characters on a page and enter them into your word processor. I discuss this process, called *optical character recognition* (or OCR, for those who crave acronyms), in detail and show you how to use it later in this book. Another good example of a "rogue" scanning application is the familiar barcode, which has appeared on just about every inanimate object in your local shipping office and grocery store.

Most of the work you do with scanners these days, however, is performed as I describe in my definition: For example, you want an image from a magazine in a form you can use with a document you've created with Microsoft Word. Or perhaps you want to send that picture of Aunt Martha through e-mail to your folks living a thousand miles away.

What Can I Scan, Mr. Spock?

You won't be scanning the surface of an alien planet from the bridge of the starship *Enterprise*, so you won't hear me say "Fascinating!" Instead, we humans here on planet Earth scan these types of materials:

- Books
- Photographs
- Magazines
- Business cards
- Printed text
- Flat objects
- Fabric
- Photograph negatives
- Sketches and original art
- Cereal and pizza boxes

You get the idea: If it's reasonably flat and it has any type of image on it, it's likely to be scanner material. Scanners can record surface detail, too, but the results vary widely according to the material that makes up the object. (Naturally, the darker the material, the harder it is for your scanner to deliver a clear image.)

Different Breeds of Scanner

Over the past few years, different types of scanners have evolved for different jobs. Some types provide a better-quality scan, some take up less room, and some are designed especially for one type of original media. In Chapter 2, I get into the specifics of which type of scanner is perfect for you. For now, take a moment for a scenic overview of what's available. Sit back and enjoy the tour. (Have an hors d'oeuvre!)

- **Flatbed:** Imagine the top of a copy machine. Cut off the rest of it, and you have a flatbed scanner, as shown in Figure 1-1. With a flatbed, you're likely to get the best resolution with the least distortion, and you can easily scan pages from a magazine or book.

Figure 1-1:
The flatbed
scanner.
Have you
ever seen
anything so
beautiful?

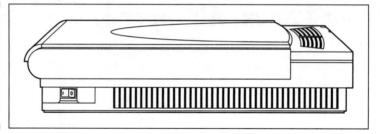

Figure 1-1:
The flatbed
scanner.
Have you
ever seen
anything so
beautiful?

✔ **Sheet-fed:** Limited space on your desk? A sheet-fed scanner may be the answer. The shortest models are about the size of a roll of aluminum foil, and other models look suspiciously like a fax machine. (As a matter of fact, a fax machine has a built-in scanner that it uses to create an image of the page.) Figure 1-2 shows you a typical sheet-fed scanner.

✔ **Photo scanner:** Many photo scanners are internal computer components, which means they fit inside your computer's case, as shown in Figure 1-3. Photo scanners are specially designed to read individual pictures taken with a film camera (or even small printed items, such as business cards or a driver's license).

✔ **Handheld scanners:** These portable scanners come in different shapes and sizes, ranging from a handheld model that can scan three or four inches at a time to a pen scanner that reads a single line of text. Handheld scanners don't offer the picture quality and convenience of a flatbed scanner. They can fit in a laptop case (or even a pocket), though, so they have their place with the road warriors among us. Barcode scanners are also typically handheld. Figure 1-4 shows a handheld scanner.

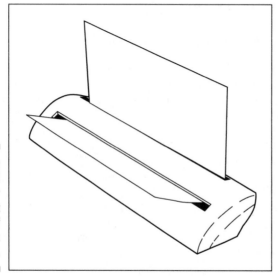

Figure 1-2:
A sheet-fed
scanner
does a great
imitation of
a fax
machine.

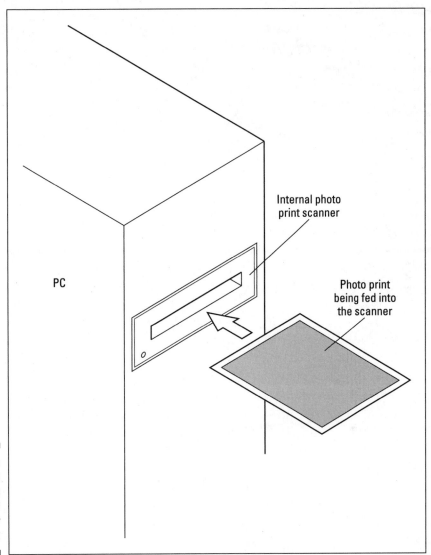

Internal photo
print scanner

Photo print
being fed into
the scanner

PC

Figure 1-3:
Photo
scanners
are installed
inside your
computer.

✔ **Negative scanners:** The snobs of the scanner world, negative scanners are designed for only one purpose: to scan photographic slides and negatives. Although these scanners are usually hideously expensive, if the images you need are on slides or you want the best possible scan of a photographic negative, a negative scanner is the only way to produce a high-quality image. Figure 1-5 provides glimpse of a negative scanner.

Quite a lineup, eh? Darwin himself would have been proud of the way in which scanners have adapted to their environment.

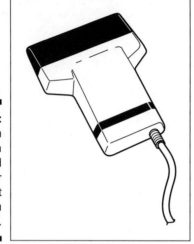

Figure 1-4:
If you're on the road, a handheld scanner doesn't weigh you down.

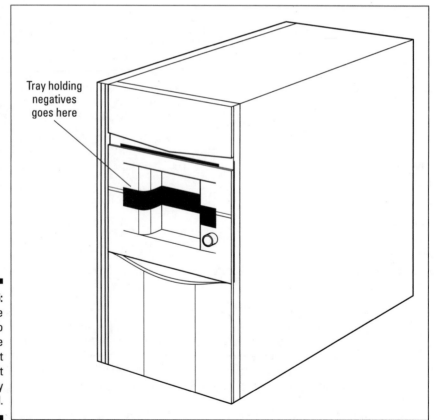

Tray holding negatives goes here

Figure 1-5:
Negative scanners do only one thing, but they do it very, very well.

Examining the Innards

Okay, I know what you're thinking. (Didn't know that little tidbit about computer book authors, did you?) You're wondering, "Do I *really* have to read about my scanner's anatomy?" Ladies and gentlemen, the answer is a big, emphatic "No!" None of the material in this section has any cosmic meaning, so if the closest you want to get to your scanner's mechanical side is plugging in the power cord to the wall outlet, feel free to jump ahead to the next section (which, come to think of it, you can skip as well)!

Hey, if you're still reading, you're curious about mechanical mysteries, like I am. Did you disassemble alarm clocks when you were a kid, too? (Dad eventually had to lock his up in the garage.) Read on while I explain the common parts shared by every scanner.

The sensor

Crack open your scanner — no, don't grab a hammer, it's just a figure of speech — and you'll find that the sensor is the star of the show. The scanner sensor is comprised of an array of individual photosensitive cells. Wait — don't drift off yet — it gets better! Each of these cells returns a certain amount of electrical current to the scanner's brain; how much current is determined by the amount of reflected light the cell receives as it passes by the original image. Figure 1-6 illustrates how this process works.

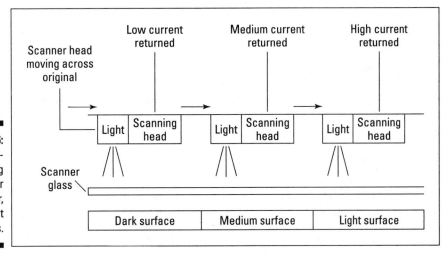

Figure 1-6: One hard-working scanner sensor, churning out the pixels.

If you're knowledgeable about your human anatomy (or, like me, you were able to stay awake in high-school biology class long enough to pass), you can see the parallels between this process and how the human eye works. In the eye, the photosensitive nerves perform the same function: They send impulses to your brain that depend on the amount of light they receive.

Each of the cells in the scanner's sensor reads a single dot of the image. And that basic building block, the *pixel,* is a unit of measure I return to time and time again in this book. Your computer monitor is also measured in pixels, as are digital cameras. All digital images are made up of individual pixels. Your eye and brain work together to combine them into the image you see.

The motor

Of course, the sensor doesn't do you a tremendous amount of good if it just sits in one place on the image. You would get a single line of pixels from the original! (That makes for a very bad scan, as you can imagine.) The designers of the first scanners knew that they needed to move the sensor across the surface of the original so that they could scan the entire thing, so they added the motor.

Figure 1-7 illustrates the two types of motors in today's scanners: In effect, one design moves the sensor head past the original, and the other moves the original past the scanner head (which is fixed in one spot). In later chapters, I explain which is better for you; both types of motor drives have their advantages.

The light

A sensor that's sensitive to light needs illumination, and your scanner carries its own built-in "reading lamp" — the light that's reflected from the original is picked up by the sensor. Most scanners have this light mounted right next to the scanner head.

The brain

Like just about everything in the world of computers, your scanner has an electronic brain for processing image data. The brain isn't sophisticated compared to your computer's central processing unit (CPU), which has a master's degree in several subjects. A scanner's brain has at least passed the fourth grade, though. I talk more about this processing in the next section.

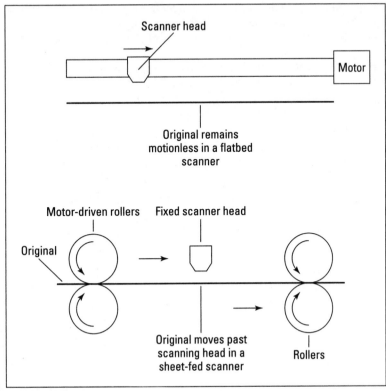

Scanner head

Motor

Original remains
motionless in a flatbed
scanner

Motor-driven rollers   Fixed scanner head

Original

Figure 1-7:
Something
has to
move in a
scanner —
either the
sensor or
the original.

Original moves past
scanning head in a
sheet-fed scanner

Rollers

The interface

Every scanner needs a connection of some sort to your computer. In all their wisdom (and their surprisingly intermittent common sense), computer hardware designers have to have a separate word for this connection. For some reason, the word *connection* didn't hack it. Therefore, they call the type of connection your scanner uses an *interface*. Although most scanners made these days use the *Universal Serial Bus* (USB, for normal human beings), I introduce you to all the connections (whoops, there I go again) — the interfaces — found on scanners. As you'd expect, I also help you determine which is best for you.

Scanning Explained (for Normal Folks)

Here I go, trying to explain the alchemist's magic box. If you don't care how the box works and you would rather jump right to the next section, I can meet you there. This stuff is *absolutely* not necessary. If you're like me, however, and you stick your head into everything electronic from sheer curiosity, keep reading!

Here's the process your scanner uses to produce that spiffy digital image (use Figure 1-8 to follow along, if you like):

1. The scanner light is turned on.

2. The sensor head moves slowly past the original, or the original is moved slowly past the sensor head. (Anyway, movement and a motor are involved, as I mention in the preceding section.)

3. The sensor reads the amount of light reflected by the original in each pixel of the current scan line and sends those signals to the scanner's brain.

4. The signals are converted to binary data and sent to your computer through the interface.

5. The sensor head moves to the next line of pixels, and the process begins again with Step 2.

This process is repeated until the scanner has read each line of pixels in the original image. Depending on the type of scanner, the sensor head typically makes as many as three full transits across the original to capture a complete, full-color image. I tell you more about this process later in this book.

Although this operation sounds lengthy, things are moving at computer speeds. For example, most scanners can read an entire page of text in fewer than 10 seconds and can read an entire full-page image in fewer than 30 seconds.

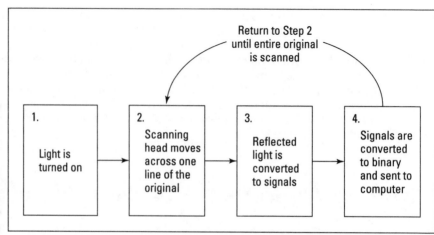

Figure 1-8:
The scanning process in all its awesome glory.

Return to Step 2 until entire original is scanned

1. Light is turned on

2. Scanning head moves across one line of the original

3. Reflected light is converted to signals

4. Signals are converted to binary and sent to computer

Resolving Resolution

If you've read the "Examining the Innards" section, earlier in this chapter, you may remember the array of photosensitive sensors I mentioned. (If not, don't worry about it; I don't give you a test on that stuff.) The sensor array in a typical scanner is comprised of hundreds of individual sensors. The density of these individual sensors leads to what's likely the most important single specification you should consider in a scanner: *resolution*.

Scanner resolution is commonly measured in *dots per inch*, or *dpi* — the number of individual dots scanned per inch of the original image. The dpi measurement is usually expressed as horizontal (the number of individual sensors in the array) by vertical (the distance the sensor head moves between individual lines), for example, 600 x 1200. I call this measurement the "common" dpi because most scanner manufacturers use it in their specifications.

Other scanner manufacturers may give you only one dpi figure. That's what I call the "true" dpi because it measures only the number of pixels horizontally. It's the resolution measurement used by professional graphic artists, service bureaus, and publishers, so high-end scanners often provide only a single dpi figure.

If you're comparing a scanner that's listed with two figures, such as 600 x 1200 dpi, with a scanner listed with just one figure, such as 600 dpi, don't panic! Just compare the first figure, which is the horizontal dpi measurement. In fact, because both scanners offer 600 dpi, they have the same horizontal resolution.

If you want to be a stickler, however, using a dpi rating to describe a scanner's resolution is technically incorrect. I tell you more about this subject in the nearby sidebar, "Positive peer pressure!"

A high-resolution picture is worth a thousand words (somebody famous said that, I'm sure) — and the next two figures are a good illustration. In Figure 1-9, you see the same photograph of an apple printed at 300 x 300 and at 600 x 600 dpi. Figure 1-10 shows a close-up of one edge of the same two images (illustrating why a higher resolution results in sharper edges in your digital image).

Figure 1-9:
Tell the
truth: Which
apple would
you rather
eat?

Figure 1-10:
Those extra
dots really
make a
difference.

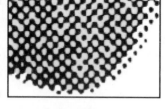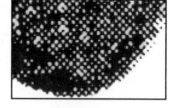

300 x 600 dpi   600 x 600 dpi

As you may expect, the *general* rule calls for a higher dpi: The higher the resolution, the better the quality and the higher the detail of your digital image. However, a higher resolution also results in much larger image files, and not every original benefits from an astronomically high resolution. Therefore, you probably don't need to spend the extra $100 to buy a 1200 x 2400 dpi model when a 600 x 1200 dpi scanner will satisfy just about any PC owner or office worker. I discuss this subject in more detail in Chapter 2.

Positive peer pressure!

If I'm going to be completely accurate here, I should use a different measure of resolution, called samples per inch rather than dots per inch. *Samples per inch,* or spi, refers to the number of individual sensors in the array. A scanning purist would say that dpi is a term that belongs with computer printers, which print — rather than scan — dots.

You may be saying, "Now, wait a second. Isn't samples per inch *effectively* the same method of measuring as dots per inch?" You bet! That's why virtually every manufacturer of scanners on the face of this planet uses dpi when referring to resolution in their advertisements and specifications.

It may not be strictly accurate, but everyone (and I mean *everyone*) uses it. In this book, I've caved in to peer pressure and elected to use dpi rather than spi.

Scanning purists can complain all they like. As long as I'm writing this book, I think that it's more valuable for you to know what people really use, not a technical term that you'll probably never see in an online store or on the side of a scanner box. (Besides, this way, you can discuss scanners with the "in" crowd at your next cocktail party while the technonerds sulk in the corner and grumble about spi.)

Before I leave the subject of resolution, however, I want to familiarize you with the difference between raw and interpolated resolution. Here are the definitions:

✔ The *raw resolution* value (also called the *optical resolution*) is the optical resolution at which the scanner reads an image — in other words, the number of dots the scanner reads from the image.

✔ The *interpolated resolution* (also called the *enhanced resolution*) is an inflated figure delivered by the software provided with the scanner. The interpolated value adds a large number of extra dots to the scanned image by using a mathematical formula, *without* reading them from the original material. Interpolation is supposed to improve the quality of the image, which is why the interpolated resolution advertised for a particular scanner model is always higher than the raw resolution. (Those additional dots are ghosts!)

Here's the payoff: I *strongly* recommend that you judge scanners by their optical resolution while shopping. Forget about the interpolated value. It's nothing more than a guess made by a program, and in my experience it doesn't visibly improve the image. If an advertisement doesn't list the raw or optical resolution, find it on the manufacturer's Web site or the specifications on the box. This factor is important when comparing two different scanners.

How Deep Is Your Color?

I have one other massively important scanner topic to introduce here: color depth. The whole concept of color depth probably hasn't been a featured topic of conversation around your table (I know that it has *never* been mentioned around mine), although it can dramatically affect the appearance of your final scanned images and is the other criteria that will probably help you decide between those two or three different scanners on your shopping list.

In the computer world, *color depth* refers to the number of colors in an image (whether that image is on a computer monitor, captured by a digital camera, or captured by a scanner). Color depth is referred to in two ways:

✔ The maximum number of discrete colors (as in 256 colors or 16 million colors).

✔ The number of bits of information required to store color information for a single pixel (as in 8-bit or 24-bit color). This form of measuring color depth is also called *bit depth*.

Will that be Web color or print color?

When it comes to color depth, "higher is better" is not the rule of thumb used on the Web! If you're experienced at building Web pages that feature full-color images — especially large ones — you've probably decided to use a color depth of 256 colors, or 8 bits. Why? The answer is simple: The lower the color depth, the less time it takes a 56-Kbps modem to download the image to your visitor's Web browser. (Downloading a huge 16-million-color image over a telephone modem connection brings new meaning to the name "World Wide Wait.") Also, some computer owners still set their display color depth to 256 colors, so a 16-million-color (24-bit) image is mostly wasted data. Until more people have high-speed Internet connections, such as cable modems or DSL, 256 colors is probably the best choice.

On the other hand, if you're printing your images, anything less than 24-bit color is simply unacceptable. The fewer colors in your image (and the fewer colors your printer can deliver), the more your beautiful high-resolution digital photograph looks like a Sunday comic strip printed on cheap newspaper.

Which is best? That depends on two things: your output device (such as your monitor or your printer) and your own eyes. Only you can determine whether the quality of the finished image is acceptable, so experiment when you create Web pages with scanned images or print your scanned photos.

Most scanner manufacturers use the second method to describe the color depth of their products. Again, the general rule is the higher the bit depth, the better the color because your scanner is better able to capture subtle differences in color and shading from the original.

The scanner you select *must* capture a minimum of 24-bit color, although most models sold these days can reach 30-, 32-, 34-, 36-, 42- or 48-bit color. (The higher bit depths allow a more accurate color capture, even if the final image is printed at only 24-bit color.) That's all there is to color depth — no confusing acronyms, no exceptions, and no gimmicks. Refreshing, isn't it?

In Chapter 2, I describe other features and specifications you should look for while shopping for your scanner.

Chapter 2

The Joys of Buying a Scanner

*A*ll right, as my dad used to say, "Let's get this show on the road!" You can buy a scanner in one of two ways:

- ✔ **Method One:** Jump in your car, head directly to the Lots o' Wires super-store near you, ask a salesperson to point at his or her favorite scanner, and buy it.

- ✔ **Method Two:** Research the scanner models with the features you want (either through the Web or through computer magazines), compare them, and buy your choice through an online or local store.

Which technique is easier? Oh, I agree — Method One is as simple as it gets. On the other hand, which approach is practically *guaranteed* to save you money and identifies a scanner with more features that closely match your needs and your computer system? Definitely Method Two!

I know that you've already guessed which procedure I use — and which one I discuss in this chapter. (After all, if I preferred Method One, you wouldn't need this chapter.) I cover everything you need to know to decide for yourself which scanner is right for you and tell you how to buy that scanner for the lowest price possible! Keep a notepad and pencil handy to jot down what you need as you read.

A Game of Five Questions (Actually, Just Three)

Buying a scanner isn't as difficult as buying an entire computer system (which requires an entire *For Dummies* book all to itself), nor is it as simple as buying a new hard drive (which boils down to capacity, connection type, and price for everyone other than technotypes). Although a scanner falls somewhere between the two extremes, you *absolutely* need to ask yourself only three questions before you continue reading about the other features and luxuries you should understand.

King size or hideaway?

Before you start shopping, you have to decide how big is too big: Can you dedicate the desk space for a flatbed scanner, which can actually take up more room than a typical computer? Or will you stay lean and mean with a sheet-fed scanner? Although I briefly mention this dilemma in Chapter 1, you need to settle on a design before you go any further. To help you determine which to choose, I cover the advantages of both.

Reasons to choose a flatbed scanner

To be honest, I'm about as biased as I can be: *I want you to buy a flatbed scanner.* Why the enthusiasm? Here are my reasons:

- **A flatbed scanner is far more versatile.** With a flatbed model, you can scan materials and three-dimensional objects *other* than paper, such as a piece of fabric or a TV remote control (or even that new tattoo on your arm). Basically, if you've ever made copies of something on a copy machine, you can scan it with a flatbed.

- **A flatbed scanner doesn't cannibalize your material.** With a sheet-fed scanner, you can't scan pages from books or magazines unless you tear them out, and don't even think about scanning the surface of your arm for that tattoo. Plus, you don't have to worry about material that's too stiff (such as your driver's license) or too small (such as your driver's license). With a flatbed, like the Hewlett Packard ScanJet 5530 scanner shown in Figure 2-1, material of reasonable thickness and just about any size can be scanned without fear of jamming the mechanism or losing something in the bowels of the machine. (This USB superstar even features an automatic photo feeder, so you can scan several photographs unattended in one session.)

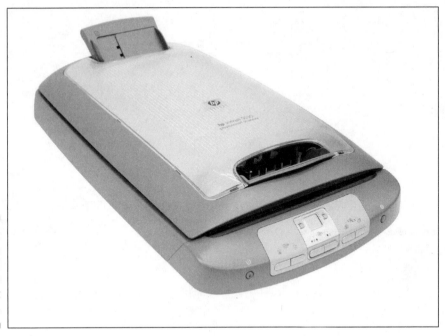

Figure 2-1:
A modern
flatbed
scanner: the
HP ScanJet
5530.

✔ **A flatbed scanner produces a better scan.** With a flatbed scanner, the scanning head moves past the material, a process that's inherently more stable than having the material move past the scanning head (as in a sheet-fed model). This is why just about any flatbed scanner features higher resolution (and often better color depth) than a sheet-fed scanner.

The reason to choose a sheet-fed scanner

"Now, wait a second, Mark. There must be *some* reason to buy a sheet-fed scanner!" You're right — and here it is:

It takes up less space. A sheet-fed scanner takes up only a fraction of the area used by a flatbed scanner on your desktop. In fact, many sheet-fed models are portable enough to be used on the road with your laptop computer. Some all-in-one printer/scanner/copier/fax devices use sheet-fed scanning engines for this reason. Other models, such as the Hewlett Packard OfficeJet 6110 multifunction device shown in Figure 2-2, now offer a built-in flatbed scanner.

Figure 2-2:
The HP
OfficeJet
6110 multi-
function
device.

Unless size is a primary concern (and you're not seduced by the advantage I just mentioned), choose a flatbed — and be happy.

Note: If you're interested in a specialized scanner, such as a photo scanner or negative scanner, remember that these exotic varieties are designed especially for a particular media. You can't scan *anything* else on them.

When you need to get really portable

If you're looking for a scanning solution that's easy to carry with you, a portable sheet-fed unit may do the trick — but what if you need to scan text from books or magazines? If you tear pages from those periodicals, don't bet on being a welcome visitor to your local library. And what about barcodes on products? Can you imagine trying to scan a plastic DVD movie case with a sheet-fed scanner?

Enter the road warrior's hero, the handheld scanner. Today's handheld scanners make it easy to capture individual lines of text from any document, but that's just the beginning. Businesses can use barcode scanning applications to track inventory without typing a single character, while collectors of DVD movies and audio CDs can effortlessly add titles to their collection database.

The $200 IRISpen Executive from I.R.I.S. Inc. (www.irislink.com) is a great example of a portable handheld document scanner. It connects to your laptop's USB port and works the same way as an old-fashioned highlighter. (Remember those?) Move the scanner over a single line of text, including rows of troublesome numbers, and the software automatically enters the characters into your favorite application. (It even reads the text aloud, which helps you ensure the accuracy of the scan.)

If you're running Mac OS X and you're a collector of books, audio CDs, DVD movies or game software, I recommend IntelliScanner Collector, from Intelli Innovations (www.intellisw.com). This package helps you build a database for your collection. You get a handheld USB scanner and the IntelliScanner Collection software, as shown in the figure. When you scan a barcode, Collection automatically retrieves detailed information about that item from Internet data sources and enters it for you. (Think "instant impressive information.")

Edit Movie   UPC: 014381428223

Info | Features | Artwork

Title
Mystery Science Theater 3000: The Movie

Starring
Trace Beaulieu, Michael J. Nelson

Media
DVD

Director
Jim Mallon

Price
$14.99

Distributor
Image Entertainment

Release Date
10/17/00

Genre
Comedy

MPAA Rating
PG-13

Theatrical Release
4/19/96

Comments
The cult television show (in which a hapless space explorer and his robot pals are forced to watch and deliver a hilarious running commentary on bad movies) makes a successful transition to the big screen as Mike and the 'bots lay waste to the '50s sci-fi yarn This Island Earth (a painfully stiff would-be epic that's actually a cut above the usual MST3K fare). While ardent fans may be a little miffed that

Copies 1 | **Purchase Date** 2/18/04 | **Location** | **My Rating** ★★★★★

Delete | Cancel | OK

How many dots are enough?

As I explain in Chapter 1, the higher the dpi, the better. How high a dpi does an average person *really* need, though? Table 2-1 shows the breakdown I use in recommending resolution. Remember that the "common" dpi is expressed as two numbers (horizontal x vertical). Remember also that I'm talking about optical resolution, not a resolution figure that has been enhanced or interpolated through software.

Table 2-1		Selecting the Right dpi	
"Common" DPI	*True DPI*	*Common Applications*	*Suitable For*
600 x 600	600	School projects	Kids
600 x 1200	600	Line art, photographs	Scavengers
1200 x 2400	1200	Almost anything	Most computer owners
2400 x 2400 and higher	2400	Design and graphic art	Photographers, artists, designers

Note: By the way, if you're wondering what I mean by a *scavenger* (see the "Suitable For" column in the table), don't be offended! That's a term I coined in another of my For Dummies books, *Building a PC For Dummies* (published by Wiley & Sons Publishing). The term refers to someone (like me!) who acquires older hardware. For example, if your Uncle Milton gives you his old 600 x 600 scanner because he has just bought a new model, you're a scavenger. This concept also applies to hardware bought at a garage sale or on eBay. In Table 2-1, it means that you're not likely to find a new scanner on the market now with a resolution of less than 1200 x 1200.

Naturally, a model with a higher resolution can do everything a lower-resolution scanner can do. Also, the figures in the table are the minimum: If you find two scanners with the right features and one delivers 2400 x 4800 resolution for only $50 more, you may want to spend the extra money.

A bit more about bit depth

Again, the higher the bit rate, the better the scanner. Should you spend extra cash, though, for a 42-bit or 48-bit scanner? Look out: Here's another of my patented, high-tech tables to help you decide this issue, too (see Table 2-2).

Table 2-2	Choosing a Bit Depth	
Bit Depth	*Common Applications*	*Suitable For*
24, 30, 32, 36 bit	Basic color scanning	Kids, scavengers
42 bit	Almost anything	Most computer owners
48 bit	Design and graphic art	Photographers, artists, designers

Although 24-bit scanners technically produce more than 16 million colors, you won't find one in a store. If you're buying a new scanner these days, stick with a scanner that offers at least 36-bit color. Anything more than 36 bit is usually overkill for a typical home computer owner. But, then again, I wouldn't turn down a 48-bit model if someone gave it to me!

Have 1 Got an Interface for You!

For technowizards, discussing the pros and cons of hardware interfaces often results in passionate arguments that last for hours. In fact, I've dodged several floppy disks and a mouse pad or two thrown in the heat of the moment. Enough variety exists in the number of cables, ports, and different connectors to fill several catalogs. What's worse, many computer salespeople suffer from CECSAUB (short for *Confusing Everything with a Collection of Silly Acronyms Used as Buzzwords*).

Here's a promise: I reduce the interface confusion to a minimum! (You can thank me with an e-mail to mark@mlcbooks.com, if you like.) I present the four common connections you can use to add a scanner to your system, and help you determine which is right for your system. I even try to keep the acronyms down to four or fewer letters.

Moving in parallel

Even the oldest IBM-compatible computers are virtually guaranteed to have a *parallel port* (often called a *printer port*). Although the parallel port was originally used only to provide a connection for your printer, the port is sometimes used to provide a connection for external devices, such as scanners. Figure 2-3 illustrates a parallel port in all its 25-pin glory.

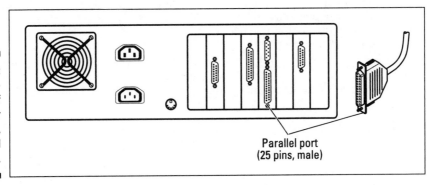

Figure 2-3:
The old-timer of scanner connections, the parallel port.

Parallel port
(25 pins, male)

If your PC was built within the past ten years or so, you can probably use a parallel port scanner. If your machine is older, check the manual to determine whether the parallel port is bidirectional (or offers ECP and EPP modes). If so, it should work with a scanner.

- ✔ **Pros:** The universal nature of the parallel port means that you can use your parallel port scanner on just about any computer, including laptops. Parallel port scanners are usually the least expensive models you can buy.

- ✔ **Cons:** Parallel scanners are very slow compared to the other connection options I cover in this chapter. Also, if you're already using a Zip drive or other external device on your computer's parallel port, you may experience problems if you try to daisy-chain a scanner by hooking it up at the end of a connected series of parallel devices (for example, a scanner connected to a Zip drive, which is in turn connected to the computer's parallel port).

If your computer doesn't have one of the other connections or you have an older laptop, a parallel port scanner may be your only choice. If you can use a USB model, however, you should pass on a parallel port connection.

The ultimate in usefulness

Here's an acronym I can appreciate: USB is short for *Universal Serial Bus.* (Personally, I think the *U* stands for *useful,* or perhaps *ultimate.*) The USB port is the Holy Grail of computer owners everywhere: It's a medium- to high-speed, easy-to-use connection for attaching all sorts of peripherals to your computer, and it has proven as popular a piece of technology as the wheel. A USB port can support as many as 127 devices. Tell the truth here: Have you ever seen a computer with 127 external devices connected *at one time?* (I couldn't even fit a system like that in my basement!)

The latest version of USB (USB 2.0) can transfer data from a scanner to your computer at speeds as fast as 480 megabits per second . . . plus, it's also backwardly compatible with older USB 1.1 hardware. "Holy connection, Batman!" But, wait! You get more: A USB device is automatically recognized and installed by Windows 98, Windows Me, Windows 2000, Windows XP, Mac OS 9, and Mac OS X. You can even connect and disconnect that USB scanner without rebooting your computer, as shown in Figure 2-4.

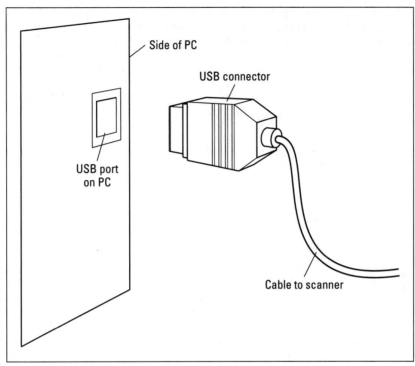

Side of PC

USB connector

USB port
on PC

Cable to scanner

Figure 2-4:
Man, is this
USB a great
port, or
what?

✔ **Pros:** USB 1.1 scanners are as inexpensive as their parallel port brethren, and they're much faster. A USB scanner is so simple to use that even a politician can connect one to a computer. That's what I call user friendly.

✔ **Con:** If I had to list a disadvantage of USB scanners, I would have to mention that USB is not available on PCs and Macintosh computers that are more than five or six years old.

Cheap, simple, and powerful — you can see why USB is the connection choice for most scanner shoppers. I heartily recommend it!

For those in the fast lane

If you've invested in a more expensive scanner that delivers 36-bit color or higher, you may want to consider the speedy IEEE-1394 High Performance Serial Bus or, as power users and computer types would rather call it, a FireWire port. FireWire has all the capabilities of USB technology, although the original FireWire bus is a little slower than the latest version of USB and can handle only a measly 63 devices. The latest FireWire standard (called FireWire 800 in the Mac world) is significantly faster than even USB 2.0, but it's not likely to appear on scanning hardware anytime soon — plus, using older FireWire hardware with a new FireWire 800 port requires a special connector or cable, because the new FireWire 800 ports are a different shape.

- ✔ **Pros:** FireWire shares the same user-friendly features as USB 1.1 and is much faster than computers with older USB ports.

- ✔ **Cons:** FireWire ports are much more rare than USB in the PC world, so your computer may not have the ports to use one of these scanners. (If you like, you can add a FireWire adapter card to your computer.) Plus, FireWire hardware is usually significantly more expensive than USB.

Unless the scanner with the features you want demands a FireWire connection, I recommend that you select a USB scanner instead.

Forget SCSI? Never!

The final candidate in the connection beauty pageant has been a favorite of computer hardware hackers for decades: *SCSI* (short for Small Computer Systems Interface) technology is used in computers for everything from hard drives to CD recorders and scanners.

- ✔ **Pros:** SCSI is fast, and as many as 15 devices can be added to your system through a single SCSI adapter card. Unlike USB and FireWire, SCSI supports both internal and external devices.

- ✔ **Cons:** SCSI is harder to install and configure than any other connection types I cover, and SCSI scanners are typically more expensive than their USB counterparts.

If your computer already has SCSI onboard, you may want to consider a SCSI scanner. For complete details on SCSI, turn to Chapter 4.

TWAIN (Not the Tom Sawyer Guy)

Hey, don't get me wrong — Samuel Clemens (also known as Mark Twain) is my favorite author! In this case, though, TWAIN is a computer term you should remember. Although it appears in all uppercase letters, it's not an acronym — TWAIN actually stands for *absolutely nothing!* You could make up an acronym, calling it "technology without an interesting name," the only acronym in this book coined by folks who understood what normal people think of computer technobabble.

The TWAIN standard was conceived and developed to ensure that your scanning hardware, image capture software, and editing software all talk the same language, no matter who made what. As long as everything is TWAIN compatible, you know that everything you use to scan recognizes everything else. Both Windows and Mac OS support TWAIN.

Check any scanning hardware or software you're buying to make sure that it's TWAIN compatible and save yourself a headache.

Scanner Features to Covet

In this section, I talk about the other features that can separate a good scanner buy from a great one. Although none of these extras is a requirement, each of them is nice to have.

One pass, one scanner, one king

In scanning terminology, a *pass* is a single sweep of the scanning head across the material. Therefore, a *single-pass* scanner takes only one trip across your photograph or document, digitizing the entire image at one time. Although a *triple-pass* scanner may be cheaper, it has to make three complete passes to capture the same data. These extra passes can result in distortion in the image because even a slight bump can shift the source material between passes (especially if you're trying to scan a three-dimensional object, such as a book cover or a canned ham).

That's not all. Naturally, a triple-pass scanner also requires at least three times the scanning time, which means that you have more time to spend wishing that you had a single-pass scanner! I heartily recommend that you save yourself those minutes and concentrate your comparison shopping on single-pass models.

Let your finger do the scanning

Most scanners are controlled entirely from the computer. In other words, you have to run the capture software that comes with your scanner before you can do anything. On the other hand, if your scanner features *one-button* scanning, you don't have to load any program.

You simply press the button on the scanner, and it automatically turns on, runs the capture software, and starts scanning! As you can imagine, this feature is quite a time-saver. In fact, one-button scanning has become such a popular feature that many higher-priced scanners also throw in one-button copying and faxing features.

Feed me!

Can you imagine a printer without a paper tray? You would end up loading sheets of paper into your printer by hand! Some people feel the same way about scanners. Personally, I don't scan that many documents in one day. But if you're working in an office environment or your work involves heavy-duty scanning of dozens of documents, a document feeder is a good idea. Your scanner may come with a document feeder already installed, but this feature is typically offered as optional equipment. Check a scanner's specifications on the manufacturer's Web site to see whether it can accept a feeder.

Adapt to transparency

As I mention earlier in this chapter, you can buy a scanner that's specially designed for slides and negatives — and many high-end flatbed scanners can do a fine job of digitizing transparent material. Just look for a scanner that includes its own light source; these models can backlight a transparent original, allowing the scanning head to correctly interpret the colors. With a *transparency light* (sometimes also called a *transparency adapter*), you can scan 35mm slides, photographic negatives, and the transparencies used in overhead projectors.

Your warranty is your shield

Most scanners now on the market have a one-year warranty, although it never hurts to check for extras (that you hope you won't need). For example, does the manufacturer offer free technical support over the phone? Is the company's Web site up-to-date, with software patches and driver updates posted regularly? Some companies also provide e-mail technical support from their Web sites.

While you're visiting any hardware manufacturer's Web site, look for *FAQ* files (FAQ is Internet savvy-speak, short for Frequently Asked Questions) that you can download about the product you're considering or a scanner you've bought. These files are usually chock-full of information, tips, and solutions to customer complaints.

Software You've Just Gotta Have

Okay, you may be familiar with the hardware, but the software you receive bundled with your scanner is just as important. If you have the wrong software, even the most expensive scanner model turns out a poor-quality image.

Also, scanner applications such as OCR, faxing, and copying depend on software. Without the right software, your scanner can't perform these tasks.

In this section, I discuss the software you need to keep your scanner healthy and happy.

Note: Your scanner may combine several programs into a software suite that can perform some or all the tasks in this section. If so, that's a powerful advantage to consider when you're comparing one scanner with another.

The image editor

For most scanner owners, the image editor is the primary program used every day. Not only can it control the scanner during the actual image acquisition, but you can also edit and improve the scan after it has been saved to your hard drive. (Plus, you can go totally wacky in an artistic sort of way.) The image editor is to digital photographs what a word processor is to written documents.

I can't think of a better example of an image editor than Paint Shop Pro, from Jasc, Inc. (www.jasc.com), which I use extensively in examples throughout this book. I first started using this great program in its shareware days, back in the hoary 1980s and early 1990s. (I know that makes me a microprocessing Methuselah, but no cracks about my age, please.) The latest version of this program packs the same power as Adobe Photoshop but for hundreds of dollars less. Naturally, Paint Shop Pro is TWAIN compatible, so it's a good match for just about any scanner. Figure 2-5 illustrates an image I'm editing in Paint Shop Pro 8.

What can you do with an image editor? I discuss this subject in depth in Chapters 9 and 11, but let me run through the top ten tasks quickly:

- ✔ Crop
- ✔ Rotate
- ✔ Change colors
- ✔ Add special effects
- ✔ Add text
- ✔ Resize
- ✔ Change contrast and brightness
- ✔ Fix individual pixels
- ✔ Convert to other image formats
- ✔ Convert color to black and white

As I said, you can do a great deal with a good image editor!

Figure 2-5:
Paint Shop
Pro, the
all-in-one
Swiss Army
knife of
image
editors.

The OCR program

Next in our cavalcade of scanning software is the *OCR*, or *optical character recognition*, program, which can "read" the text from a scanned document and insert it into a word processor, just as if you had retyped the text yourself. Many OCR software packages can also handle photographs and line art as well as simple text, creating a virtual copy of the original scanned document in Microsoft Word or Corel WordPerfect.

This feature sounds cosmically neat, and it can be. However, I think it's important to remember this important Mark's Maxim:

No OCR software is perfect.

The accuracy of the recognition depends not only on the program you use but also on a host of other conditions, including

- ✔ The font used in the original material.
- ✔ The quality of the original. (Naturally, a pristine sheet of paper scans better than a crumpled sheet you've rescued from your trash can.)

✔ The dpi resolution you selected during the scan.

✔ The color of the text on the page and the page itself.

For this reason, the page you scan from a library book may produce only one or two errors in the final Word document, but a color brochure from your company may be practically incomprehensible to your OCR program. You can fix these errors by individually correcting words the software couldn't recognize, although I don't want you to think that the process is foolproof.

The faxing program

As Frank Gorshin may have asked Adam West in my favorite classic TV series, "Riddle me this, Batman: Why is a fax-modem *not* like a fax machine?" Allow me to answer that, Caped Crusader: A fax-modem can send only documents you create electronically, such as a résumé or a digital photograph. If you want to send Aunt Harriet a copy of a recipe from the newspaper, however, you're out of luck. You have no way to fax from a physical original (called a *hard copy* by technotypes and media types alike).

But, wait! With a scanner, a program such as WinFax PRO (see Figure 2-6) can turn your computer system into a true fax machine that's as good as the expensive model you have at work. If you're using Mac OS X 10.3 — popularly called "Panther" — you don't even need a separate application! These lucky Mac folks can fax a document from an application, or fax a scanned image from Panther's Preview application. This, my friends, is the definition of *sassy*.

The copying program

Need a full-featured copier for your home or office? To be honest, you can't find the answer in this book. Although the addition of a scanner can turn your computer system into a basic copy machine, the scanner still can't deliver the versatility and features of the real thing.

If all you need, however, is the occasional copy of a document, your scanner fits the bill perfectly. You can even do basic resizing. This feature usually isn't built into the software, though, so you probably have to zoom in or zoom out manually with your image editor.

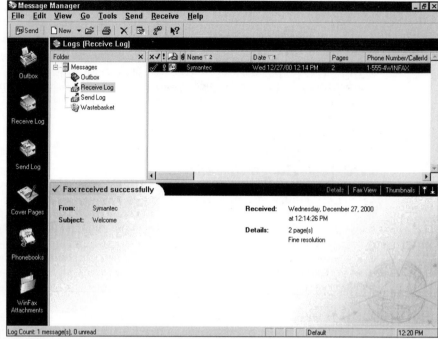

Figure 2-6:
WinFax PRO
can use
your
scanner
to fax
documents.

And the Winner Is . . .

It's totally up to you! Look over any notes you may have made as you've read this chapter, and you have the complete picture of the scanner you need. For example, suppose that you've written down the following:

> Flatbed, 1200 x 1200, 36-bit, USB, TWAIN, one-pass, one-button scanning, image editor, OCR

With those specifications, you can go comparison shopping — on the Web or in a real, live brick-and-mortar store — confident that you know exactly what you need.

Note: Are you wondering, "Where can I compare?" I recommend that you browse through the electronic versions of the major computer magazines if you have an Internet connection. Finding reviews is easy, and the awards that a particular scanner wins in a magazine comparison indicate that it's a good buy. I also like www.pricewatch.com and www.computershopper.com — two sites that offer online comparisons and help guide you to the lowest price online.

"Should I Buy on the Web?"

Speaking of online shopping, have you ever bought anything on the Web? If not, you may be a little nervous about providing your credit card number, and you may be wondering why so many people are shopping with their computers these days. Let me take a moment to fill you in on the advantages of buying your scanner online:

- ✔ **Prices are lower.** Of course, this is probably Reason Number One that most folks shop online. You can't beat the prices.

- ✔ **Shopping online is a time-saver.** After you're familiar with your favorite online stores, you can compare models, find the lowest price on the model you choose, and buy it, all within an hour or two. (You save gas as well.)

- ✔ **You may save on sales tax.** Depending on your location, you may not have to pay sales tax on your online purchase.

- ✔ **It's in stock!** You can not only find any scanner on the market online but also always find a store with one in stock.

When you're using your credit card online, follow the Mark's Maxim that I consider the golden rule of Web shopping:

Never entrust your credit card to any Web site that doesn't use a secure connection!

Reputable online stores use this encryption to safeguard your credit card data as well as your sensitive personal information.

Netscape Navigator and Microsoft Internet Explorer (the two big guns in PC Web browsing) support secure sessions, as does Apple's Safari browser for the Macintosh. When a locked padlock icon appears on the status line at the bottom of the browser window (or at the top of the window, if you're using Safari), you know that the session is secure.

Also, check the amount the store charges for shipping. Many stores use second-day shipment as a default option, which is much more expensive than regular ground shipment. If you can afford to wait a few days for your new toy, you can save a significant amount of money by choosing the slowest shipping method.

Supporting Your Local Hardware Hut

I should mention the advantages of the dull, boring, oh-so-'90s trip to your local Mess 'O Wires computer store. Yes, you still have reasons to buy from a salesperson! They include

- ✔ **Hands-on shopping:** Although the selection may not be the same as an online store, you can try out the scanner you're considering and check out the software before you buy.

- ✔ **Easier returns:** If you buy online and you end up with the famous Lemon Scanner, it's a quick trip back to the store for a replacement. If you order online, however, you're stuck with the hassle of obtaining an RMA (return merchandise authorization) and sending the scanner back. You end up waiting for the replacement, too.

- ✔ **Personal help:** With luck, you can talk to a knowledgeable salesperson who can answer your questions. (Without luck, you're stuck with a blank stare.)

Okay, that's the bright side. Here are the possible scams you may encounter at your local store:

- ✔ **The hidden surprise:** Your local store may charge a restocking fee if you return your scanner, even if it's unopened. This trick is a particularly insidious one that I despise. In effect, the store is charging you 15 or 20 percent just to put a box back on the warehouse shelf. If the store does charge this fee, make very sure that you're buying the right scanner. And don't forget to give the manager a piece of your mind before you leave the premises.

- ✔ **Whatever *you* call it, *I* call it used:** I also recommend that you avoid a *refurbished* scanner. Stores call them by different names — the important thing is that they're *used.* Although you may save a few bucks, is it worth buying a used scanner to save $20? A refurbished piece of hardware has already malfunctioned once, and you have no way of determining how the previous owner treated it. Plus, you're likely to receive a very short warranty or no warranty.

- ✔ **What's wrong with the free warranty?** I should warn you about the so-called extended warranty that most stores like to sell you — generally at an inflated price. If you're buying an expensive laptop or an entire computer system, an extended warranty may make sense. A scanner has very few moving parts, though, and they're not prone to failure. Besides, your new scanner is already covered by the manufacturer's warranty (usually a year). Why spend $20 to $40 extra when the cost of a brand-new scanner is only $100 to $150?

After you buy your scanner, you're ready to Plug and Play. In Chapter 3, I cover how to install a scanner.

Part II
Surviving the Installation

In this part . . .

1 demonstrate how to connect several types of scanners (including complete coverage of SCSI technology), and I help you test your scanner. In addition to information on installing your software, you'll find coverage of additional hardware that may make your scanning much easier.

Chapter 3

"Will That Be Parallel, USB, or FireWire?"

*W*hat do you find scarier: leaping off a bridge with a flimsy-looking rubber hose attached to your ankle or connecting a new peripheral to your computer?

If you chose the latter, don't head for Bungee Village quite yet. Besides, I've heard that they use *refurbished* cords. (Sorry. I couldn't resist.) Scanners are somewhat unique in the computer world: They belong to that elite group of external computer hardware that can boast a truly *easy* installation process! (Other members of this club include the external USB modem and all breeds of printers.)

As you can see from the relatively short length of this chapter, installing a scanner with a USB, parallel, or FireWire interface is so simple that you should be finished in five minutes flat.

Just in case your chosen path takes you in a different direction — namely, SCSI — I had better provide a signpost. SCSI scanners are a different animal entirely. In fact, the installation of a SCSI device takes an entire chapter to cover completely. If you picked a SCSI scanner, do *not* panic. Instead, take heart and turn to Chapter 4. Although SCSI may be a little more complex than the connections in this chapter, I make sure that you're well prepared.

The Plug and the Play

USB and FireWire are Plug and Play connections, which means that you simply connect them to your PC or Macintosh, and the computer automatically recognizes them. No hassles! If you're running out of USB ports, you can disconnect your USB scanner after you're finished with it and plug in another USB peripheral. (Note that a parallel port connection isn't Plug and Play, so if you've just connected your parallel scanner, you have to reboot your PC before you can use it.)

If you have only two USB ports and four USB devices you want to keep connected all the time, you need a USB hub. A *hub* functions just like a multiple-outlet AC adapter for your wall socket. Most hubs split a single USB port into four ports so that you can connect all four of your USB toys at one time.

Luckily, most of us can just connect and go, but if your system has a problem recognizing your USB or FireWire scanner, you may have to consider these three requirements for proper Plug and Play operation:

- ✓ **Your computer must support a Plug and Play operating system.** Most PCs built within the past five to six years support Plug and Play, so this issue probably isn't a problem. However, if your machine is older, check your manual to see whether your machine can handle Plug and Play. Older Macintosh computers built before the days of USB need an expensive SCSI-to-USB converter (or a USB card installed in one of the computer's PCI slots) to add USB support. If you have an older Macintosh, it may actually be a better idea to buy a SCSI scanner than to add USB ports.

- ✓ **Plug and Play must be turned on in your BIOS if you're using a PC.** Your BIOS holds a number of important settings that control your PC, and one of those settings usually controls whether your PC uses Plug and Play. This setting is almost always enabled by default, although not every computer is a winner. To check this setting and change it (if necessary), you must press the correct key when you first turn on your computer — usually Delete or F1. When you press this magical key, your computer displays its BIOS configuration menu. The key to press should be listed in your manual and is probably also displayed on your monitor when you first turn on your PC. If you have to turn Plug and Play on, don't forget to save your changes!

- ✓ **You must be running at least Windows 95 with USB support or Mac OS 8.** Windows 3.1 (and System 7 on the Macintosh) just don't cut it. They were designed long before the days of USB, FireWire, and Plug and Play, so if you're still running an older operating system it's time to upgrade. Also, USB support was not provided on the first versions of Windows 95, so if your Windows CD-ROM doesn't say that it has USB support built in, you should upgrade to Windows 98 (or make that determined leap to Windows XP or Windows 2000) before trying to install your scanner. Mac folks should be running at least Mac OS 8.

Before You Begin . . .

If you're sitting next to your computer desk, ready to rip open the box and scan up a storm, *stop!* — at least for a second — and let me remind you of three important steps you should take while unpacking any piece of computer hardware!

Your box is your castle!

Why do I say that your box is a castle? For a start, the original box can protect your scanner if you need to move it, but there's much more:

- ✔ If you sell your scanner later, it's generally worth more if it's in the original box.

- ✔ If your scanner is a lemon, it should be in the original box when you take it back to the store (or send it back through the mail) for a replacement.

- ✔ If you need to send your scanner back for servicing, the original box is worth its weight in gold.

How long should you keep your original box? I recommend that you hang onto it for at least a year (and toss it then only if you need the room)!

Register, register, register!

Believe me, I know that nothing is worse than filling out a registration card, besides being abducted by aliens, that is. However, I still fill out those cards and send them off, and you should too. No, I really do register my stuff. You've got to believe me!

Without registering, you may not be eligible for technical support, and you may have problems obtaining warranty or service on your scanner. You can avoid all that with a few minutes' worth of effort, so resist that strong temptation to install until you've registered.

Check for packing materials!

Don't forget to read your scanner manual to determine whether you need to remove any packing materials from the unit before you turn it on. For example, many manufacturers have a locking mechanism that holds the scanning head motionless during shipment, and you can *seriously* screw up your new hardware if you turn it on before unlocking the scanning head. Better safe than sorry later!

Docking at the Parallel Port

Did you decide on a parallel port connection for your new scanner? If so, follow these instructions to connect your scanner to your PC running Windows:

1. **Find the 25-pin parallel port on the back of your computer case. It may also be labeled Printer Port.**

2. **If your computer printer is already connected to the parallel port, disconnect the printer cable and set it aside for a moment.**

3. **Align the connector on the end of your scanner's cable with the parallel port and push it in firmly.**

   Note that the connector has angled edges to ensure that it goes on the correct way.

4. **Turn the knobs (or screws) on the connector clockwise to tighten it.**

   You may be tempted to leave the cable hanging if it's firmly connected, but it's always a good idea to take a few extra seconds to tighten things down; if you move your computer, you also risk moving the cable enough to cause an incomplete connection. (This problem is often the cause of this classic PC owner's comment: "I swear — this thing works half the time, and the other half it sits there like it's disconnected!" That's because it is.)

5. **If you also have a printer for your system, connect the parallel cable from the printer to the Printer port on your scanner.**

   This is the daisy-chaining process I speak about in Chapter 2.

6. **Connect the power cord from your scanner to the wall socket and turn your scanner on.**

7. **Restart your PC.**

USB or Bust (and FireWire, Too)

USB and FireWire scanners are installed in the same fashion, so I give my keyboard a break and show you how to connect a USB model. Refreshingly enough, both Windows and Macintosh use the same steps, too. Eerie, isn't it?

Follow these steps to install a USB scanner under Windows or Mac OS:

1. **Some USB scanners have their own cables permanently attached, and others accept standard USB cables. If your scanner fits in the latter category, connect the USB cable to the device.**

   If your scanner uses a separate cable, that cable should be included in the box.

2. **Plug in your scanner and turn it on.**

3. **Allow Windows or Mac OS to boot normally.**

   I love the phrase "boot normally." What's the definition of an *abnormal* boot? Your computer starts belching smoke, perhaps, or you find that your PC abruptly thinks it's a toaster? Such is the computing life.

4. **Plug the USB connector on the cable into a USB port (or your USB hub) on your computer.**

   Your computer suddenly notices that you've added a USB scanner and decides to welcome the new kid on the block.

5. **If your computer requests files from the manufacturer's installation CD-ROM, feed it accordingly.**

   The first time you connect your scanner, you're prompted to load the manufacturer's CD-ROM so that it can install the correct drivers. If you're installing under Windows, you may also be prompted to load your Windows CD-ROM. If you run a software installation program from the manufacturer before you connect your scanner, the program may load these drivers beforehand.

Don't Forget Your Driver!

I wonder whether Tiger Woods owns a scanner? Anyway, golf fans, the *driver* I'm talking about here isn't a club. I mean a *software driver* — a program, written by the manufacturer, that allows your operating system to use your new scanner.

As I say in the preceding section, the manufacturer of your scanner should send you a driver for use during installation — either by itself or as part of a complete software installation program. You should use this driver whenever you're prompted by Windows, as I show you in the preceding section. For most PC owners, that's it. They immediately forget about the driver and put the CD-ROM away.

That's not the end of the tale, though. If you want to become a scanning power-house, *update your drivers!* Most scanner manufacturers periodically release new versions of their drivers, which may include one or more of the following:

- ✔ Bug fixes
- ✔ Improved performance
- ✔ New features
- ✔ Compatibility with new versions of the operating system

To keep an eye on your drivers, visit the manufacturer's Web site. If you have scavenged an older scanner and can no longer find support on the Web from a scanner manufacturer, I can heartily recommend a trip to these popular Web sites:

- ✔ www.driverzone.com
- ✔ www.windrivers.com
- ✔ www.drivershq.com

These sites are great for all your hardware. You should check on video card drivers at least once a month, for example.

All right, troops, if you've had your fun with the three types of connections described in this chapter, you may want to check out Chapter 4, where I show you how to attack SCSI and win!

Chapter 4

And Then There's SCSI

I'll be honest with you. Back in the days of DOS and Windows 3.1, adding SCSI to a PC used to be somewhat akin to building the Hoover Dam with a toothbrush (and a broken one, at that). If you were a novice PC owner, nothing about a first-time SCSI installation went easily, and even a veteran hardware technician, like yours truly, often encountered problems. (I woke up screaming after more than one SCSI installation, back in those DOS years.) After you did get things working, though, you couldn't help but appreciate the performance and versatility of a SCSI system. And yes, you do pronounce it "skuzzy."

With the introduction of Windows 95 and Windows NT, however, everything changed for the better. Support for SCSI is now built into Windows XP and Windows 2000, and things are *practically* automatic. Why the one-word disclaimer? Because you still have to make decisions and perform configuration tasks correctly, or else your SCSI scanner still won't work. Unlike with USB and FireWire, things are definitely not Plug and Play in the SCSI world.

Now, nothing is wrong with simply hauling your computer, your new SCSI card, and your scanner to your local computer store and having a hardware technician do the work I describe in this chapter — or working that old family magic on a technosavvy relative and asking him or her to help. If you decide that you're ready to install SCSI yourself, however, I'm here for you.

Note: Here's an ironic side to this quest for Macintosh owners: Until about five years ago, all Macs used SCSI hard drives and offered SCSI external ports as standard equipment! With the introduction of the iMac and "blue-and-white" G3 machines, however, Apple turned away from SCSI and embraced USB and FireWire (which the company developed). Therefore, if you own a newer Macintosh computer and you're reading this chapter, you have to follow the same guidelines. Sorry about that.

In this chapter, you and I face the task of a SCSI scanner installation together, without the need for weapons or armor! King George would be proud — and probably a little surprised to boot.

The Way Things Should Work

Okay, before I tell you how to configure your SCSI scanner, I want to give you an overview of how things are *supposed* to operate in the SCSI scheme of things. In other words, if your SCSI device chain isn't working to begin with, configuring your scanner is entirely pointless.

If you're installing a SCSI adapter card only for your scanner, the scanner connects to the external SCSI port on the card. If you're also adding a SCSI hard drive or internal CD/DVD recorder, it's connected to the adapter card by a separate cable inside the computer. So far, so good.

Here's where you turn up the heat: Your SCSI scanner and adapter card (and any other SCSI devices you have) must meet two important requirements before everything hums:

- ✔ Each device on your SCSI cable (or cables) has to be "named" so that it doesn't argue with the other SCSI devices. You must therefore assign a *unique SCSI ID number* to each of your SCSI devices (including the adapter card itself). If you assign the same ID number to your scanner and your SCSI adapter card, they argue about who's who and your entire system freezes.

- ✔ The combination of a SCSI adapter card and your SCSI devices — both internal and external — is called a *chain.* Your SCSI adapter, however, doesn't know how long the chain is, so the two ends of the chain need to be terminated. You can think of a terminator as a stop sign for your SCSI adapter card. In effect, the terminator is telling your SCSI adapter card, "Hey, no other devices are connected to the chain past this point." If your SCSI devices (including the SCSI adapter itself) aren't properly terminated, your SCSI adapter card continues to search for new devices forever and your computer again freezes or steadfastly refuses to recognize your new scanner.

You probably noticed that the word *freeze* just occurred twice. A frozen system is one reason that SCSI can be so frustrating to install if you don't watch your hardware settings. If you've chosen your ID numbers carefully and set termination correctly, however, the process should go smoothly.

Look Out, It's the Terminator, er, Governor of California!

Although this particular terminator is much less dangerous than the film (or political) variety, it can still wreak havoc on your system if you don't handle it correctly on both your SCSI adapter card and your scanner.

It's an end thing, man

If you're adding just a SCSI card and a SCSI scanner, you're in luck: This SCSI chain arrangement is the simplest because you need to indicate only one external device through termination. Because your adapter card and scanner are both at an end of the SCSI chain, both need to be terminated, as shown in Figure 4-1.

Figure 4-1: This is the life — just your SCSI adapter card and your scanner.

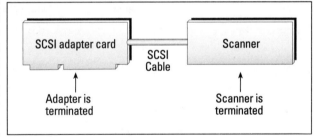

But what if you have a second SCSI device, such as a hard drive? I was afraid that you'd ask that. No, I'm kidding. It's really no big deal! Figure 4-2 shows a properly terminated chain. Note that the hard drive is internal, which puts the adapter in the middle of the new chain.

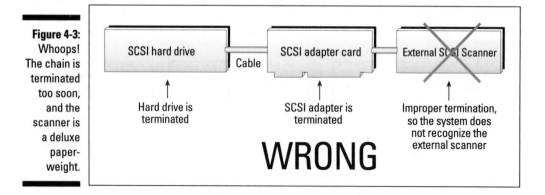

Figure 4-2:
A typical
chain with
one internal
device, an
adapter
card, and a
scanner.

Terminated   Not terminated   Terminated

Internal SCSI   SCSI adapter card   External SCSI
hard drive   scanner

Now suppose that you forget to disable the termination on the SCSI adapter.
Do not try this at home! Figure 4-3 illustrates the problem: Because the SCSI
adapter card is improperly terminated, it thinks that the chain ends with itself
and never even attempts to find the scanner. Your computer simply ignores
the scanner until you change the termination on the SCSI adapter card.

Figure 4-3:
Whoops!
The chain is
terminated
too soon,
and the
scanner is
a deluxe
paper-
weight.

SCSI hard drive   SCSI adapter card   External SCSI Scanner

Cable

Hard drive is   SCSI adapter is   Improper termination,
terminated   terminated   so the system does
                                               not recognize the
                                               external scanner

WRONG

So, what have you found out? If your computer doesn't recognize your SCSI
scanner after you connect it, incorrect termination is probably the culprit.

On a truly huge SCSI chain with five devices or more, it may help to map
things out on a piece of paper so that you can keep track of what device is at
the end of both the internal and external portions of the chain. (Of course, if
you've already installed a chain that large, you could write this chapter. But
this trick works for any chain, no matter what size, so I stick by my tip!)

Setting termination can be fun (almost)

Three methods are typically used on SCSI hardware to set termination:

- ✔ **Change the DIP switch.** Using the tip of a pencil, slide or press the switches to the combination listed in the manual to enable or disable termination. The On direction for the switch should be marked to make things easier, as shown in Figure 4-4.

- ✔ **Use the resistor pack.** Older SCSI devices usually use a resistor pack like the one shown in Figure 4-5, which is simply a plain, electronic resistor you either plug in (to enable termination) or remove (to disable termination). For directions on locating the socket, refer to the device's manual. And for goodness' sake, if you remove a resistor pack from an older SCSI device, hang onto it like it's made of pure gold! (They're practically impossible to find — take it from someone who knows.)

- ✔ **Change the jumper.** To change the ID number on a device that uses a plastic *jumper,* like the one shown in Figure 4-6, use a pair of tweezers to pull the jumper off the original set of pins and press it on the correct sequence of pins. This enables or disables a hardware feature (in this case, termination). For example, you may move a jumper connecting pins 4 and 5 to pins 5 and 6 instead.

Figure 4-4:
Two types
of DIP
switches.

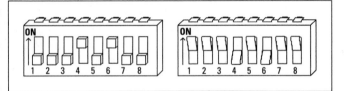

Figure 4-5:
That is one
boring
looking
resistor
pack.

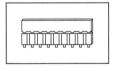

Figure 4-6:
Use a pair of
tweezers on
a jumper.

Be on your guard when installing a new SCSI toy. Some SCSI devices on the market now default to terminated status right out of the box, and you may need to disable that termination setting if you change the arrangement of your SCSI device chain.

Can I See Some ID, Please?

How do you set a unique SCSI ID for your scanner, adapter, and other SCSI devices connected to your computer? Most SCSI cards use a range of numbers from either 0 to 7 or 0 to 14, depending on the variety of SCSI you're using. The ID number 7 or 14 (respectively) is usually assigned by default to the adapter card itself. You can use all the other ID numbers for other devices, including your scanner. Your card's manual tells you which number has been reserved for your card, your scanner, and any other devices you're installing.

Figure 4-7 illustrates a typical SCSI device chain with the SCSI ID numbers set — three unique values, no problem.

Figure 4-7:
This simple
SCSI chain
is set
correctly
with three
different
IDs.

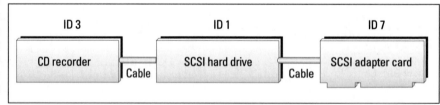

If all the defaults in this cozy arrangement are unique already, you can rejoice and count your blessings. If not, you have to change the SCSI ID numbers that match so that all the ID numbers are unique. Your SCSI adapter card should stay at the default, if possible. (If not, you probably have to run the manufacturer's software to change it.)

Many SCSI adapter cards can set their own SCSI device IDs automatically. If you have one of these and your scanner supports this feature, let the hardware do the work! Your SCSI adapter card and all your devices must support SCAM (a nasty-sounding acronym that stands for SCSI Configured Automatically).

If you have to do things manually (sigh), you use one of two methods to set the number on a device:

✔ **Spin the wheel or throw the switch.** To change the ID number, using a thumbwheel as shown in Figure 4-8, turn the wheel until the unique number you want appears. Your scanner may also have a simple sliding switch you can set.

✔ **Move the jumper.** As with termination, your SCSI device may use a jumper to select an ID number. Move the jumper to the correct set of pins, as instructed in the manual for the device.

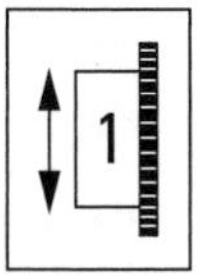

Figure 4-8:
The thumbwheel looks innocuous, but don't forget to set it!

Installing Your SCSI Card

All right! If you've been following along in this chapter, you undoubtedly have come through it unscathed, and now you're ready to grab your magnetic screwdriver and install your SCSI adapter card. Again, *make sure that you've set the termination correctly before you install the card.* Setting a jumper or adding a resistor pack is much easier now than after you've installed the card. As I mention earlier in this chapter, you should leave the SCSI ID number for your card set to the default, if possible.

Here we go! Follow these steps:

1. **Turn your computer off and unplug the power cable.**

2. **Remove the cover from your case.**

   Don't be ashamed to refer to your computer's manual to determine how to do this step. All cases used to be fastened from the back with screws; these days cases are held on with connectors of many types.

3. **Select an open adapter card slot for your SCSI card.**

   These slots are located at the back of the case. Most motherboards have a selection of PCI and ISA slots, which are different in layout. Any open slot of the right size and connector configuration works with your card.

4. **Touch the metal surface of your computer's chassis before you touch your card.**

   This step dissipates static electricity from your body, which can destroy computer components like Darth Vader destroys X-wing fighters.

5. **Remove the screw and the metal slot cover adjacent to the selected slot, as shown in Figure 4-9.**

6. **Align the card's connector with the slot on the motherboard, as shown in Figure 4-10.**

   The external connector should be visible from the back of the computer, as shown in Figure 4-11.

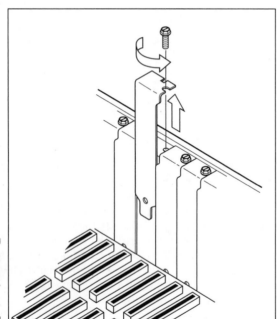

Figure 4-9:
Removing
a cover
from a slot.

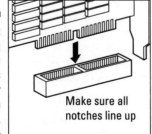

Figure 4-10:
Matching
the
connectors
on your
card with
the slot.

Make sure all
notches line up

Figure 4-11:
Hello, I'm an
external
SCSI port.

7. **Apply even pressure to the top of the card and push it into the slot.**

   With a snug fit, the bracket should be resting tightly against the back of your computer's chassis.

8. **Add the screw you removed in Step 5 and tighten the bracket.**

9. **If you have internal SCSI devices, attach the cable from the internal portion of the device chain to the proper connector on the card. Check the manual for the location of the connector.**

10. **Replace the cover on your computer.**

11. **Plug the power cord back into your computer and turn it on.**

12. **Check your card's manual for specific steps you need to follow to load the SCSI driver software for your card.**

A testing procedure should be outlined in your card's manual to help you determine whether the adapter is working properly.

Connecting Your SCSI Scanner

After your SCSI adapter has been installed and is working properly, you're ready to connect your SCSI scanner to your system. Make sure that someone is standing by with a camera to capture the moment! Here we go:

1. **Make sure that your termination and SCSI ID number have been correctly set for your scanner!**

2. **Locate the external SCSI port on the back of your case.**

   Are you adding your scanner to an existing external chain? If so, connect the cable from the scanner to the secondary SCSI port on the external device that used to be last on the chain. (Don't forget to disable termination on that device too because it's no longer at the end!)

3. **Check the alignment of the connector and the port (notice that the connector can go on only one way), and push the connector on firmly.**

4. **Lock the connector in place by snapping the wire clips toward the center of the cable, as illustrated in Figure 4-12.**

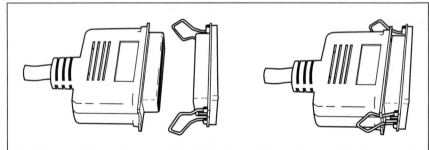

5. **Connect the scanner's power cord to the wall socket and fire that puppy up.**

Uh . . . It's Not Working

How can you tell whether your scanner is working? You may have to visit the end of the next chapter (when you've installed all your imaging software) to determine whether everything is working right. Even at this point, though, your scanner should at least be recognized and listed as a SCSI device by your card during the boot sequence (or from the SCSI testing software provided by the manufacturer of your SCSI adapter card).

If you continue to experience problems with your SCSI installation, however, here's a list of troubleshooting tips that may help you track down the cause:

- ✔ **The *T* word.** Yes, I know that you may be sick to death of my harping about termination, but check to make sure that the last devices on both the internal and external portions of the SCSI chain have been terminated. Nothing between them should be terminated!

- ✔ **Is your scanner plugged in and turned on?** Hey, it happens.

- ✔ **Are all SCSI IDs unique?** Keep your scanner from participating in petty arguments over ID numbers with other SCSI devices.

- ✔ **Have all drivers and support programs been installed?** If not, don't panic. Loading the software that your SCSI adapter card and scanner need may do the trick.

If you're still having problems after reviewing this checklist, I recommend a call to the manufacturer of your SCSI card and the scanner itself for technical support.

Chapter 5

Installing the Extra Stuff

· ·

· ·

*T*he title to this chapter says it perfectly: Although you've installed your scanner and added the necessary drivers to the computer's operating system, you have more to do:

✔ Install the right software, so you can capture an image or edit it for use in other applications.

✔ Find out about additional storage requirements and extra hardware you may need to consider.

✔ Run through a quick test of your entire installation to make sure that everything's working.

In this chapter, I lead you through the steps you need to take to finish your scanner's installation (after you've followed the instructions in Chapter 3 or Chapter 4, whichever one you may have used). I also describe some extras you may want to add that can improve your system — after which, I'm happy to say, you will *indeed* be a lean, mean scanning machine!

Installing Your Scanner Software

Because some scanner manufacturers combine their hardware drivers and scanner software in one installation, you may have already taken care of installing your scanner software in Chapter 4. If you can already run a scanning-control program (it probably looks something like the window shown in Figure 5-1), you can skip this section and move on.

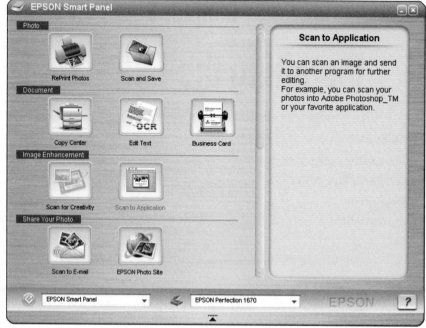

Just in case, though, let me walk you through the installation of a popular scanning-control software package — in this case, EPSON Scan and SmartPanel, which run under Windows, Mac OS 9, and Mac OS X.

Note: Remember that software that runs like a dream under Windows 98 and Windows Me may not work at all under Linux, Windows XP, and Windows 2000! If you discover that your scanner software is incompatible with your operating system, contact the manufacturer's Web site to determine whether you can download the correct version or contact technical support.

Make sure that your scanner is turned on, and then follow these steps:

1. **Load the EPSON software CD-ROM into your drive.**

   If you're running Windows 95 or a later version, Setup should start automatically. Under Mac OS, double-click the EPSON CD icon, and then double-click the EPSON installer icon.

2. **Agree with the legal stuff.**

   Read the license agreement and click Agree to continue.

3. **Choose the applications to install.**

   On the screen shown in Figure 5-2, click Custom. Then enable the check boxes for the applications you need, and click Install.

This CD-ROM has all the software and information you need for scanning. Click the Install button to get started.

☒ **EPSON Scan**

☒ **EPSON Smart Panel**

☒ **ArcSoft PhotoImpression**

☒ **Scanner Reference Guide**

If you need to reinstall individual items, click Custom.

EPSON   Custom   License   Exit   Install

Figure 5-2:
It's time
to play
Choose Your
Applica-
tions! Is that
your final
answer?

4. **Specify a program folder.**

   The EPSON default is usually a good choice here, although you can click an existing program folder if you would rather have the program icons appear in another folder.

5. **Click Next to begin copying the files.**

   Note that Epson's scanning software includes more than one application, so be prepared for a little repetition if you decide to install everything from the CD-ROM. Follow the on-screen instructions, which will vary according to what you install.

6. **Click Finish to return to Windows.**

   That's it! You've installed all the basics you need to control your scanner.

7. **When prompted to register the software you've just installed, go ahead.**

To see if your scanner software and your computer recognize your new toy, follow my simple step-by-step test later in this chapter.

Pile On an Image Editor

Okay, turn your attention to installing an image editor — and I can't think of a better example than my old friend Paint Shop Pro, which I use later to illustrate the fun you can have with your images. (In fact, I was using this great image editor when I wrote my first book in 1994!)

Note: The following step-by-step instructions apply to the commercial Windows release of Paint Shop Pro Version 8. If you're installing the trial version from this book's CD-ROM, follow the instructions displayed by the CD-ROM menu program instead. Macintosh owners can skip this section. (Or, if they really want to follow along, run Virtual PC for Mac from Microsoft and then install Paint Shop Pro!)

Follow these steps to install Paint Shop Pro:

1. **Load the Paint Shop Pro CD-ROM into your drive.**

   Under Windows 95 and later versions, the Setup program starts automatically and displays the screen shown in Figure 5-3.

2. **Click Next on the opening Setup screen.**

3. **Agree to the software license, and then click Next.**

   If you do not agree to the terms of the Jasc, Inc., software license, the installation ends. Read the terms carefully — you can scroll the window to read the entire text of the license. If you like what you've read, click the I accept the terms in the license agreement button.

4. **Enter your information, and then click Next.**

   Type your name and organization name in the appropriate fields. If you're sharing this PC with others, you can choose to install Paint Shop Pro in what I call "selfish mode" — only you get to use it — by clicking Only for me. If you're the only person who'll use this computer, just leave the option set to Anyone who uses this computer.

Figure 5-3:
Paint Shop
Pro bids you
welcome.

5. **Select a configuration.**

   You can choose whether you want the complete install (where every-thing is copied) or a custom install (where you can choose the "pieces" of the program you want to copy). See Figure 5-4. I install everything. Although a complete installation takes additional space, it includes sample files and much more functionality than attempting a bare-bones custom installation. (You may need that stuff someday.)

6. **Select a location, and then click Next.**

   On the same screen, you can specify the location where the software will be installed. I recommend that you use the default location. It helps when you upgrade or patch your copy of Paint Shop Pro — although you can click the Change button and select a new location on your hard drive, if necessary.

7. **Click Install to begin copying files.**

8. **When Setup displays a completion dialog box, click Next.**

   If you like, you can enable the check box that displays "important infor-mation" (the program's README file) or the check box that creates an icon on your desktop for Paint Shop Pro. Heck, if you like, you can even elect to run Paint Shop Pro right now!

9. **Click Finish to return to Windows.**

Now you're ready to use Paint Shop Pro later in this book for all sorts of cool stuff. But don't skip to the back of the book quite yet — you still have work to do.

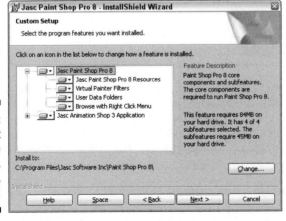

Figure 5-4:
You want
the whole
enchilada,
right? Sure,
you do!

"Do I Need More Storage?"

Most technotypes are always ready with the maxim "There's no such thing as too much storage!" Of course, that's only if you have no monetary constraints and can easily afford a 500GB RAID storage array. (Forget that I even said that.) I can't — and you don't need 500 gigabytes to use your scanner, no matter what Bill Gates tells you.

So how much is *really* enough? In this section, I'm here to help you answer the two questions that determine how much storage (and what type of storage) you may need to add to your computer system.

Query one: What's your free-space situation?

Within a certain range of free space, your system doesn't need additional storage to use your scanner. Table 5-1 is another spectacular member of my arsenal.

Table 5-1	How Much Free Space Is Enough?
Scanner Usage	*Desirable Free Space*
Light: Two or three images per week	300MB
Medium: Two images every day or so	500MB–750MB
Heavy: Five images every day or so	1GB
Bodacious: Ten images per day	2–3GB

If you're thinking that I'm padding those amounts somewhat, you're right. From experience, I'm adding extra space for conversion, image editing, and the room you need for multiple or truly huge scans. (Honestly, a scan at a very high dpi level can easily top 100MB all by itself!) Plus, I tacked on additional megabytes for those who store more than one copy of an image for different purposes.

To check how much free space a drive has under Windows XP, double-click My Computer to display your drive icons. Right-click the drive and choose Properties to display its Properties page, as you can see in Figure 5-5.

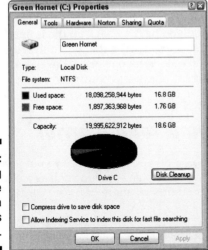

Figure 5-5:
Checking
out the free
space on a
Windows
drive.

Under Mac OS X, click the drive on the desktop and press ⌘-I to display
the General Information Pane, as shown in Figure 5-6. (Mac OS 9 works the
same way.)

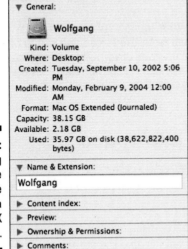

Figure 5-6:
Displaying
the
available
space on a
Mac OS X
drive.

If your system has enough free space to provide the amount of room you need without feeling pinched, you really have no need to add more storage at this time. However, remember that you have to back up those images, and you have to maintain that much space to ensure that you don't run out. Plus, you can't send an internal hard drive to someone else halfway across the country in a Priority Mail envelope.

Query two: Are you a road warrior?

Are you on the road with a laptop, or do you need to carry your images with you? If so, you'll find that an external storage solution such as a portable USB flash drive, a CD-RW drive, or a hard drive is more of a necessity than a luxury. Here are the reasons:

- **Teeny-tiny drives:** Laptop computers are notorious for their smaller-capacity hard drives (especially older models). If you've stuffed Microsoft Windows XP and Microsoft Office (or Mac OS X and Office v.X) as well as all sorts of business applications on your laptop system, you may find that you don't have enough elbowroom available for your scanning software and several high-resolution images.

- **Removable is good:** A portable drive that uses removable media — for example, a Zip drive or a CD-RW drive — is perfect for storing your images in a form you can easily carry, send through the mail, or hand to a customer.

- **To serve and protect:** Storing your images by using a CD-RW drive is a great method of protecting them from the stress and strain of a long trip (and clearing 650MB–700MB from your cramped laptop drive). As long as you protect CD-RWs from heat and scratches, they can easily resist magnetism and your average baggage-handling robot.

Three easy ways to add space

If you've decided that you need more space — or you just want the convenience and security of removable storage — you can buy one of three great solutions. To wit:

- **CD-RW:** I'll be honest: A $50 CD-RW drive is my personal-favorite pick for an image data repository. After all, I'm also the author of *CD & DVD Recording For Dummies,* 2nd Edition, conveniently published by Wiley. (Gee, what a plug!) Anyway, a CD-RW drive can provide as much as 700MB of reusable storage — and you can record both CD-ROMs for use on other computers and audio CDs to play in your car or home stereo. Both internal and external CD-RW drives are available in USB, FireWire, IDE, and SCSI configurations. Figure 5-7 illustrates a typical external CD-RW drive.

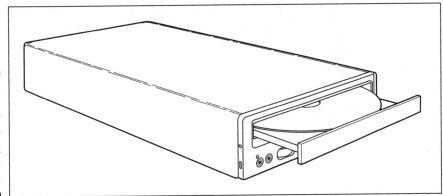

Figure 5-7:
An external
CD-RW
drive, ready
for a blank
recordable
disc.

You may be wondering why I'm not recommending a DVD+RW, DVD-RW, or DVD-RAM drive instead of an old-fashioned CD-RW recorder. Although you can indeed burn rewriteable DVDs to hold your data, I don't know of many computer owners who would actually *need* almost 5GB of space just to store scanned images and digital photographs! (Most of the semi-professional photographers I know don't need that kind of room to back up their entire *collection* of images.) Instead, I recommend that you opt for a less expensive CD-RW drive for storing images. You'll find that CD-RW discs are much cheaper than recordable DVD discs, too.

✔ **Zip:** The Iomega (www.iomega.com) Zip drive, as shown in Figure 5-8, can hold anywhere from 100MB to 750MB per cartridge (depending on the model), and the disks aren't much bigger than a typical floppy disk. However, a Zip drive can read and write data much faster than an archaic floppy drive, and the disks themselves are much sturdier and more reliable. Zip drives are available in both internal and external form, using USB, parallel port, IDE, and SCSI interfaces.

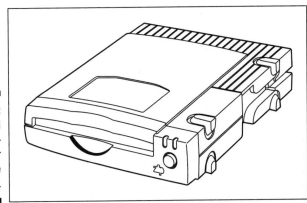

Figure 5-8:
An external
Zip drive —
a popular
storage
solution.

> ✔ **Hard drive:** Of course, nothing can stop you from adding an additional hard drive (either internal or external) or replacing your existing drive with a larger-capacity model. Hard drives are inexpensive these days, and they're available with USB 2.0, FireWire, IDE, and SCSI connections.

Printers, Printers, Printers

Granted, a printer isn't necessary to operate your scanner — but then, a helmet isn't necessary for skateboarding, either. (I know, I know, one is a piece of computer hardware and the other is a safety requirement.) The point is, if you don't already have a printer on your system, you're going to want one sooner or later. Why not use your scanner as an excuse?

In this section, I outline the features you should look for in a printer that delivers photo-quality hardcopy from your scanned images. (If you want more details about the world of computer printers for your Windows PC, pick up a copy of my book *PCs All-in-One Desk Reference For Dummies,* 2nd Edition, published by Wiley. Yes, another shameless plug!)

It has to be an inkjet (unless you're really well off)

Why do I say that you have to get an inkjet? Because two common types of printers these days weigh in at less than $300: the *inkjet* printer (which can produce both color and black-and-white pages) and the monochrome *laser* printer (which can produce only black-and-white). If you spend $600 or more on a laser printer, you can indeed buy a color laser model — but why not buy an inkjet model that delivers the same (or better) quality and save your cash for other things, such as food and your mortgage payment?

For once, that's it — no exceptions, no confusing acronyms, and no decisions to make! For virtually every home computer owner, the inkjet is simply the right choice. On the other hand, if you're buying a printer for your home office or your business and you can afford the price of a color laser, you benefit from its speed.

It has to have these features

Here's a quick rundown of the features a scanner owner should look for in an inkjet printer:

- ✔ **Resolution:** There's that word again! Like your scanner, the higher the resolution figures on your printer, the better your scanned images look on paper. I recommend a printer model with a minimum resolution of 4800 x 1200 (which should cost you less than $200), although you can pick up a 5760 x 1440 model by spending $300 instead.

- ✔ **Speed:** Everyone loves a sports car, and a printer that delivers eight pages or more per minute in color has the pickup you need.

- ✔ **Interface:** Because I go into detail about USB and parallel port connections earlier in this tome, I don't discuss the details here. Either method works, but I've been using a USB printer for three or four years now (there's a broad hint for you). Also, be sure to check out what I say in Chapter 2 about troubles you may encounter in daisy-chaining a parallel port printer and a parallel port scanner. If you have USB, save yourself the potential headache.

- ✔ **Cartridges:** If you want quality results, invest in a printer that has at least two ink cartridges onboard at all times (that's one with black ink and at least one other cartridge for color). A single-cartridge system forces you to swap the cartridges when you want to print color — not a good thing.

Better printers now have several cartridges, allowing you to change just the ink colors you need. For example, if your business logo is printed in purple on every document, you run out of magenta before any other color. In general, you'll get better results with an inkjet printer that features more colors, so I'd give the nod to a six-color inkjet printer over a four-color model.

Testing the Whole Doggone Thing

Some scanner controller programs may not test your hardware as part of the installation — therefore, in this section I lead you through a general checkup you can follow, using Paint Shop Pro under Windows XP. If you're using a Mac with the controller software that accompanied your scanner or Photoshop Elements, don't worry — you should be able to follow along.

Follow these steps:

1. **Turn on your scanner.**

   Remember that if you're using a parallel port scanner and it wasn't powered on when you booted, you should reboot after turning on your scanner so that Windows can recognize it.

2. **Place an original document in your scanner.**

   If you have a flatbed model, lift the cover and place the original face-down on the glass at the corner indicated, and then lower the cover. If you have a sheet-fed scanner, load the original into the scanner; the document should be pulled slightly into the machine by the scanner's motor.

3. **Run your scanner control program.**

   In this case, you run Paint Shop Pro by choosing Start⇨All Programs⇨ Jasc Software⇨Jasc Paint Shop Pro 8.

4. **Choose your TWAIN source.**

   In Paint Shop Pro, choose File⇨Import⇨TWAIN⇨Select source. The program displays the dialog box shown in Figure 5-9. In the example, I'll choose the Epson scanner and then click Select.

Figure 5-9: If only Samuel Clemens could see you now.

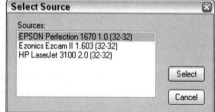

5. **Choose the Acquire command.**

   In Paint Shop Pro, choose File⇨Import⇨TWAIN⇨Acquire. Your scanner should make a noise somewhat reminiscent of a hive of angry bees being poked by a stick. Don't panic: You're not in danger of being stung; your scanner is simply resetting itself and moving the scanning head to preview the material. After the bees have escaped (whoops — sorry about that — I mean after the *preview* is finished), you should see a screen with some sort of preview window and a toolbox full of controls and buttons. (You may have to click Preview or something similar, however, before your scanner digitizes an image of the original material.)

6. **Close the scanning program.**

   Okay! If you've received similar results and a smaller version of the original document appears in the Preview window, the test is complete, and your scanner is working fine. Click File and choose Exit to leave the program and return to Windows.

If, on the other hand, things *don't* go as planned, here's a checklist of possible troublemakers:

✔ **Are the cables connected?** Check the cabling between your scanner and your computer.

✔ **Did you reboot?** You shouldn't have to reboot for a USB scanner, but a parallel port model likely needs to be restarted under Windows.

✔ **Did you unlock the scanning head?** If your scanner has a lock that can hold the scanning head in place, check to make sure that you've disabled it.

✔ **Did you choose a TWAIN source?** Your scanning software needs to know the source of the incoming image before it recognizes your scanner.

✔ **Did your scanner activate when you clicked Preview?** If so, the driver itself is probably working, so the problem may be with the scanning software. You may try removing the scanning software and reinstalling it.

If your answer is "Yes" to these questions, try running any diagnostics software that accompanied your scanner. The program may be able to determine where the problem lies. The scanner's manual also may provide the information you need.

Remember that technical support for your particular scanner should be no further than a telephone call away, so don't despair if things don't run smoothly at this point. Overlooking something when you're installing new hardware is easy to do. I also recommend visiting the manufacturer's Web site, where you may find FAQ information and troubleshooting information specific to your model.

Part III
Bread-and-Butter Scanning

The 5th Wave   By Rich Tennant

"Of course graphics are important to your project, Eddy, but I think it would've been better to scan a _picture_ of your worm collection."

In this part . . .

*F*ind out all about the basic scanning techniques you'll use each time you fire up your scanner. In addition to giving you a tutorial of the scanning process, I discuss how to scan different types of original material and how to configure your scanning software. I also give you the basics of image editing under Windows using Paint Shop Pro.

Chapter 6

Just Plain, Basic Scanning

. . . .

In This Chapter

▶ Preparing your scanner

▶ Aligning the original

▶ Configuring the settings

▶ Previewing the scan

▶ Selecting a scan area

▶ Saving the scanned image to disk

▶ Using a one-button scanner

. . . .

At this point in your quest for scanning excellence, you may have suc-
cessfully chosen a scanner, paid for it (I hope), and installed both the
necessary hardware and software. Life is good. Take a break, refill your cup
or glass, and pat yourself on the back for a job well done.

Wait! I know that I'm forgetting something. Leave it to me to get all caught up
in the hardware and software side, and . . . wait, I've got it! You probably
haven't *scanned* anything yet!

Let's fix that right now; this chapter covers all the basics you need to know to
operate your new scanner. You use the default settings and configuration in
this chapter, so don't worry about optimizing this or fine-tuning that. I wade
into those deeper waters in Chapter 7, when you find out how to scan different materials for different purposes.

Note: I have another reason for covering basic scanning in a separate section.
The default settings used by your software are probably correct for a wide
range of jobs, so what you discover here may well be all you need to know
for a typical scanning session!

Before You Scan

You should take four important steps before leaping into a scan; call them the four *C*s, if you will:

- ✔ Clean the glass
- ✔ Check the original
- ✔ Consider using a sleeve
- ✔ Clear some disk space

Skipping one or more of these steps saves you time, but you may also significantly reduce the quality of your finished image. Even if you don't take care of each one of these preparations each time you use your scanner, at least consider whether they're needed.

Clean that glass

Yes, you guessed correctly, there's a Mark's Maxim in store:

Grime, dust, and fingerprints do not add flavor or artistic touches to your scans!

This situation isn't as much of a problem with a sheet-fed scanner, but a layer of accumulated crud can cause a problem with a flatbed scanner, often resulting in visible smudges and specks that even the best image editor would find challenging to fix. The higher the resolution, the more a dirty glass affects the final image.

Therefore, I recommend that you wipe your flatbed scanner's glass at least once every five or so scans. Keep these guidelines in mind when scanning:

- ✔ **Never touch the glass.** If you're scanning a periodical, document, or page from a book, lifting the original off the glass without touching it after you're done scanning is usually pretty easy — although a photograph or card-size original is a different matter. (Don't even think about scanning a body part.) Of course, you end up with a fingerprint or two from time to time, but a good wipe takes care of such problems.

- ✔ **Keep your flatbed's cover closed.** The best way to maintain your flatbed scanner's glass is to keep the cover closed whenever possible; virtually all scanners have a padded underside that locks out dust and protects the glass from fingerprints.

✔ **Never use abrasive or household cleaners.** I can tell you about this one from experience. As a consultant, I have seen what happens when someone wiped a scanner down — *inside and out* — with a famous-name, all-purpose household cleaner. A close examination of the glass revealed dozens of tiny scratches, some as thick as a human hair. With the scanner set to average resolution, you could even see many of them in the final image. My advice to the person was to buy a new scanner. I'm also talking about typical household glass cleaners here. They may work on your kitchen window, but they can leave behind deposits that affect your scan.

✔ **Use antistatic lens or monitor wipes.** "Okay, Mark, what should I use to wipe my scanner's glass?" I'm glad you asked! I recommend one of two choices: a photographer's lens wipe or a computer monitor wipe. Whichever you choose, make sure that the product is antistatic, which helps repel dust from the surface of the glass.

✔ **Never wipe the glass in circles.** Wipe your scanner's glass directly from side to side in a straight motion, as shown in Figure 6-1. This motion helps to prevent scratches that can be caused by repeated circular buffing (or, as scanner jockeys like to call it, RCB).

Figure 6-1:
Wipe your
scanner's
glass the
cool way,
man.

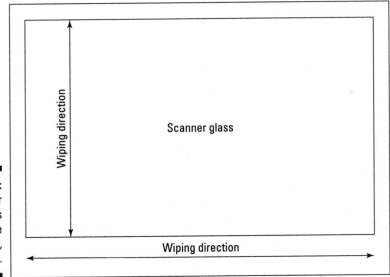

Today's computer hardware is well built, although your scanner was not manufactured to be a weight lifter. Use common sense! While you're cleaning your scanner, *never apply more pressure to your scanner's glass than you would to a typical window in your home.* And never try to scan an object that weighs more than a pound or so. If the glass shatters, it's time for a trip to the dumpster — and perhaps a trip to the hospital as well.

Check your original

You often need to prepare your original beforehand to improve the quality of your scanned image. At higher resolutions, the most minor surface imperfection is magnified, and you don't notice the problem until you've loaded the image (which usually results in having to repeat the entire scanning process, usually accompanied by a few choice epithets). Why not save yourself that trouble?

Here are a number of tips you can follow to prepare an original document:

- **Remove staples.** Three reasons apply here: First, staples can scratch your scanner's glass. If you're using a sheet-fed scanner, staples can come loose inside or cause a paper jam. And if the staple appears in the body of the document (like that Britney Spears jumbo poster in the center of your latest fan magazine), touching up the scanned image can be harder. (As you see in Chapter 11, editing out the two holes that remain when the staple is removed is easier than editing the staple itself.)

- **Smooth creases.** By smoothing down a crease or wrinkled area in the original document, you preserve the image with as little distortion as possible.

- **Add a backing, if needed.** Is your original printed on translucent paper or transparent film? If your scanner has a black backing pad, a white sheet of paper works wonders as a backing that brings out the details in the document.

- **Remove "invisible" tape, plastic wrap, and glue.** Because clear tape is nearly transparent, many scanner owners make the mistake of thinking that it doesn't need to be removed. However, your scanner is sensitive enough to record both the surface covered by the tape and its boundary, so remove it whenever possible before you scan. (Watch out because you can rip the original while removing the tape.) The same is true for plastic wrap and glue — your scanner picks them up as well.

- **Wipe off fingerprints.** Photographs pick up fingerprints like a dog picks up a bone. Fingerprints can show up against both matte and gloss finishes. You can use a soft cloth to remove fingerprints and streaks from an original before scanning it.

Consider a sleeve

Will you be using a sheet-fed scanner? If so, you probably need a transparent plastic sleeve for original items that are smaller than a sheet of paper; for example, a business card or a school photo. The sleeve looks something like a resealable plastic bag, although it's stiff enough to hold its shape while moving through the rollers of a sheet-fed scanner (as shown in Figure 6-2). Every sheet-fed scanner I've ever used has come with at least one sleeve.

Unless the manufacturer of your scanner specifically states otherwise in the manual, *never attempt to scan a small original item without a sleeve;* otherwise, you risk a paper jam (or worse).

Clear the space

Another *C* in the list of things to do before you scan stands for *clearing* — as in freeing up the necessary disk space on your hard drive to hold the images you're about to scan. Check your target drive (whether it's your main hard drive or a removable media unit, such as a USB Flash drive) and verify that you have enough room to handle the workload.

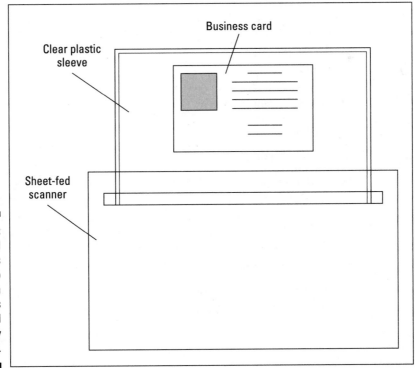

Figure 6-2: A sheet-fed scanner is poised to scan a business card protected by a sleeve.

Business card

Clear plastic sleeve

Sheet-fed scanner

As I mention earlier in this book, leaving enough space for Windows or Mac OS to use as virtual memory while you're editing your image is a good idea also. It's not uncommon for an image-editing program to lock up or close with an error when you're trying to resize a 70MB high-resolution image with only 100MB of free space on your hard drive!

How much space does an image take? Although your scanner's capture software may be able to guesstimate the final size, you really have no way to tell for sure. However, you can control five settings you make in your scanning-capture software to help keep file sizes to less than 200MB:

✔ **dpi:** At 75 dpi, an entire page of a document may take only 10MB; at 300 dpi, that figure jumps to more than 100MB. (That's why I've never scanned at the maximum interpolated mode with my scanner. I've never needed such a level of detail, and you can imagine how big a 9600 dpi image may be!)

✔ **Selected area:** Later in this chapter, in the section "Choosing a Chunk," I show you how to specify exactly how much of your original document you want to scan. Scan only what you need, to save yourself both time and hard drive space!

By the way, a common misconception exists that scanning a blank piece of paper produces a very small file. After all, nothing is on it, right? Ah, but don't forget: Unless you're using an OCR program, your faithful scanner doesn't care about what's on the paper and doggedly spends many, many megabytes of space and lots of wasted time digitizing that blank page! You'll probably end up with an artistic (and realistic) 20MB image of a blank piece of paper.

✔ **Color depth:** If your scanning software allows you to choose the color depth of your final image (and most do), you can reduce the size of the file by choosing 8-bit or 16-bit color rather than 24-bit (or higher) color. Remember, though, that anything less than 24-bit color doesn't look as good on paper or on your screen, so you may not want to use this trick often. It comes in handy when you're scanning material for the Web or your OCR application.

✔ **File format:** I cover file formats in depth in Chapter 10. Suffice it to say at this point that the JPEG (or JPG) image format is always the best choice when space is at a premium.

✔ **Scale:** The scale of your image determines the size of the finished scan. I give you more info on this topic in the "Make with the Settings" section, later in this chapter.

If you do need to clear space on your drive, it's a good time to remove things such as applications you no longer need and accumulated Internet temporary files. Some programs can help you free up room on your system: Windows folks can use CleanSweep from Symantec or the Windows Disk Cleanup wizard, and Mac owners can turn to Spring Cleaning from Aladdin.

Lining Things Up

All right, it's time to ready your scanner! Go ahead and turn it on, and run your scanning-capture software on your computer. After everything is on and idling nicely, I show you how to align your original for the best scan.

If you have a flatbed

Aligning an original on a flatbed scanner is much like using a copy machine: One corner of the glass is designated what I call "home corner," and one of the edges of your document or object should always meet this corner as closely as possible (as shown in Figure 6-3). Lift the cover of your scanner and look for markings on the area surrounding the glass that help you locate the home corner on your particular model.

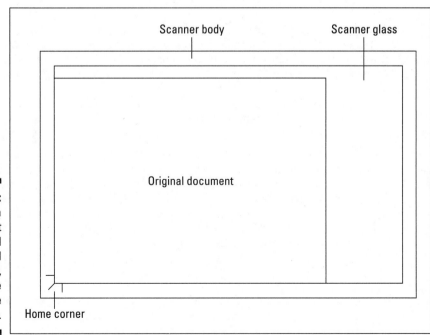

Figure 6-3:
Aligning a document on a typical flatbed scanner, using the home corner.

Scanner body

Scanner glass

Original document

Home corner

If your document overlaps the glass, it's decision time:

- ✔ If the area you want to scan still fits completely within your model's scanning range, you have to adjust the original so that the material you want to scan is positioned over the glass.

- ✔ If you need to scan the entire area of the original and it's larger than your scanner can accommodate (usually the case with older hand scanners), try the next best thing: Scan the original in "pieces" (using multiple scanning sessions) to produce a number of images and then use your image editor to "stitch" them together. However, I have to warn you that it doesn't always work perfectly.

Make sure that you close the cover carefully to avoid moving the original. Many scanners feature an adjustable cover that can be "raised" for thick items, such as books and three-dimensional objects.

Ever wondered whether you really need to lower the cover on your scanner before you use it? The answer is definitely "Yes!" Leaving the cover up can result in washed-out colors or a contrast and brightness problem. Close the cover, even for originals that completely cover the glass.

If you have a sheet-fed

Aligning an original on a sheet-fed scanner is different than doing so on a flatbed scanner. Naturally, you're not going to "overlap" the scanning surface, although it's still possible to feed the original incorrectly. Keep these alignment tidbits in mind:

- ✔ **Face the document in the right direction.** Your scanner's manual provides more information about which direction the original should be facing when you feed it.

- ✔ **Don't feed an original askew!** Avoid tilting your document when you're feeding it into the scanner. Loading an original as shown in Figure 6-4 is bound to cause problems (ranging from a bad scan to an outright paper jam, which is harder to solve and potentially more damaging to the unit than a similar paper jam in a printer). As shown in Figure 6-5, the orientation of the original should be as straight as possible, even if the item being scanned has irregular edges.

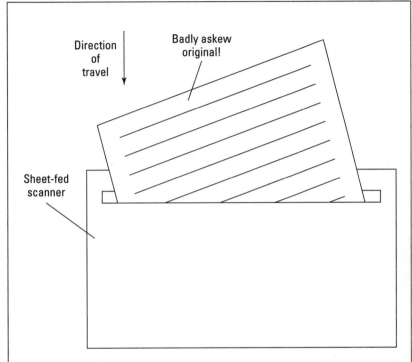

Direction of travel

Badly askew original!

Sheet-fed scanner

Figure 6-4:
Never load
a tilted
original into
a sheet-fed
scanner.

Remember that you may have to press a button to feed the original on a sheet-fed scanner, especially if you're the proud owner of a multifunction (or all-in-one) unit that can print, scan, copy, and fax. The manual explains what you need to do when you're loading your document.

If you have something else

Using a negative scanner? These scanners are generally easy to load because slides and photographic negatives are always uniform in size and shape; you typically mount the original in a sliding tray, or you may slide the original into a slot on the front of the machine. If your scanner loads originals through a slot, remember the same rule that applies to sheet-fed scanners: Don't feed an original askew.

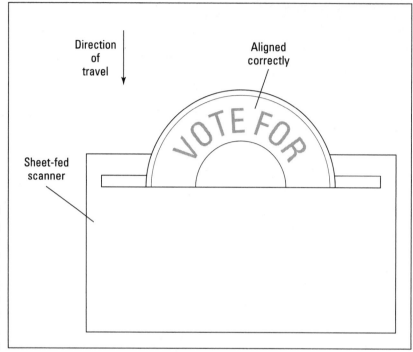

Figure 6-5:
Even an
irregularly
shaped
original
works fine
when fed
correctly.

On the other side of the coin, you have no need to align a handheld or pen scanner. You move the scanner itself across the surface of the original (usually matching the edge of the region you want to scan with a pointer or marker of some kind on the body of the unit). With one of these scanners, it's necessary to remember only the edge of your last image if you're "stitching" together multiple scans. As I say earlier in this chapter, lining up and connecting multiple scans is both tiresome and less precise than using a flatbed scanner, so I'm assuming that you're a road warrior and using your hand scanner with a laptop.

If someone has given you an older hand scanner from the misty dawn of time (that is, the early 1990s), use it with your laptop while you're on the road, or use it to scan barcodes. However, if you want to scan a full page of text or graphics at a high resolution, I *implore* you to invest in a flatbed model. Join the rest of us in Convenience City and leave the hassle behind! Even the latest-model hand scanners can't deliver the color depth or resolution of a modern flatbed scanner. And scanning an original any larger than about 4 inches across is likely to drive you nuts, which is why hand scanners are now used exclusively for barcodes or scanning a few lines of text at a time for OCR.

Make with the Settings

With the original aligned and your cover closed — that is, if you have a cover — it's time to turn your attention to the software end of things. Your first task at the keyboard is to properly tune a handful of settings that control your scanning-capture software. As I mention earlier in this chapter, the default settings may work fine, although I want to cover the bare necessities here just in case. (That's the kind of guy I am. I'm the type who has an eyeglass screwdriver handy when he needs it.)

In this section, I use the Windows version of Hewlett-Packard's Director application in league with an HP ScanJet 5530 scanner. Believe it or not, the Mac version of this great scanner-control program is similar to the Windows version; this makes it especially valuable to us rogues of the computer world who give both platforms equal time. Therefore, you should be able to follow along easily if you use this scanning application, no matter which breed of computer you favor.

If you use a different brand of scanner and don't use this program, this discussion is still valuable, so don't go away! Your program's buttons, levers, dials, and associated sliding things may be called something slightly different, but they should be there somewhere and have the same effects on your scanned image. If you need help in locating a particular sliding thing, use the program's online help or check the software's manual.

Note: If you have a one-button scanner, you can skip forward to the section "Look, Ma — One Button!" After all, most one-button models try to automate things as much as possible, so you may not have to change any settings or select a region to scan. I prefer that you go ahead and read through this section, however, because you have to use these procedures if you switch to your scanner's more advanced modes (where everything automatic suddenly becomes manually controlled, and you separate the tourists from the locals).

For my first scanning demonstration, I chose a common original: a color print from my collection. This print is a great photo of a secluded mountain stream in Rocky Mountain National Park . . . and brother, that water is clear and *cold*. I show you how to scan this photograph in preparation for sending it acrossthe Internet through e-mail to a friend. Follow these steps to choose your settings:

1. **Click the HP Director icon on your desktop to run the program.**

   Like most of today's easy-to-use scanning-control programs, HP Imaging Director first displays a task-oriented quick menu (Figure 6-6) to lead you through common procedures, such as scanning a document, printing a copy, or sending a scanned image through the Web or as an e-mail attachment.

Figure 6-6:
Your
scanner
asks, "So
what shall
we do
today?"

2. **This time, we're intent on scanning an image and saving it to disk, so click Scan Picture.**

   After making that curious noise, your scanner makes a quick pass over the original and the window shown in Figure 6-7 appears; notice that the program has already selected the area of the original it thinks you want to scan. (Don't worry if the selected region surrounded by the animated dotted rectangle is incorrect. Later in this chapter, in the "Choosing a Chunk" section, I show you how to select what you want.)

Figure 6-7:
The HP
Image
Director is
ready for
action.

3. Choose the Output Type menu item and select your first setting.

This step specifies what type of original material you're scanning and helps the program determine a default for the other settings. In this case, choose Millions of Colors — we're scanning a color photograph, and we want the best possible image quality.

The option you'll likely choose most often is Millions of Colors (also referred to as true color, 16 million colors, or 24-bit), but you have other color options. For a smaller file size — or for better results when you view the image on a PDA or cell phone screen — choose the Full 256 Colors, 8-Bit option. Webmasters can specify a Web Color Palette option that's also 256 colors or 8-bit (but displays better in a Web browser). The 256-color System Palette option is optimized for use with older versions of Windows, and the 256 Gray Shades option is good for scanning grayscale or halftone images. Finally, you can even choose the old-fashioned Black & White option for text documents (I guess some things never change).

The more colors, the larger the image file. If you want your digital image to look its best, however, choose your program's True Color setting or Millions of Colors setting.

4. Choose Advanced⇨Resolution, and set the dpi range for your image.

You can select from a wide range of dpi settings or simply type a value to set your own dpi. By default, Director assigns what it thinks is the best value; to reset your dpi to this value, click the Auto button. Because this image is destined for display on the screen (and we want a smaller file size so that the image can be sent through e-mail), click the drop-down list box and set the dpi to 75.

5. Choose Basic⇨Resize, and specify the size of the scanned image.

By default, the image Output Dimensions are set to inches, but you can switch to pixels by clicking the Units drop-down list box. To maintain the aspect ratio of the image (which is always a good idea, unless you actually want to distort the appearance of the image), click the nifty padlock icon next to the Output Dimensions to "lock" them.

The Scale Output button determines the relative size of the scanned image relative to the original. Leave this button set to 100% unless you're scanning something particularly small, such as a postage stamp, where you need to dramatically increase the size of the original in the scanned image.

That's all you need to set — at least for a quick scan using the basic settings. At the bottom of the Director window, you see a summary box that presents the following settings information:

✔ The output type you chose

✔ The output dimensions you chose

> ✔ The approximate size (just an estimate) of the image file to be created with these settings
>
> ✔ The dpi you chose
>
> ✔ The scale you chose

You may have noticed that you didn't mess with the other settings in the Basic and Advanced menus. These are tricks that I describe in detail in Chapters 8 and 9. Usually, you don't even need to adjust them anyway, as long as your original is sharp and the colors are bright. Remember, we're talking basic scanning here. Most of the scans you'll perform will need only the tweaks I've just described.

Let me mention one more menu item in this section. The Reset Tools item under the Basic menu resets all the values the program uses to their defaults. So if you need to start over, choose Reset Tools to clean your digital slate.

Previewing on Parade

That small thumbnail image of your original is called a *preview*. You use it to select the region of the original you want to scan. However, it doesn't have to stay thumbnail sized. Director allows you to zoom in on the original for a closer look, which also gives you finer control over the region you select. For example, you may want to scan a single piece of clip art from an entire sheet. Why scan that entire page when you can simply zoom in on the one drawing you want and select it?

To zoom in on your original, click the magnifying glass with the plus sign. The more you click, the more you zoom. To zoom out, click the magnifying glass with the minus sign.

To rotate the preview image, click the counterclockwise and clockwise buttons at the left of the window (above the zoom controls); the preview rotates 90 degrees in the desired direction.

Figure 6-7, presented previously, shows the default preview. Compare that figure with Figure 6-8, in which I've clicked the zoom key and clicked the rotate counterclockwise button to center the preview on the center section of the stream so that I can scan just that area of the original photograph.

If you decide that you need to switch originals, you don't have to restart Image Director to preview the new material. Just click the New Scan button, and your scanner makes another pass and displays the new original.

Figure 6-8:
With the
Zoom
feature, you
can get up
close and
personal
with your
preview.

Choosing a Chunk

Okay, you've set everything and your preview is centered right where you need it. But what if the animated dotted box (called a *selection box*) is not over the right area? Director takes its best shot at guessing what you want to scan on your original, although that's sometimes not the right region. You can select a new square or rectangular region of the original to scan in three ways:

✔ **Click and drag the existing selection box:** If the box is the right size and shape but in the wrong place, you can move it to a new spot on the original. Move your mouse cursor over the box, and it turns into a special cursor that points in all four directions. Click and drag the cursor to move the box where you want it, and then release the mouse button to drop the box in its new location.

✔ **Resize the existing selection box:** If the box is in the right place but too big or too small, you can resize it. Move your mouse cursor over the edge of the box you want to change. This time, the cursor turns into a special cursor that indicates the two directions in which that edge can move. If you click over a corner, you can resize both edges (just like you can resize a window in Windows or Mac OS). Click and drag the cursor to move the edge or corner to the desired size and release the mouse button.

✔ **Create a new selection box:** You can also discard the existing selection box and create a new one. Move your mouse cursor anywhere outside the box, and it turns into a crosshair. Click and drag to open a new box.

In most cases, you simply want the selection box to cover the entire original from edge to edge, and this is the assumption the program makes when it creates the default selection.

Doing the Scan Thing

Houston, everything is go! The original is in place with the cover down, the settings are correct, and you've chosen the region of the original you want to scan. It's time to do the Scanner Dance. Follow these steps:

1. **Click the Accept button at the bottom of the Director window.**

   The program displays a progress bar to update you on what's being done.

2. **When Director asks whether you need to perform another scan, click No.**

   In this case, we're scanning only one image. Director loads the Photo & Imaging Gallery application, a program that HP supplies with its scanners. If you've used Photo Gallery 4 from Jasc Software, you'll be very comfortable with this application. You can use Photo & Imaging Gallery to view, organize, and send your scanned images to different applications, such as your printer, your e-mail program, or your Web site.

3. **Double-click the thumbnail for the image you've just scanned.**

   By default, Director saves your new image in JPEG format in your Windows XP My Pictures folder. (Under Mac OS X, the image is stored in your Pictures folder in your Home folder.) Figure 6-9 illustrates the thumbnail that represents the new image. When you double-click the image, it appears in HP's Image Editor application, which can fix a number of problems that commonly crop up in scanned images. (Pun intended.)

However, you don't really need to use the HP Photo & Imaging Gallery just to view your image. To admire your new work of art in Windows Explorer (as shown in Figure 6-10) or Mac OS Finder, just double-click the image icon. This trick works if you're running Windows 98 (or later) or Mac OS 8 (or later). Figure 6-10 shows off my image in the Windows XP Picture view, ready for my e-mail Outbox. The image is a whopping 400K, so it fits as a message attachment with room to spare!

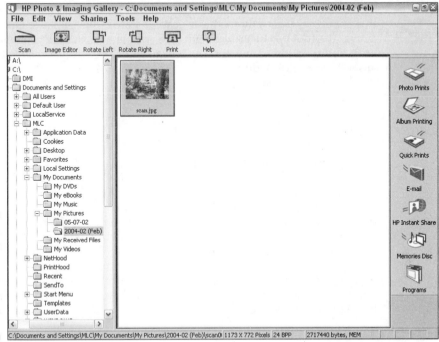

If your first scanned image isn't quite perfect, don't worry. Remember that this chapter covers only the basic scanning procedure. In later chapters, I cover the tool you can use to enhance your images and fix problems (both great and small) in your work: the image editor, tool of scanning veterans around the world!

Look, Ma — One Button!

Before I close this chapter, I want to talk about one-button scanning, which I introduce in Chapter 2. In purely automatic mode, which is the default for most of these scanners, you can forget most of the steps I cover in the last four sections, if you've read them. The software for a one-button scanner takes care of configuring settings and usually checks the entire original to make sure that all text and graphics are included, so you probably don't even have to select a region to scan.

Although the basic scanning procedure naturally varies by manufacturer, here's a typical scanning procedure on a one-button model after you've loaded the original document and pressed the automatic scanning button on the scanner:

1. A program running in the background in Windows or Mac OS detects that the button has been pressed and loads the scanner's control software.

2. The scanning software automatically previews the original and selects what it considers the major area (or areas) of text and graphics.

3. At this point, you may be given the chance to adjust the selection box to better fit your needs, or the software may blissfully continue without any intervention from you. (This option depends on the manufacturer's idea of what the phrase "one-button" *really* means.) You may be able to configure your scanner software to work both ways.

4. After the scanning has finished, the software usually concludes with one of five actions (depending on what you pressed and how you've configured the scanning software):

   • The program displays the Save As dialog box. You're given the chance to save the image to disk.

   • The program runs a word processor. As I mention earlier in this chapter, many of these scanners advertise that they can create a nearly perfect duplicate of a printed document as a document in your word processor (using simple scanning for images and a simple OCR program for the text). With this option, your computer runs Word, WordPerfect, AppleWorks, or a page-layout program and "pours" the document directly into it. From there, you can modify and edit the document just as you would do with a page you write yourself.

- The program creates a copy. If your scanner has a one-button copy function, the image it scans should shoot directly to your printer without any intervention from you.

- The program runs a fax program. Some scanners deliver one-button faxing as well, although this isn't, of course, a completely automatic procedure. You press the fax button on your scanner, which runs your fax program and sends the document, using your computer's modem.

- The program runs an e-mail program. Here's another wrinkle on the one-button idea: Pressing the e-mail button on your scanner runs your e-mail program and attaches the scanned image to a new message. Neat!

All this is neat, as long as your scanner's software allows you to do more. If you find yourself unable to use a fully automatic, one-button scanner in other chapters because of the programs you received with it, use another TWAIN-compatible scanning-capture program (such as Photoshop, Photoshop Elements, or Paint Shop Pro 8). You still have your buttons when you need 'em, but you can also explore the advanced image-editing and creative techniques I demonstrate in Chapters 9, 11, and 13.

Chapter 7

Examining Your Original: The Sequel

. . . .

In This Chapter

▶ Understanding how originals differ

▶ Scanning line art

▶ Scanning color and grayscale photographs

▶ Scanning halftone images

▶ Scanning 3-D objects

▶ Scanning text

. . . .

I t's time to expand your horizons and move into more advanced material. Translated, that reads "Ready for another of my maxims?" Okay, here it is:

All originals are not scanned equally.

(If Shakespeare himself had owned a scanner, he would have included this weighty thought in one of his plays.) Different types of original material need different treatment to provide the same quality in the finished image. For example, if you use the same settings when scanning three different originals — a color photo, a pencil drawing, and a military shoulder patch, for example — you end up with three dramatically different results, and two of those images are probably of poor quality.

In Chapter 6, I tell you that you should always examine your original. In this chapter, I discuss how to expand that examination a step further than simply checking for tape, staples, or creases by studying the media used to create the image itself.

So What's the Difference?

Why do originals created using different media have different requirements? You can sum up the variation between media by using three criteria:

- **Shading:** Shades, tones, graduations — call them what you will, some originals have them (such as photographs) and others don't (such as line drawings).

- **Texture:** If you're scanning a three-dimensional object — and by that term, I mean any original that's not as perfectly flat as a plain piece of paper — it likely has some sort of texture. A certain depth to the texture is desirable, although a texture that's too deep can produce heavy shadows. Also, if a portion of the original is significantly farther away from the scanner glass, such as a dinner plate, you end up with fuzzy spots in your image. (Why scan a dinner plate? I've done it: Ever attempt to describe a china pattern that's not in the book?)

- **Color:** Originals have more variety than you may think when it comes to color. Besides handling just simple color and black and white (or *monochrome,* as graphic artists call it), you also have to deal with grayscale and halftones. I get into these topics later in this chapter, in the "Halftone Images" section.

Three scanner settings also vary between these different media. (Weird how that works out that way, doesn't it? Perhaps those theories of visits from ancient astronauts have some truth to them.) The settings are shown in this list:

- **Color depth:** You may have read the point I make previously in this book about scanning a blank piece of paper in stunning 24-bit color. You get a huge image file filled with more than 16 million possible shades of white, of which your image likely uses only a handful. The same rule applies here: If you're working with a monochrome original (such as a black-and-white line drawing or a blueprint), you don't need the same color depth as in a color photograph. That savings translates into a smaller image file at any resolution.

In one case, more colors with a monochrome document may make sense: You can often improve the performance of an OCR program slightly by scanning a page of text in 24-bit color, *if* the original page was printed on an inkjet printer. Why? Two reasons: First, a typical inkjet printer often doesn't produce a true black, especially if you're printing black with a color cartridge on an older printer. Second, subtle differences in color often exist across the text on a page, especially if your printer's cartridge is low on ink. On the other hand, because a laser printer produces a true black character, you can use fewer colors when you're scanning OCR text from a page produced by a laser printer.

✔ **dpi:** It's generally true that the higher the dpi, the better the image — but what if you're going to view your scanned image only on your computer's monitor? Most computer monitors can display a maximum of around 72 to 90 dpi (depending on how much you spent on that high-resolution screen). Anything more is overkill.

✔ **Color balance:** The third setting that helps tailor your scan to your original image is a relatively new setting in consumer-level scanning software. If your scanning application does not offer this setting, you may have to adjust color balance with an image editor after the scan is complete. If your original image includes colors that are not true to life — for example, a color print taken under harsh fluorescent light, a faded or sepia original, or a printed image produced without color correction — you need to adjust the balance. This process is handled differently depending on the software: Some programs can perform automatic color balancing, others let you make the changes manually, and a few require you to specify the color of absolute white in your image before you can make adjustments.

That covers the scanning settings used in this chapter. One or two affect only one type of original material, and I point those out when necessary.

Without further ado, then, I want to cover each major type of original material you're likely to encounter and demonstrate how to configure your scanning software for the best possible results with each material. (If you don't want me to do this for some reason — for example, if you were frightened by a piece of line art when you were a child — you can certainly turn to Chapter 8, although you'll miss some great stuff.)

Line Art

By the strictest definition of the graphics world, *line art* is material drawn in black and white with no shading or tones, like the ink-on-plain-paper masterpiece shown in Figure 7-1. (I'm no critic, but I know what I like, and anything my kids turn out is art.)

However, what's interpreted as line art in the real world can include a host of other possibilities:

Figure 7-1:
Look out,
Leonardo —
a piece of
"true" line
art.

- ✔ **Blueprints and diagrams:** If you scan traditional white-on-blue blueprints, you should follow the same guidelines for line art.

- ✔ **Charcoal, felt-tip pen, and colored pencil:** Regardless of the two colors used, I usually scan these as line art (as long as the contrast between the colors is high).

- ✔ **Cartoons:** A cartoon produced without shading (for example, a classic *Dilbert* or *Peanuts* cartoon) looks best when it's scanned as line art.

Perhaps a better definition of line art would be an original with images drawn in contrasting colors, featuring crisp borders, heavy lines, and little or no shading. With this definition, the familiar graphics of a playing card that I've scanned in Figure 7-2 also (rightly) qualifies as line art.

Figure 7-2:
Although it's
not black
and white,
this playing
card counts
as line art.

Here are the guidelines you should follow in choosing settings for scanning line art:

✔ **Color depth:** A maximum of 256 colors (or 8-bit color) should be suffi-cient for virtually all line art. As I mention earlier in this chapter, this setting should also result in a smaller image file.

✔ **dpi:** I recommend a setting of 72 dpi for on-screen display. If you're sending your image to your inkjet or laser printer, 200 to 300 dpi is a good pick.

✔ **Color balance:** If you follow that strict definition of line art, color bal-ance is not applicable: You have only black lines on white or one color on another.

However, if you're scanning an original that uses multiple colors on a white background that's really *not* white — perhaps it's oyster or cream — you may need to adjust the color balance if you want a true white background. I run into this extra step most often with originals destined to be transparent GIF images for Web pages. For example, if the page has a pure white background, an image scanned without this correction is surrounded by an obvious border of a slightly darker white.

Color and Grayscale Photographs

Full-color photographs are probably the most popular class of originals for the majority of people. This category includes

- **Film prints:** Before digital cameras dropped so much in price, I got several years' worth of experience in scanning color prints. For example, Figure 7-3 is the scan I made of a scenic photograph I took atop Hoover Dam.

   Note: Please bear with me for just a second — it's time for another plug! If you want a complete guide to digital cameras for the novice or intermediate photographer, pick up a copy of my *Hewlett-Packard Digital Photography Handbook,* published by Wiley.

- **Continuous-tone images:** This type covers everything from originals created by expensive, thermal wax printers to oil paintings. *Continuous tone* means that the colors and detail in the image are, well, blended and continuous! To be more specific, a continuous-tone image isn't created by grouping dots together — that's the definition of a halftone original, which I cover later in this chapter, in the section "Halftone Images." Most photographs produced in books and magazines are halftone images. As you may have guessed, inkjet and laser printers don't fall into the continuous-tone category because they create images by using dots.

- **Slides, transparencies, and negatives:** As I mention earlier in this book, you need either a negative scanner (for just slides and photograph negatives) or a slide/transparency adapter (for all three types of transparent originals) to properly scan these materials. The reason? Slides, transparencies, and negatives have to be illuminated differently than an opaque original; hence, the hardware.

If you're configuring your scanning software to capture a color photograph, I recommend these settings:

- **Color depth:** Here's where you need the full-color-depth firepower of your scanner. Use the true color setting, which should result in a minimum of 24-bit color. Naturally, your image file will be larger, but that's the penalty you pay for a photo-quality color scan.

Figure 7-3:
A scanned
image from
a color
photograph.

✔ **dpi:** For the same reasons as line art, a setting of 72 dpi for on-screen display (which includes Web page display) is fine for your color photographs. However, I always recommend at least 300 dpi for a good-quality scan, and I have taken my system to as high as 1200 dpi for some materials.

✔ **Color balance:** If the colors in the original are appreciably out of balance (a green cast to a person's face, perhaps), it's time to correct the color balance in the finished image. As I said earlier in this chapter, you may be able to accomplish this balance by using your scanning software; you can also look for a control that sets white balance or performs hue correction. If your scanning software can't correct a color-balance problem, you have to load the scanned image into your image editor and fix it there.

I should also mention grayscale photographs. They're the familiar black-and-white film counterparts to the color photographs I've been discussing. Grayscale images also provide continuous tones, although the tones are 256 shades of gray (8-bit) rather than color. Grayscale images can also be printed with colored inks (typically gray, sepia, or blue as well as black) as a special effect. These "tinted" images are called *duotones*.

✔ **Color depth:** If your scanner allows you to capture grayscale as a selection for color depth (for example, the Microtek software I use offers Gray as a scan type), you should use this setting. However, if you're forced into a color depth, I recommend that you use 24-bit color and convert the image to true grayscale, using your image editor.

✔ **dpi:** dpi settings for grayscale remain the same as with a color photograph; use 72 dpi for on-screen display and at least 300 dpi for a good-quality scan for printing or archiving.

✔ **Color balance:** Naturally, you don't have to bother with balancing color in a grayscale image, although you may decide to experiment with brightness, contrast, and gamma correction. They can have a similar effect on the shades of gray. For example, you may use a combination of gamma correction and contrast to rescue an original grayscale image that's overexposed — too light. (Read more about this subject in Chapter 8.) Unfortunately, if your grayscale image is underexposed — too dark — you may not be able to save it at all because increasing the brightness doesn't add detail to a muddy image.

Halftone Images

As I explain in the preceding section, halftone images are composed of thousands of tiny dots of varying sizes, which the human eye perceives — at least, at a distance — as a continuous range of color or monochrome shades. (Notice that I don't call them photographs. This distinction helps keep halftone originals separate from the continuous-tone originals I discuss earlier in this chapter.)

Here are three classic examples of halftones:

- ✔ **Output from your inkjet printer:** If you read Chapter 5, do you remember that I talk about resolution when I discuss printers? Like your monitor, today's inkjet printers produce an image with dots. These dots are so fine that they're smaller than the point of a pin, but they're there.

  "Wait just a second, Mark — you said a page or so ago that something called a thermal wax printer could print a continuous-tone photograph! How does it do that?" The answer is in the semifluid nature of the wax dye that's applied to the paper. The dye flows together to blend into continuous shades, whereas the ink from an inkjet printer dries immediately. (This is the reason that printing color images on your inkjet using glossy photo paper produces better results: The ink spreads slightly before it dries instead of soaking into the paper.) Of course, a good-quality thermal wax (or dye sublimation) graphics printer is liable to set you back $500 or more, so you pay for that quality!

- ✔ **An image in a newspaper or magazine:** Does Figure 7-4 look familiar? It's a magnified example of the kind of halftone you've come to expect from the front page of your newspaper — no continuous tones here! The glossy pages of your favorite magazines are also halftones, although you may have to use a good magnifying glass to see them (depending on the quality of the paper and the type of press that produced the page).

Figure 7-4:
Nice kitty —
at least,
I *think* it's
a kitten.

✔ **Images in books:** That's right — check out any of the figures in this book with a magnifying glass (except for 7-4, or else you'll wear your eyes out). Of course, the presses that produce the book you're holding are state of the art, so most of us never notice.

Scanning a halftone image calls for these settings:

✔ **Color depth:** Like a continuous-tone photograph, a halftone benefits from 24-bit color. Anything less can accentuate the dots in the original and produce a truly ghastly image. (I've seen this done on purpose, although only as a special effect!)

✔ **dpi:** Here's where things get dicey. Because of the dots that make up a halftone image, scanning at too high a resolution *degrades* the quality of the image rather than improves it. I typically choose 150 dpi or less when I'm scanning a halftone. Depending on the quality of the original, you may have to experiment before you hit on a value that properly preserves the appearance.

✔ **Color balance:** Although the shades of color aren't continuous, they can still be fine-tuned in a color halftone, using the same techniques as in a photograph. In other words, use the built-in color-balance controls in your scanning software or the color-balance controls offered by your image editor.

3-D Objects

You may not scan solid 3-D objects very often — how many people buy a scanner to create gargantuan, high-resolution images of a toothbrush or a floppy disk? However, scanning an object can also save you the trouble of digging through your collection of clip art, trying to find the perfect picture. If the object is sitting on your desk, why not scan your own clip art?

Friends of mine have used their scanners to capture images of items for eBay auctions and to create photos for their home inventory records. A woman I know even uses her scanner as a tool in her hobbies by scanning interesting fabric patterns and objects for her photo collages. In fact, forget what I said a second ago. If you don't have a digital camera, you *may* end up scanning solid, 3-D objects often!

Are you the proud owner of a sheet-fed scanner? **IF SO, SKIP THIS SECTION.** (By the way, that's the only sentence in this entire book that's completely capitalized.) No matter how tempting, scanning anything that's not perfectly flat and thicker than card stock is likely to result in a *seriously damaged* sheet-fed scanner!

What makes a suitable object for scanning? Three general requirements apply:

✔ **At least one reasonably flat surface:** You won't be scanning the Venus de Milo any time soon — Figure 7-5 illustrates what happens when you try to capture a 3-D figure with deep crevices. (My bust of Samuel Clemens, also known as Mark Twain, provides me with inspiration while I'm writing.) A scanner can't focus on surface details that are far removed from the glass, so your object needs one recognizable surface that can rest fairly close to the glass, such as the floppy disk shown in Figure 7-6. Use a digital camera for the Venus.

Figure 7-5: Sorry, Sam. You're my favorite author, but you're just not scanner material.

High Density

Figure 7-6:
Hey,
remember
when
software
used to
come on
these?

    ✔ **Surface detail:** "Ach, Cap'n, I just don't think the scanner can see any-
    thing. I need more power!" Scotty's got a point: Without at least some
    surface detail, your scanner can't capture anything more than a general
    outline. As an example, scanning a bar of soap gives you a really nice
    rectangle, and because it has little or no surface detail, that's it. Scanning
    the label on a compact disc, on the other hand, captures the text and
    design. Other favorite originals include textured paper products and
    cloth, like the woven item shown in Figure 7-7.

    ✔ **Little or no reflectivity:** Even a perfectly flat original with reflective
    regions causes some problems because the reflected light tends to over-
    whelm the scanner's sensor head, producing phantom light spots in the
    scanned image (an effect I like to call *white-out*). Therefore, scanning a
    highly reflective 3-D item, such as a piece of jewelry or a shiny toy, defi-
    nitely doesn't work. Adding distance to the mix creates a mixture of
    shadows and reflections as the scanner head moves across the original.

If you do have to scan an original with reflective areas, you can use one of
two workarounds to avoid white-out. You can reduce the brightness setting in
your scanner software — or, if you don't need the reflective area, simply
resize the selection box and don't scan that area.

Figure 7-7:
Textiles can produce interesting patterns for Web page backgrounds and such.

Although scanning a 3-D object probably requires more experimentation than just about any class of original in this chapter, I can at least steer you in the right direction with these guidelines:

- ✔ **Color depth:** Even if your 3-D original is made of a single material, I recommend that you use 24-bit color to capture the image — especially if the surface detail is textured, embossed, or inscribed rather than painted or printed, so that the shading can help define the surface.

- ✔ **dpi:** Unlike scanning a "herd of dots" (as my college journalism professor used to call a halftone), scanning a 3-D object calls for a higher dpi setting. You need the higher setting to capture fine detail, especially if the surface is textured.

- ✔ **Color balance:** Not a problem here. Your scanner produces a pure white light, so the colors of a 3-D object should be spot-on.

Most flatbed scanners now come equipped with a cover that can be elevated to accommodate 3-D items that are several inches thick. Even though a space may exist between the glass and the cover, lowering the cover when you're scanning a thick object is still a good idea.

Text

Welcome to my discussion of that perennial office favorite, the text document. I discuss and demonstrate OCR in Chapter 13. For now, consider what types of text originals you're likely to encounter:

- **Office documents:** Although inkjet printers are making inroads into the business world, the laser printer is still the workhorse around most offices, and that means sharp, consistently black text at a snappy 600 x 600 dpi. It's not too shabby, and it's easy to scan, as you can see in Figure 7-8!

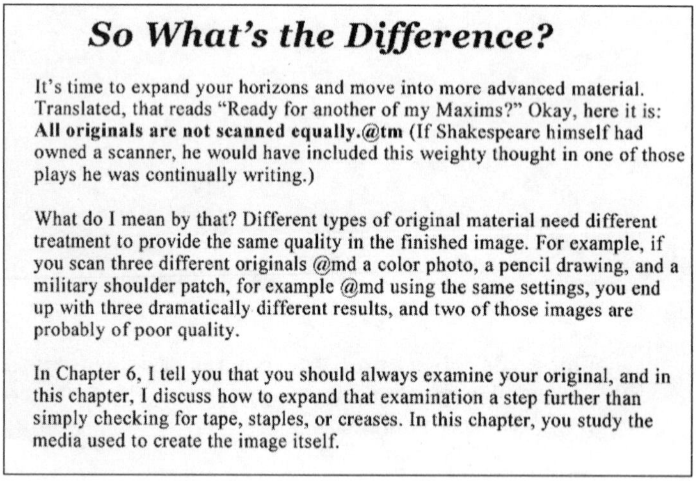

Figure 7-8:
Crisp text
and nice,
dark,
uniform
black — it
must be
laser-
printed text!

So What's the Difference?

It's time to expand your horizons and move into more advanced material. Translated, that reads "Ready for another of my Maxims?" Okay, here it is: **All originals are not scanned equally.@tm** (If Shakespeare himself had owned a scanner, he would have included this weighty thought in one of those plays he was continually writing.)

What do I mean by that? Different types of original material need different treatment to provide the same quality in the finished image. For example, if you scan three different originals @md a color photo, a pencil drawing, and a military shoulder patch, for example @md using the same settings, you end up with three dramatically different results, and two of those images are probably of poor quality.

In Chapter 6, I tell you that you should always examine your original, and in this chapter, I discuss how to expand that examination a step further than simply checking for tape, staples, or creases. In this chapter, you study the media used to create the image itself.

- **Faxed material:** Documents you've received by fax are more akin to halftone photographs than they are to typical text documents. Most folks have noticed that transmitting a document results in a grainy appearance on the receiving end and that text printed in all except the largest font sizes generally loses its sharpness. (This is one reason that it's often difficult to use a faxed document for OCR work.)

- **Business cards:** Generally, you have no problem scanning a traditional business card with black lettering on a white background. You may need to adjust the color balance and contrast level, however, if you're scanning a card with a colored background or colored text to yield a "white" background or "black" letters. For example, my business cards are printed with raised green lettering on a green background. By adjusting the color balance and contrast level before I scan the card, however, I can produce clean black characters on a white background.

Logos and other artwork on a business card should be scanned as line art.

✔ **Books and magazines:** Scanning text from a book or a page from a thick magazine can be challenging, especially if the text falls in the middle pages of a thick book, where the page curls away from the binding and you can "lose" characters. (Try to flatten the original as much as possible, but don't put too much pressure on your scanner's glass.) Also, you may have to adjust the brightness and contrast settings to pick up colored text in a magazine or text that's printed with a photograph as a background.

When you're scanning the most common text — black characters on a white background — use these settings:

✔ **Color depth:** As I mention earlier in this chapter, use 24-bit color for scanning text (even if you're not planning on using the image for OCR). One exception exists: If you're planning to fax the image of a document you're scanning, drop your image to 8-bit color to minimize the size of the file. It takes less time to transfer, and (unless the receiving end of your transmission is a color fax machine) those extra colors are wasted.

✔ **dpi:** I recommend 75 dpi for scanning a text document, which is all the resolution you really need. If photographs are included along with the text in the same document, however, there's no reason that you can't crank up the dpi setting as necessary.

✔ **Color balance:** You can use the same color-balancing techniques I suggest for color photographs to change the appearance of colored text. (In an extreme case, such as hot pink letters mixed with olive drab, a grayscale scan can do the trick as well.)

If you want to use all the advanced features of your scanning software to make the adjustments I talk about in this chapter, see Chapter 8, where I cover the process of manually changing settings.

Chapter 8

Attack of the Fine-Tuning Monster

. . . .

In This Chapter

▶ Understanding when to use advanced settings

▶ Specifying resolution

▶ Setting colors and color depth

▶ Adjusting brightness and contrast

▶ Choosing an image size

▶ Balancing color

▶ Applying filters

▶ Flipping and rotating

▶ Inverting colors

. . . .

*I*n Chapter 6, I show you scanning in its simplest form, using the default settings. That chapter is fun, but now it's time to tackle originals that need fine-tuning before you can scan them properly. To do that, you have to explore the true power of your scanning software by using its advanced features.

In this chapter, I do just that with HP Image Director: I move from the basics into the more complex and powerful advanced settings, which offer you complete control over the scanning environment. I demonstrate each of the advanced controls, and you see their effect on a representative scanned image.

Are All These Advanced Settings Really Necessary?

I can hear you asking, "Are all the advanced settings necessary?" The answer, in a word, is "No," but *only* if one or more of the following criteria is met:

✔ **Your original happens to be well suited to the default settings used by your scanning software.** This situation is often the case. However, as you find out in Chapter 7, a wide range of originals require special attention to achieve the best results.

✔ **Your scanner sets these controls automatically.** Some scanner-control programs try their best to deduce which settings are right for the original, but I can't say that I've seen them do better than a smart monkey with a dartboard. Besides, if the software can't automatically correct a problem, you have to know how to change the settings described in this chapter anyway.

✔ **You don't care about the quality of your scanned image.** I know that this statement isn't true, or else you wouldn't be reading this book!

I obviously consider this chapter to be required reading. However, it's fine if you want to use your scanner's default settings (or rely on your software's automatic settings and scanning profiles). Just use these advanced manual settings whenever necessary.

Note: What I say in Chapter 6 about the basic controls in HP Director is true here, too: Your scanning software's controls may be labeled differently, but most programs do have these features, and they have the same effect on the final image. If you're uncertain as to what does what, use the program's online help or check the software's manual to determine whether you can make a similar setting change in your program (and where that setting is located on the menu).

Setting Your Resolution

Figure 8-1 shows another favorite photograph from my album: the beautiful, scenic skyline of Chicago, complete with one of the world's tallest buildings. I chose this image because it has a wide range of shading and plenty of detail you can use.

I scanned this photograph, using the default settings for a color photograph in HP Director so that you have a frame of reference for the different effects produced in this chapter. The settings were

- ✔ 24-bit color
- ✔ 200 dpi
- ✔ No adjustments to brightness, contrast, sharpness, color, or saturation

HP Director provides a number of preset dpi resolution values, or you can choose your own. However, you can't choose a different unit of measurement, such as lpi (lines per inch) or pixels. Personally, this is not a problem in my little corner of the world. Even if your software supports lpi, it's a good idea for you to stick with dpi or ppi (short for pixels per inch, which, as you already know, is another moniker for dots-per-inch). Again, dpi is the commonly used standard for resolution.

To select a measurement from the program's preset levels, choose Advanced⬧ Resolution to display the resolution settings at the right side of the window, then click the drop-down list box to select a value. Depending on the scanner you're using, HP Director offers 75, 100, 150, 200, 300, 600, 1200, 2400, 3600, 4800, and 9600 dpi.

Figure 8-1:
The fair city
of Chicago,
as scanned
with
untouched
default
settings.

You can also click directly in the Resolution drop-down list box and enter a specific resolution.

To illustrate a range of resolution, Figure 8-2 shows the Chicago skyline at a whopping 20 dpi, and Figure 8-3 shows it off at 600 dpi. Boy, those extra dots do make a difference, don't they?

By the way, I should mention that I had to resize both these images for reference so that they match the size shown in Figure 8-2. In reality, 20 dpi produced an image with a total size of only 105 x 78, and the 600 dpi image was 3012 x 2251!

Now, really, why would anyone in his or her right mind want to scan something at 20 to 40 dpi? Well, I give you two good reasons, both related to the Web. First, you may want to use a low resolution if you want to use images as buttons on your Web page. This trick also comes in handy if you want to offer an index of *thumbnails* (small versions of images that are about the size of your thumb); a visitor to your page clicks the thumbnail to download a larger version of the same image. Your images are still recognizable, although they're tiny, and they load in a Web browser much faster than larger images. (To create a thumbnail with a higher dpi — say 75 to 100 dpi — after the image been scanned, use your image editor's Resize feature to reduce the size of the image and save a copy of it.)

Figure 8-2:
Man, talk about rough edges — 20 dpi is barely recognizable!

Figure 8-3:
At this
image size,
no
difference
exists
between
200 dpi and
600 dpi.

Note that Figure 8-3 looks exactly the same as Figure 8-1, which you may remember was scanned at 200 dpi! What effect did all those 400 extra dots per inch make? The final image at 600 dpi was much bigger, but after it's resized to the same image size of 800 x 600, the human eye can discern literally no difference. However, the difference in file sizes is incredible: The 200 dpi image is a mere 1.3MB, and the 600 dpi version is more than 21MB!

Colors and Bits, Colors and Bits

Although HP Director cleverly disguises the color depth control as Output Type, the result is the same: Choose this menu to set the color depth for your scan.

I recommend that you use the Millions of Colors setting for most work. That's yet another way of saying 24-bit or true color, which provides as many as 16.7 million colors. Here's a list of other color depth options offered by today's scanner software (including a number of common names for each color depth setting).

- ✔ **Grayscale/256 Gray Shades:** Use this option for 8-bit, 256 shades of gray.

- ✔ **Web/Internet/256 Colors (Web palette):** Choose this option for a 256-color image that's optimized for use on a Web page. HP Director uses a special selection of colors (called a *palette*) that's supported by Netscape, Safari, and Internet Explorer.

- ✔ **8-bit/256 colors:** Use this option for your average, standard 8-bit color depth.

- ✔ **Line Art/Black & White/Text:** As I explain in Chapter 7, you use this setting for black-on-white drawings (or any other high-contrast color on a solid background color).

- ✔ **Halftone/B&W Diffusion:** You and I know this option as a black-and-white halftone that simulates shades of gray — not to be confused with true grayscale. Figure 8-4 shows the demonstration photograph scanned with this setting.

Figure 8-4:
A black-and-white halftone version of the photograph.

The Light and the Dark

I don't say much elsewhere about brightness and contrast because your scanning software may not allow you to adjust these two settings. However, I have good news: If you find that your scanning program doesn't support them, you can always use your image editor to make changes to them instead!

If you're using HP Director, you can lighten or darken an image before the scan. Follow these steps:

1. **Choose Basic⇨Lighten/Darken (or click the down arrow next to Lighten/Darken in the pane at the right side of the Director window).**

   The settings shown in Figure 8-5 appear.

2. **Move the desired slider control by clicking and dragging it. Alternatively, you can click in the field and enter an exact value.**

   Notice that HP Director automatically updates the image on the right as you change the value, allowing you to gauge the effect the setting will have on your scan.

3. **To reset the values, click Auto to return to the original settings chosen by Director.**

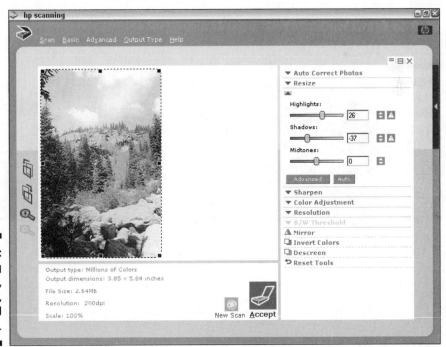

Figure 8-5: Changing highlights, midtones, and shadows.

The brightness of an image indicates the concentration of light (in the positive) or the intensity of dark (in the negative) throughout the entire image. Raising the brightness level can accentuate details in the dark areas of an image, and lowering the level can cancel the effects of overexposure (a photographer's 10-cent term for "too much light").

If your scanning software provides a contrast setting, you can use it to control the contrast between light and dark shades in your image. This feature is a great tool for bringing out detail in an image, although you shouldn't overuse it because it can degrade the overall quality of your image at higher contrast settings.

Some scanning programs (such as HP Director) express brightness and contrast as three values: highlights (the bright areas), shadows (the dark areas), and midtones (the middle range). This allows a finer level of adjustment. For example, Figure 8-6 illustrates our skyline image with a full 100 percent shadow setting, and Figure 8-7 shows the effects of a 100 percent highlights setting.

Figure 8-6:
Lowering brightness (or increasing shadow) darkens the entire image.

Figure 8-7:
Increasing
brightness
(or
increasing
highlights)
yields a
lighter scan.

Size Really Does Count

Now consider height and width — no, not *yours*. I'm talking about your
scanned image! (Sorry. I couldn't help that one.) The image dimensions and
size controls are probably the most straightforward settings you can make in
your scanning software, but sometimes you may find yourself wondering if
you have *too* many options. For example, HP Direct uses five values to com-
pute the final size of your scanned image (as shown in Figure 8-8):

- The width of the region you've chosen with the selection box
- The height of the region you've chosen with the selection box
- The width of the output image
- The height of the output image
- Scaling

Figure 8-8:
This puts
things in the
proper
scale.

Scaling works just like the size-percentage control on a typical copy machine: 100 percent yields the same size, 50 percent yields a scanned image half the size of the original (both the horizontal and vertical dimensions are reduced by 50 percent), and 200 percent doubles the size of the original, for example. Click the Scale drop-down list box to choose one of the standard scale levels or click directly in the field and enter your own. Notice that Director automatically adjusts the output size if you specify a different scaling value.

In most cases, you want to keep the proportions (also called the *aspect ratio*) of the image the same so that the image you scan doesn't turn out pinched or pulled, like a piece of taffy. To make sure that the proportion stays the same even if you make a change to the height or width, click the Lock aspect ratio padlock icon to enable it before making any modifications to the image dimensions. Notice that the program automatically adjusts the other dimension to provide the same aspect ratio.

By default, the measurement units are inches, although you can also choose the following units:

- ✔ Centimeters (cm)
- ✔ Points
- ✔ Pixels

To change the unit of measure, click the Units drop-down list box to the right of the output fields and click the unit you want.

After you've set your image size, Director does its best to estimate the total file size. The estimate is displayed in the File Size field. For example, selecting a 50 percent scale may drop an image from 2.9MB to 725K.

Making Green Bananas Yellow

It's time to balance that color! Again, you can take care of color balancing before the scan (using your scanning software, if it supports this feature) or after the scan (using your image editor). In Chapter 11, I show you how to alter the color of a single element in your scanned image. This procedure alters the color range for the entire image, making it the perfect method of fixing an original with a tinge from fluorescent or colored lighting.

Note: I think that it's important to keep in mind that if your original uses a well-balanced palette of colors (for example, if you're scanning a simple text document, a page from a magazine, or a photograph taken in sunlight), your color levels shouldn't require any adjustment. You should use these controls only if you need to correct an obvious color defect in the entire image (such as a greenish cast caused by fluorescent lighting) or if you want to exercise your creativity.

Follow these steps:

1. **Choose Advanced⇨Color Adjustment (or click the down arrow next to the Color Adjustment section of the pane at the right side of the window).**

   Director displays the Color Adjustment settings shown in Figure 8-9.

Figure 8-9:
Adjusting
the entire
color range
of an image.

2. **Click and drag the pointer in the center of the palette circle in the direction directly away from the color you want to reduce.**

   For example, if the image has too much red in it, you move the pointer to the left, toward the cyan area of the circle. You can see the results immediately as Director updates the preview.

   For more precise movement in a specific direction, click the colored arrows on the outside of the palette circle; this draws the pointer directly toward that color.

3. **To reset the values, click Auto to return to the original settings chosen by Director.**

I don't show you an example of color correction here; the sample image was taken outside on a somewhat overcast day, yielding an almost perfect color palette (and this book uses black-and-white halftone figures, so it would be hard to tell the difference). Suffice it to say that you should try this using your own scanning software. You'll be surprised by the results!

"I'm saturated with color!"

Don't have a Color Adjustment control within your scanning software? It may be there under another name: color saturation, for example. You may want to try adjusting it before you scan an original. In a similar vein as color adjustment, color *saturation* controls the intensity of a specific color (or, in other words, the amount of color in a single hue of the original's palette). If that sounds like verbal spaghetti, think of it this way: The more saturated a color, the more you see of that particular color in the image. Green grass looks greener, and a blue sky looks bluer, for example.

Basic Filters 101

First, here's a definition of *filter*: It's a mathematical formula applied to an image in an image editor, a digital camera, or a scanning program. A filter can make both subtle and dramatic changes in the appearance of a digital image.

I'll be honest with you: I don't use the filters that are built into scanner-control programs. Why? I like to apply filters and effects to an image *after* it has been scanned, using Paint Shop Pro, which gives me more precise and powerful tools. I show you how to do just that in Chapter 11. (I also display a gallery of my ten favorite filters and effects in Chapter 17.)

However, I also like to be thorough, so here's a quick rundown of what the filters provided by most scanning applications can do for your image:

- ✔ **Blur:** Yes, believe it or not, sometimes you want a scanned image to turn out blurry and hazy! This filter gives an image a soft, out-of-focus look by lightening the pixels next to any sharp border in the original.

- ✔ **Edge enhancement:** This filter increases the contrast level along the boundaries of gray and color regions in your image. The results can be spectacular from a graphic artist's point of view.

- ✔ **Emboss:** Turn your original into an embossed metal work of art! I like this one.

- ✔ **Sharpen:** I discuss how to use the Sharpen filter in detail in Chapter 9. Suffice it to say that this filter is the opposite of the Blur filter, darkening the pixels next to the borders in the original instead. A wide range of images benefits from at least a small amount of sharpening, so you'll probably use this filter often.

To apply the Sharpen filter in Director, follow these steps:

1. **Choose Basic⇨Sharpen (or click the down arrow next to the Sharpen section of the pane at the right side of the window).**

   Director displays the Sharpen list box and Auto button.

2. **Click the Sharpen list box and choose the desired level of sharpness.**

   The effects of the filter are displayed automatically in the preview image.

3. **To return to the original settings chosen by Director, click Auto.**

Flipping and Rotating: The Scanner Dance Craze

Naturally, your scanner has no idea which end is up on your original. That's why your scanning software has the capability to rotate or flip *(mirror)* the image. The mirror feature is particularly useful when the original is reversed or you have to reverse an original. For example, when you're creating a T-shirt design and you're scanning a photograph to use, you may have to flip it; either the entire design has to be reversed, or your inkjet printer has to print it in reverse. After you've figured out which way is up when aligning your originals with your scanner's home corner, this stuff doesn't come up often, although being able to flip or rotate when you need it is handy.

To mirror the image, choose Advanced⇨Mirror (or click the Mirror button in the pane at the right side of the window). To rotate the preview image 90 degrees, click the counterclockwise or clockwise Rotation buttons at the left side of the Director window.

As an example, look at the image shown in Figure 8-10 — we'll use this as the original orientation. Clicking the top Rotation button produces an image that's rotated to the left 90 degrees, as shown in Figure 8-11. Clicking the Mirror button produces the mirrored image shown in Figure 8-12.

Figure 8-10:
A favorite
still life in
its original
orientation.

Figure 8-11:
Applying a
90-degree
rotation to
the left.

Figure 8-12:
Is this a
clone? Or is
it all done
with
mirrors?

You can also take care of rotating and mirroring an image with Paint Shop Pro; I show you how in Chapter 9.

Let's Invert

If you're looking for a startling effect that still allows the viewer to recognize the subject of your image, consider inverting the colors in your image. Inversion also works with a grayscale image, producing an effect just like a photographic negative. (Compare the preview image in Figure 8-13 with the preview image in Figure 8-9.)

To invert the image, choose Advanced⇨Invert Colors (or click the Invert Colors button in the pane at the right side of the window).

To undo a single-click operation such as mirroring or color inversion, just click the button or choose the menu command a second time.

Figure 8-13:
An inverted
grayscale
image can
deliver quite
a punch.

If you're familiar with both the basic controls and the more powerful
advanced settings I've covered here (whatever your scanner-control software
calls them), you can turn your attention to another tool on the scanning
expert's belt: the image editor. In Chapter 9, I introduce you to Paint Shop
Pro, and you use it to adjust and improve your images — *after* you've
scanned them!

Chapter 9

Image Editing the Easy Way

A scanner is indeed a wonderful piece of equipment, and, if you've read the previous chapters in this book, I think that you'll agree with me. I rank my scanner right up there with inventions such as the light bulb, the baseball, and the Rolling Stones. Yet, even with all the tips and tricks you may have discovered, you can do only so much with a "raw" image saved straight to your hard drive. Often, an image still needs a bit of tweaking (even with the scanning software adjustments I discuss in earlier chapters) before you can use it.

Ladies and gentlemen, you're no longer raw recruits. In this chapter, I introduce you to the *image editor*. Consider it your development lab, creative digital easel, and versatile cutting board, all rolled into one! After you've experienced the power of an image editor, I think that you may find it hard to imagine a mundane scanning existence without one. Personally, I like to manipulate pixels like a composer manipulates musical notes.

Throughout this chapter, I use my favorite image editor under Windows XP — Paint Shop Pro 8, from Jasc Software, Inc. — to demonstrate how you can apply the necessary finishing touches before importing your scanned image into a document, sending it through e-mail, or preparing it for use on your Web page. As in Chapter 8, I provide step-by-step procedures and show you their effects.

Mac owners will find that iPhoto includes most of these functions as well. You may take a slightly different road, but you'll end up with similar results.

But don't mess with perfection! If your scanned image is already *exactly* as you need it, or if perfection isn't a necessity (for example, if you've scanned a document to send it with your computer's fax-modem), you have no need to use an image editor, and you can march proudly onward.

However, other images *do* require first aid. You may need to edit an image for a number of reasons:

- ✔ **Something is wrong with the composition.** In some cases, the problem may be one of *composition* — something that's there isn't supposed to be there.

- ✔ **The image requires a post-scanning process.** Perhaps you decide that a post-scanning process (such as an orientation procedure or a mirror procedure) needs to be performed after scanning an original.

- ✔ **The image needs enhancement.** You can make simple aesthetic changes to enhance a scan, too, such as converting it to grayscale or adding a picture frame.

- ✔ **You get a creative urge.** Finally, an out-and-out creative urge may bring a wild look to your eyes — and wild results to your hard drive! With filters and special effects (which I discuss in detail in Chapter 11), you become a true artist.

In this chapter, I stick with the first three types of image-editing work, including the problems that you may be able to fix from within your scanning software (as I show you in previous chapters).

Introducing the Tool of Choice: Paint Shop Pro

Paint Shop Pro (www.jasc.com) has been a fixture on my PC since the days when it was a simple shareware program available on bulletin-board systems.

Today, Paint Shop Pro ranks with Adobe Photoshop as one of the best-known image editors on the market. Paint Shop Pro provides most of the same features as Photoshop, although it costs many hundreds of dollars less. Also, readers of my other books have told me that they find Paint Shop Pro much, much easier to understand and use than Photoshop. (Like anyone else who has to program a VCR when the power goes out, I'm in favor of simplicity.) The trial version of Paint Shop Pro is included on the companion CD in this book.

Figure 9-1 illustrates the Paint Shop Pro main window, which is comprised of four major parts:

- ✔ The familiar menu system
- ✔ The toolbars at the left side and top of the window
- ✔ The color palette at the right side of the window
- ✔ The editing area

I refer to these areas (and the controls you see) throughout the rest of this book.

Figure 9-1:
Displaying
an image in
Paint Shop
Pro.

I want to mention one other feature of the program: Paint Shop Pro includes a great online help system that provides complete details on every function, feature, switch, and setting. Plus, you also find additional image-editing tips and tricks for just about everything the program can do. Dig into this gold mine whenever you try out a new procedure.

Opening a File

Every journey begins with a first step. In this case, tweaking a scanned image begins when you open the file. Follow these steps to open an image in Paint Shop Pro:

1. **Double-click the Paint Shop Pro icon on your Windows desktop to run the program.**

   Alternatively, in Windows XP you can click the Start button and choose All Programs⇨Jasc Software⇨Jasc Paint Shop Pro 8.

2. **Choose File⇨Open to display the Open dialog box, as shown in Figure 9-2.**

Figure 9-2: The Paint Shop Pro Open dialog box lets you preview an image — pretty doggone convenient, eh?

3. **Navigate to the folder where the scanned image is located and click it once.**

   A thumbnail preview and basic information about the size and color depth of the image appear.

Need even more information on an image without opening it? You can display the full description of an image — including compression level, exact size, and the creation or modification date — by clicking the Details button.

4. **Click Open to open the highlighted file within Paint Shop Pro.**

The image is displayed in a new editing window.

By the way, if you allow Paint Shop Pro to configure itself as the default viewing program for image files during installation, you can simplify things dramatically. Open an image file from an Explorer window by simply double-clicking it! You know that Paint Shop Pro 8 is registered in Windows as the default application for an image if the scanned file is represented by an artist's palette icon with a tiny number *8*. The file also carries the Paint Shop Pro Image type in Windows Explorer.

Shall We Browse?

As you continue to build your library of scanned images, you'll eventually find yourself digging through a folder containing hundreds of files for a particular scan of a llama next to a grass hut. It's a frustrating chore that brings new meaning to the tired, overworked, worn-out cliché "looking for a needle in a haystack." (You would *think* that a picture like that would stand out, but to your computer, everything's ones and zeros.)

Paint Shop Pro includes a feature that can save you from spending hours opening images. You can browse a folder's worth of files by viewing a catalog of thumbnail images. It's much easier to locate that llama visually than try to remember the filename.

Here are two methods of browsing a folder using Paint Shop Pro:

✔ The easiest method is to right-click a folder in Windows Explorer; one of the menu items is Browse this folder using Paint Shop Pro 8. Choose this menu item, and the program automatically starts and opens the Browse window, as shown in Figure 9-3.

✔ If Paint Shop Pro is already running, choose File ➪ Browse (or press Ctrl+B). Then select the folder you want to browse.

Figure 9-3:
Browsing a
folder of
image
thumbnails
using Paint
Shop Pro.

After the contents of the folder are displayed, you can load any image by double-clicking the thumbnail. A highlighted border surrounds it, and Paint Shop Pro loads it into a separate editing window.

Fence those images in, pardner!

I always recommend that folks dedicate a folder on their hard drive to store their scanned images (rather than save them here and there or simply dump them in the C:\ root directory). Why? It helps you keep track of where your images have been saved — and, if you use Paint Shop Pro to browse that directory, it can also save you time in the future! Here's the deal: Whenever you use Paint Shop Pro to browse a folder, the program saves a small data file, named PSPBRWSE.JBF, in that folder. This index file holds a snapshot of information about which images were included in the browsing session. The next time you browse that same folder, Paint Shop Pro can use this index file to automatically update the Browse display with any new images you've added since the last browsing session, and the update process is over with *fast!* Windows XP and Windows 2000 already address this need for organization — images are typically saved and loaded from your My Pictures folder (inside your My Documents folder).

To keep your images sorted alphabetically by filename, right-click in the Browse display and choose Sort. Then click the Name sort condition and click OK.

Cropping a Scanned Image

So you have the perfect scan from a magazine page, but all you want is the photograph, and not the text around it. (Or perhaps your finger intruded into the frame of that priceless family reunion photo.) No problem: You can *crop* the image, which removes the portion of the border you specify. (It works just like the selection-box control you use with your scanning software.) Because cropping an image also reduces its dimensions, you get the bonus of a smaller file size!

Follow these steps:

1. **Choose File⇨Open, and then double-click the desired filename to load your image.**

2. **Click the geometric selection tool (it looks like a dotted rectangle) on the toolbar on the left edge of the screen.**

   Your mouse cursor changes from an arrow to a crosshair, indicating that you're in selection mode.

3. **Use the selection rectangle to select the portion of the image that you want to keep.**

   Click the top-left corner of the area you want to save, and hold the mouse down to drag the selection rectangle to the lower-right corner of the area you want to save. Release the mouse button to select the area, which is surrounded by an animated dotted line, like the one shown in Figure 9-4.

4. **Choose Image⇨Crop to Selection.**

   For those of you who still favor the keyboard, you can also press Shift+R. The area outside the selection box is cut, as shown in Figure 9-5.

5. **To save the cropped image, choose File⇨Save (to overwrite the old image) or Save As (to save a new image).**

   You can use Save As to create a copy of the image with another filename or format.

Figure 9-4:
Selecting
the portion
of an image
to keep.

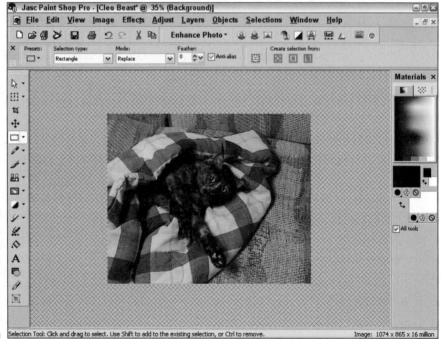

Figure 9-5:
The
cropped
image looks
much better,
don't you
think?

Need to undo something that didn't work in Paint Shop Pro? Choose Edit⇨Undo (or press Ctrl-Z) to cancel the effects of the last task you performed.

Sharpen That Line, Mister!

Paint Shop Pro provides a sharpening feature that I often use to add focus to a scan of a hazy or blurry original. In effect, this sharpening increases the contrast at all the lines and edges in the image, which usually means the subject of a photograph. Sharpening usually isn't necessary with simple line art or a text document because those types of scanned images already offer a high level of contrast.

Sharpening sounds like a cure-all for any blurry scanned image, but it just isn't so. Here's a Mark's Maxim worth its weight in gold:

Sharpening an image does *not* create additional detail!

(Creating extra detail would be a neat trick, rather like the interpolation I talk about in Chapter 1 — creating pixels out of nothing.) Too much sharpening can turn an image into a grainy mess, so use this technique sparingly.

Follow these steps:

1. **Choose File⇨Open, and then double-click the desired filename to load your image.**

2. **Choose Adjust⇨Sharpness⇨Sharpen (or Sharpen More, which significantly enhances the effect).**

3. **Save your changes by choosing File⇨Save or File⇨Save As.**

To give you an idea of the effects of sharpening, Figure 9-6 illustrates an image in need of serious focus, and Figure 9-7 shows the same image after the application of the Sharpen More operation.

Figure 9-6:
Notice the edges in this scanned image. They need sharpening.

Figure 9-7:
With Sharpen More, the image looks much better.

What is an aspect ratio?

When you're resizing an image, *aspect ratio* (the ratio of height to width) is important. A picture can be badly stretched or pinched if the aspect ratio is changed while you're resizing it. When the Lock aspect ratio check box at the bottom of the dialog box is enabled, Paint Shop Pro auto- matically enters the second value when you enter one number in either the width or height fields. Leave this box checked unless you need to force an image to a new aspect ratio. The moral of the story is "Preserve that ratio!"

It's Just Too Big!

A scanner can turn out a huge image at higher dpi settings, so you often need to resize the image before printing it, importing it to another document, or using it on your Web site. Resizing the image dimensions also helps trim the size of the image file.

Follow these steps to resize an image:

1. **Choose File⇨Open, and then double-click the desired filename to load your image.**

2. **Choose Image⇨Resize.**

   The Resize dialog box appears, as shown in Figure 9-8.

3. **Choose one of the measurement modes: pixel resolution, a percentage of the original size, or the actual size of the final image.**

   If I'm resizing an image to fit in a specific size on a Web page, I usually use pixel resolution, where you enter the new width and height for the image in pixels. If you're importing the image for use in another docu- ment, using the actual size of the final image is a good idea.

4. **Click the Resample using check box to enable it, then click the drop- down list box and choose Smart Size.**

5. **Click OK.**

   Note that the larger the change in the image size, the more time resizing takes.

6. **Save your changes.**

   Choose File⇨Save or File⇨Save As.

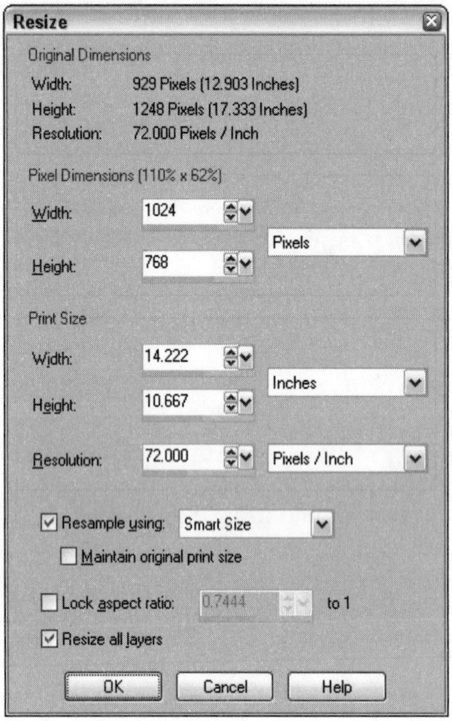

Resize

Original Dimensions
Width: 929 Pixels (12.903 Inches)
Height: 1248 Pixels (17.333 Inches)
Resolution: 72.000 Pixels / Inch

Pixel Dimensions (110% x 62%)
Width: 1024

Pixels

Height: 768

Print Size
Width: 14.222

Inches

Height: 10.667

Resolution: 72.000   Pixels / Inch

☑ Resample using: Smart Size

☐ Maintain original print size

☐ Lock aspect ratio: 0.7444 to 1

☑ Resize all layers

[OK] [Cancel] [Help]

Figure 9-8:
The Paint
Shop Pro
Resize
dialog box.

Mirror, Mirror, on the Wall

Paint Shop Pro can easily reverse or flip an image. This is a good trick when you're creating a reverse image for a T-shirt transfer. Follow these steps:

1. **Choose File⇨Open, and then double-click the desired filename to load your image.**

2. **Choose Image⇨Flip (to reverse the image from top to bottom) or Image⇨Mirror (to reverse the image from left to right).**

3. **Save your changes by choosing File and then choosing Save or Save As.**

Figures 9-9 and 9-10 speak volumes about the effect the mirror operation can have on a typical scanned image.

Figure 9-9:
An image
that needs
to be
reversed.

Figure 9-10:
After the
mirror
operation,
things look
much
better!

The Light and the Dark

Scanning an overexposed or underexposed original can result in an image that needs a contrast adjustment. The easiest way to lighten or darken an entire image is to use the gamma correction setting in Paint Shop Pro.

Follow these steps:

1. **Choose File⇨Open, and then double-click the desired filename to load the image.**

2. **Choose Adjust⇨Brightness and Contrast⇨Gamma Correction from the pop-up menu (or just press Shift+G).**

   The Gamma Correction dialog box appears, as shown in Figure 9-11.

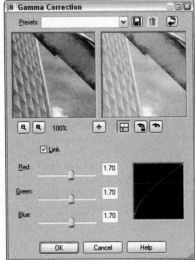

Figure 9-11:
Adjusting the Gamma Correction for an image.

3. **Enable the Link check box.**

4. **Click and drag any of the three slider controls to the right (to lighten the image) or to the left (to darken the image).**

   The upper-right window displays a preview of the correction.

5. **When you're satisfied with the correction, click OK.**

6. **Save your changes by choosing File⇨Save or File⇨Save As.**

Wouldn't a Frame Look Nice?

Paint Shop Pro 8 allows you to add a decorative frame to an image. Some frames even come with mats that can add more visual interest to your image, as shown in Figure 9-12.

Follow these steps:

1. **Choose File⇨Open, and then double-click the desired filename to load your image.**

2. **Choose Image⇨Picture Frame.**

   The Picture Frame dialog box appears, as shown in Figure 9-13.

Figure 9-12:
Note the fancy shadowed mat on this frame.

Figure 9-13:
Selecting a
picture
frame.

3. **Click the Picture frame drop-down list box and choose the type of frame you want surrounding the image.**

   Paint Shop Pro displays a preview of the frame. Depending on the type of frame you choose, you may also be able to fill transparent areas of the frame or accompanying mat with a color that you specify.

4. **Next, specify whether the frame should fall inside the edges of the image or be added outside the edges of the image.**

   Placing the frame inside the edges keeps the original image dimensions, but the frame hides more of the image itself.

5. **If you like, you can flip, mirror, or rotate the frame clockwise.**

   The effect is shown in the orientation preview.

6. **When you're satisfied with your framing job, click OK to return to the Paint Shop Pro editing window.**

7. **Save your changes by choosing File⇨Save or File⇨Save As.**

Removing Uncle Milton's Red-Eye

Although some automatic point-and-shoot cameras have a red-eye reduction feature, you may still have to remove that irritating red shine from your subject's eyes after scanning a photograph.

Follow these steps:

1. **Choose File⇨Open, and then double-click the desired filename to load your image.**

2. **Choose Adjust⇨Red-eye Removal.**

   The dialog box shown in Figure 9-14 appears.

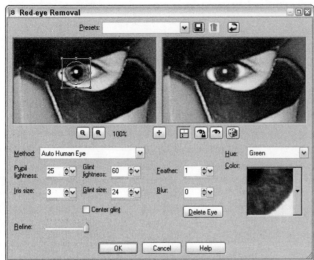

Figure 9-14:
Red-eye,
begone!

3. **Click in the right window and drag the image in the desired direction until the subject's eyes are in the selection windows.**

4. **Click the mouse cursor in the center of one eye in the left window to select it.**

   Paint Shop Pro surrounds the colored portion of the eye with a selection box.

5. **Click the Hue drop-down list box and the Color drop-down list box and choose the proper hue and color.**

6. **Click OK.**

7. **Repeat Steps 4 through 6 to correct the remaining eye (or eyes, depending on the species).**

8. **Choose File⇨Save or File⇨Save As.**

Rotating 101

If you snap a photograph holding your camera on its end, you may need to change the orientation of the image before it's displayed correctly. Follow these steps in Paint Shop Pro:

   1. **Choose File⇨Open, and then double-click the desired filename to load your image.**

   2. **Click Image⇨Rotate⇨Free Rotate.**

      The dialog box shown in Figure 9-15 appears.

Figure 9-15:
The Free
Rotate
dialog box.

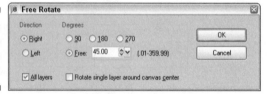

   3. **Click the Right or Left option to choose the direction of rotation.**

   4. **Click the number of degrees to rotate.**

   5. **Click OK to rotate the image.**

   6. **Choose File⇨Save or Save As to save the file.**

Who Needs Color, Anyway?

You may be wondering why anyone would convert a perfectly good color image to grayscale. More reasons exist than you may think! For example:

   ✔ **To hide mismatched colors:** There goes Aunt Harriet again, choosing a robin's egg blue kimono when the rest of the family was dressed in festive red and green for the holidays. In grayscale, though, she matches once again!

   ✔ **For artistic reasons:** If the creative bug bites you, a grayscale version of a color image may appeal to your photographer's eye.

   ✔ **For specific publications:** If you're busy publishing a black-and-white newsletter, using the office copier, a grayscale image likely looks better in the final copy.

The procedure is simple and painless. Follow these steps:

1. **Choose File⇨Open, and then double-click the desired filename to load your image.**

2. **Choose Image⇨Greyscale.**

3. **Immediately choose File⇨Save As and save the grayscale creation under another filename.**

   I recommend that you save the file under a different name right away because you can't undo a grayscale conversion.

A Little Alchemy: Changing Image Formats

Time to talk more about alchemy. In this case, I'm not talking about digitizing images but rather changing the *format* of a digital image. I don't delve deeply into image formats here because I cover them in detail in Chapter 10. However, because Paint Shop Pro makes the process of conversion from one format to another so doggone easy, I want to take the time to show you how to change a format now.

Follow the next set of steps to convert a file from one format to another. For this example, I convert a JPEG image (the native format that's produced by default by my scanner software) to a TIFF image:

1. **Choose File⇨Open, and then double-click the desired filename to load your image.**

2. **Choose File⇨Save As.**

   The dialog box shown in Figure 9-16 appears.

Figure 9-16:
Saving a
file to disk
using Paint
Shop Pro.

3. **Click the Save as type drop-down list box and choose the format for the new image.**

   In this case, choose Tagged Image File Format (*.tif).

4. **In the File name box, type a new filename if you want.**

   Again, I recommend that you type a new filename so that you save the original image, just in case.

5. **Click the Options button, and change the settings as necessary.**

   Most of the image settings are different for each format; Figure 9-17 illustrates the Save options for the TIFF format. Leave them at their defaults unless you specifically need to change them.

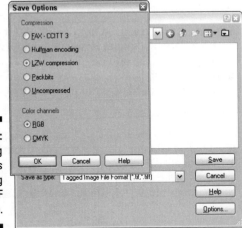

Figure 9-17:
Adjusting
settings
while saving
a TIFF
image.

6. **Click OK to return to the Save As dialog box.**

7. **Click Save to start the conversion and save the new file to disk.**

Part IV
The Lazy Expert's Guide to Advanced Scanning

The 5th Wave — By Rich Tennant

"...and here's me with Cindy Crawford. And this is me with Madonna and Celine Dion..."

In this part . . .

*I*t's time to turn your attention to more complex material, including details on image formats, producing images for e-mail messages and Web pages, and advanced image-editing techniques. I provide you with a comprehensive discussion of scanner maintenance and troubleshooting and show you how to use your scanner for craft and business projects.

Chapter 10

So You Want to Be an Internet Graphics Guru

. . . .

. . . .

"The Internet has revolutionized. . . ." Blah, blah, blah. I absolutely refuse to type that stuff. You've heard it so many times during the past few years that there's nothing left to explain! Everyone's fighting to get online if they're not already there. A business isn't truly on the fast track to success without a Web site, and your Christmas cards are just as likely to list your e-mail address as your mailing address. I don't want to waste your time by noting how the Internet started as a military communications network, nor will I describe in excruciating detail how your peanut-butter fudge recipe gets to Aunt Harriet in Boise by hopping from your modem to an e-mail server across the Internet to her ISP and back again. (If you want to pull back the curtain and see how the Great Oz does these things, I recommend buying *The Internet For Dummies,* written by John R. Levine, Margaret Levine Young, and Carol Baroudi, and published by Wiley.

What's *really* noteworthy about the Internet — and what's especially interesting to your elite group, the Scanner Owners of the World Club — is the *visual* aspect of the Grand Design! Naturally, the World Wide Web comes to mind first; it's the fastest growing part of the Internet, and it offers a chance for just about anyone to publish the information they want the world to see — in 24-bit color, no less. However, don't forget about your e-mail account; I'm just as likely to find myself transferring scanned images as e-mail attachments to my friends and family. (In fact, every figure in this book was transferred to my heroic project editor through e-mail.)

In this chapter, I turn the magnifying glass on the Internet — specifically, how you can produce images that are optimized for use on your Web pages and as enclosures in your e-mail messages. I also cover a number of subjects that are of interest to Web page designers, lawyers, and the average preschool child. (You can't say that I don't appeal to a wide audience.)

GIF Isn't a Snack Food, and JPEG Isn't Spelled Jaypeg

Although the two image formats most commonly found on the Internet are GIF and JPEG (with PNG on the rise), I want to cover the advantages and disadvantages of all the well-known formats here. After all, you may find yourself scanning images for use on that *other* operating system.

By the way, keep in mind that no hard-and-fast rule says that you have to use GIF or JPEG images on your Web site. You can just as easily offer Windows bitmap or TIFF images for display on your site. However, in the descriptions that follow, I explain why an unwritten agreement stipulates that GIF, JPEG, and PNG are the best choices for the Internet.

Joint Photographic Experts Group

Commonly called JPEG, the Joint Photographic Experts Group format is the most popular now in use. It's also called JPG because these images usually end with the JPG extension under Windows. You do indeed pronounce it "JAY-peg."

What exactly *is* an image format?

An *image format* is a standard file layout (or template) that's used to store the data that makes up the image. I could spend a chapter or two quoting the specifications for a typical format, but to tell you the truth, details about the low-level structure of a digital photograph fall into the realm of computer programmers and technowizards. (In other words, the details would likely be gibberish to you and me.) If you're interested in how the bits and bytes are stacked together, you can find information on the Web that details the standards used by programmers to read and write image files. Here are a couple of sites to visit:

For JPEG: www.jpeg.org/public/ jpeglinks.htm

For PNG: www.libpng.org/pub/png/

JPEG images deliver high resolution with very small file sizes; a typical one-page document with mixed text and graphics, for example, can take less than 300K worth of hard drive space. The savings result from the built-in compression that's part of the JPEG format. You can find out more about this topic later in this chapter, in the section "Compression in the 21st Century."

On the flip side, a JPEG image can lose detail and image quality at higher compression rates or if it's compressed repeatedly. Compression like this is commonly called *lossy* compression because pixels and colors (and therefore details) are removed to deliver better compression. (Again, I cover this topic in a few pages.)

JPEG images, with their small size and great quality, are the standard for pictures used on the Web and images sent through e-mail; smaller file sizes mean less time required to send or receive these images over your computer's modem. (Smaller attachments also mean less storage space needed on your e-mail server, too.)

It's no accident that most of today's digital cameras also save images to their RAM cards in JPEG format. Smaller files mean more exposures on a "roll" of digital film.

Graphics Interchange Format

The GIF file format is one of the oldest (and most common) image formats still used today. GIF files usually end with the GIF extension under Windows. Although many uninformed folks persist in pronouncing GIF with a hard "g" sound, as in "guffaw," the inventor of the GIF format (as well as the author of this book) pronounces it correctly, with a soft "g," as in "giraffe."

As for the other great international CTPF (that's short for computer term pronunciation flub), the word *Linux* is pronounced like "linen," and that's according to the man who wrote most of the operating system. (He ought to know.)

GIF images originated on the old king of the online services, CompuServe, and were popularized on the bulletin-board systems (or *BBSs*) common throughout the 1980s and early 1990s. At the time, the Internet was a "weird" system that colleges and scientists used and was barely known in public circles. I'm showing my age again, I admit, but I have fond memories of those times. I operated a popular multiline BBS throughout those glory years — in fact, I'm running it. (You can reach The Batboard on the Web at http://batboard.mlcbooks.com with your browser, if you'd like a taste of the BBS world.) I still have thousands of GIF images stored on CD-R. They're lurking somewhere around my office, although it would take a bulldozer to find them.

These days, GIF images are used almost exclusively on the Web. Unlike a JPEG image, a GIF image can be animated, so it appears to move when your browser displays it. Two common types of GIF images exist. The specifications are cryptically named 87a and 89a (after the dates they were released), but only the 89a GIF images can be made transparent, so they're now the most popular by far. *Transparency* means that you can see the background color or pattern of a Web page around the edges of the graphic, just as though it were part of the page itself. Many Web sites use this trick to build a Web page that looks like a cohesive whole, when it's actually a background covered with text and transparent GIF images. GIF files are also quite small because they're compressed. (A GIF image doesn't lose quality like a JPEG does when it's compressed over and over.)

"Then why aren't GIF images as popular as JPEG images?" Ah, that's a good question with an easy answer: GIF images can include a maximum of only 256 colors (or 8-bit color), so when they're displayed on-screen or printed, the 16.7 million colors supported by a 24-bit JPEG image are *far* superior. (Also, GIF images can't produce true grayscale.) Therefore, GIF images have been relegated to cartoons, basic Web graphics, and animation.

I'll miss GIF images when they finally disappear, but they're still in vogue because most people still connect to the Internet through an analog telephone modem. After the majority of folks have moved to broadband connections, such as DSL and cable modems, image quality will be the name of the game!

Windows bitmap

If you use Windows, you've likely encountered an image in bitmap format. For example, you may have changed your background image on your desktop or used clip art from some Microsoft products. These images end with the BMP extension.

Bitmap images provide great image quality, ranking with TIFF images as the best of any of the common formats. (More on the TIFF format in the next section.) Bitmaps can deliver both 24-bit color and grayscale, and the bitmap format is supported by every Windows operating system from Windows 3.1 to the latest Windows XP and Windows 2000. You can bet that another person using Windows can open a bitmap image you send.

Unfortunately, because this quality stems partly from a lack of compression, bitmap images are many, many times larger than their JPEG counterparts . . . we're talking *huge*. For example, a typical desktop background image at 1024 x 768 resolution may measure more than a full megabyte in size! For this reason, bitmaps are scarce on the Internet. (If you do download them, they're usually compressed beforehand with a program such as WinZip.)

Most folks store scanned images in bitmap format for archival purposes. These images, with their compatibility and image quality, can be read from a CD-R and converted into whatever format you need at the time.

Tagged image file format

Cross-platform appeal is the claim to fame for the TIFF format. It's recognized by just about any image editor under Windows, Mac OS, Linux, and even operating systems such as BeOS and that rascally OS/2. TIFF images end with the TIF extension in the Windows world.

The TIFF format delivers a little of the best of all formats: You can choose to apply different types of compression, although picture quality is excellent with both 24-bit color and grayscale. Graphic artists and publishers appreciate the support TIFF provides for color separations, too. On the downside, TIFF images are still larger than JPEG, even with significant compression, so TIFFs aren't a big favorite for Web or e-mail use.

Table 10-1 summarizes the image formats I discuss in this chapter. The sizes I list represent the same 24-bit color image at 1024 x 768 resolution, converted to each format.

Table 10-1	The "Compressed" Pros and Cons of Image Formats			
Format	*Compression*	*Size*	*Color Depth*	*Grayscale*
JPEG	Yes	110K	16.7 million (24 bit)	Yes
GIF	Yes	N/A	256 colors (8 bit)	No
Bitmap	No	972K	16.7 million (24 bit)	Yes
TIFF	Yes	403	16.7 million (24 bit)	Yes

What the Sam Hill Is a PNG?

A little-known image format has been threatening to burst onto the Internet scene for the past three or four years, and it's finally starting to gain a foothold. The format is named *p*ortable *n*etwork *g*raphics — or PNG ("ping") for short — and these images typically carry the PNG extension under Windows.

Why treat PNG differently? Here are three reasons:

- ✔ **PNG is the only format designed from top to bottom especially for the Internet — specifically, the Web.** PNG offers the same transparency feature as a GIF file (although a PNG image can't be animated), and it delivers the same 24-bit color as a JPEG. The first ancestor of the PNG format appeared in 1995, so it's a relative toddler compared to the other formats I discuss.

- ✔ **PNG offers a lossless compression.** Unlike with a JPEG, the compression used to shrink the file size doesn't remove pixels or detail.

- ✔ **PNG was supposed to revolutionize the very fabric of the space-time continuum.** (Yes, I'm a *Star Trek* fan, but only of the original series — well, and the first three movies. In my opinion, *any* form of the show after the third movie is a travesty.)

As you may have guessed from the direction I'm taking, that last reason doesn't hold water. The developers of the PNG format forgot that simple human nature makes people stick with what works until someone develops something better, and that something better has to be accepted as a standard by everyone or else it just doesn't get very far off the ground. Although PNG is indeed a better format than GIF, the file sizes PNG provides aren't as small as they are in JPEG format. Therefore, Web page developers still continue to use GIF and JPEG images, and PNG has spent the last few years sitting on the sidelines like a third-string quarterback.

The PNG format is supported in today's popular browsers, and it's beginning to appear on more Web pages, so there's hope for the future. After all, it took a few years for people to get excited about that Wright Brothers contraption. (Or so I've read. I'm not *that* old.) For now, though, don't hold your breath waiting for PNG to replace the Big Two.

Choosing Color Depth for Web Images

Here's where things get interesting for your preschooler: Ask the next 4-year-old you meet, "What's the best size for a box of crayons?" That little boy or girl almost certainly will grin widely and say "The biggest one, of course!" And in just about every case, that's the right answer. After all, who wants to use a measly 16-color box of crayons when you can have the 256-color deluxe box instead?

There *is* one case . . . (You just knew that I would say that, didn't you?) Like English grammar, the world of computer technology has an exception to every rule. As I say in Chapter 1, most Web developers tend to choose 256-color images for pages that are visited often. This choice cuts down on the time it takes to download images, including these types:

✔ Buttons, clip art, and borders.

✔ Three-dimensional titles. For example, Figure 10-1 illustrates one of my sites (dedicated to the classic 1960s TV series *Batman*). The title on this page is a fair-size piece of rendered three-dimensional artwork, but the image was reduced to 256 colors and loads in five or six seconds on a 56-Kbps modem connection.

✔ Thumbnails (for Web sites that allow a visitor to click thumbnails to download larger versions).

✔ Advertising banners and animated graphics.

Figure 10-1:
A title graphic is a perfect example of a Web image that should be no more than 256 colors.

On the other hand, in two cases, 24-bit color is called for on a Web page:

✓ **When quality is the thing:** If your site presents high-quality images as its primary function, you need the high-quality appearance of 24-bit color. For example, if your Web site is dedicated to medieval European tapestries of the 14th century, you *have* to deliver 24-bit color to your visitors. (If these images are 800 x 600 or larger, I recommend placing a warning on your home page explaining to those with modem connections to the Internet that downloading may be tedious. Most sites with this kind of content list the typical download time for an image at various speeds, which can help visitors decide whether downloading the image is worthwhile.)

This type of site is the perfect candidate for thumbnails. That way, your visitors can decide with a glance whether they want to download "Men in Tights" or "Knights in White Satin" *without* having to suffer through an interminable wait just to discover that they chose the wrong image.

✓ **When your visitors are in the fast lane:** If you run a business site that caters to other businesses (which are likely to be using high-speed connections to the Internet, such as a T1 line or a DSL/cable modem connection), you make a better impression with flashier, high-quality images. This statement is especially true on an office intranet, where you know that everyone accesses the site over the office network.

For most people, then, the rule is simple: Stick with 256-color images unless you have a specific need for a larger box of 16 million crayons.

Compression in the 21st Century

The topic of compression pops up in this chapter whenever I mention image formats such as JPEG and PNG. Because these image formats allow you to pack a 24-bit image into a smaller space, why not crank compression higher and reduce them even further? In this section, I show you a series of images that help illustrate what I mean by *lossy* compression (where pixels are removed by using a mathematical formula) and *lossless* compression (which compresses the image without removing pixels), and I help you to understand why too much compression is not a good thing.

The sample shown in Figure 10-2 is the starting point: It's an uncompressed Windows bitmap image, with plenty of detail and shadows you can use (and an attractive subject to boot). At 1100 x 1057 and 24-bit color, the image occupies about 3.5MB of hard drive territory.

Figure 10-2:
An uncom-
pressed
bitmap
version of a
scanned
photograph.

You can experiment with compression to convert this bitmap image into a compressed JPEG. As a first step, you apply a simple 15 percent compression (practically nothing) by following these steps in Paint Shop Pro:

1. **Choose File⇨Open.**
2. **Highlight the file you want to use and click Open.**
3. **Choose File⇨Save As.**
4. **Click the Save as type drop-down list box and choose the JPEG format.**
5. **In the File name field, type a new filename.**
6. **Click the Options button to specify JPEG settings.**

   The dialog box shown in Figure 10-3 appears.

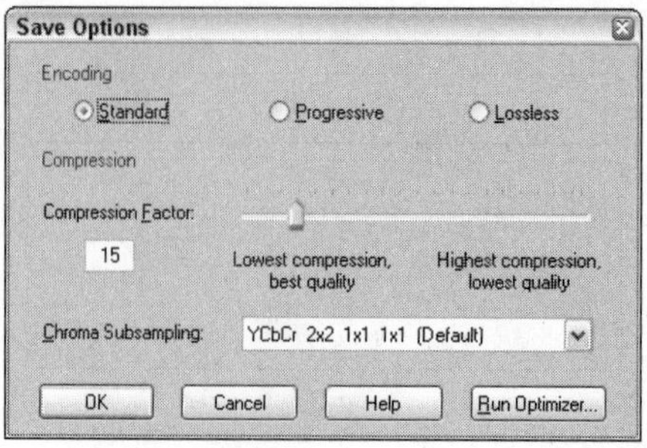

Figure 10-3:
Choosing a
mild level of
JPEG
compres-
sion with
Paint Shop
Pro.

7. **Click the Standard encoding option, and then click and drag the Compression Factor slider until it reaches 15.**

8. **Click OK to return to the Save As dialog box.**

9. **Click Save to start the conversion and save the new file to disk.**

As you can see in Figure 10-4 . . . well, you can't really see much difference (at least none that you can tell with the naked eye, or even at a significant zoom factor). I generally apply 15 percent compression to all my JPEG images, and it has never affected the quality of the images appreciably. However, check the new file size. Whoa! The same file at the same size and color depth is now (drum roll, please) a measly 196K — hence, the popularity of the JPEG format. The smaller file size results from a combination of the more efficient image format and the compression level you chose.

Crank up the compression and apply 65 percent to the sample image. Finally, you can just begin to see in Figure 10-5 the effects of lossy compression as the image starts to lose detail. The file size is reduced further, to a mere 62K.

Avoid the pit of compounding compression!

You can easily fall into the Pit of Compounding Compression. That's the case with a JPEG image you open and edit repeatedly (perhaps to add or update a piece of text or to experiment with the gamma level). If you save the image each time by using that typical 15 percent compression ratio I mention in the main text, each copy you save suffers another repetition of the compression procedure, thereby unnecessarily degrading the quality of the image a little bit further. To avoid this situation, set your image editor to reduce compression to 1 percent for successive saves. You generally can't turn off compression altogether when you're saving a JPEG, although you can reduce it to the bare minimum. Alternately, you can edit the original image in a lossless format such as TIFF or Windows bitmap, and then convert it to the JPEG format (using Save As) whenever you need a JPEG copy.

Figure 10-4:
Wait —
I know that
15 percent
compres-
sion is
applied
here, but I
can't see it!

Figure 10-5:
At 65
percent
compres-
sion, the
image starts
to lose a
noticeable
amount of
quality.

Just for kicks, go all the way and increase the compression to the maximum 99 percent. This amount is ridiculous, but as you can see in Figure 10-6, the JPEG format still provides something that's almost recognizable! At this point, the image is only 27K!

Figure 10-6:
Well, what did you expect at 99 percent lossy compression? A Rembrandt?

Now you can convert the first sample image to PNG format. Although the image looks the same as the original bitmap image shown in Figure 10-2, its size drops to about 1.7MB. The lossless compression used in a PNG image is far less effective than even a minimum 1 percent compression level applied to a JPEG image, which produces about an 800K image.

That Color Doesn't Look Right

The Web can be a colorful place — at least, if you've decided to use 24-bit color images. Then again, for all the reasons I mention in previous sections, you may decide to opt for 256 colors, which means that you've decided on the GIF format for a particular Web image. The problem is, *which* 256 colors look "right in every visitor's browser? Imagine all the different combinations of commercial, freeware, and shareware browsers out there, matched with Windows or Mac OS or Linux!

Luckily, the HTTP powers that be (read "Internet Explorer, Safari and Netscape Navigator") have decided on their own color palette that's supposed to be the best possible compromise between the Windows system color palette and the Mac OS system color palette. The result is an optimized Web palette of 216 colors that delivers a good range of colors, from a 256-color VGA display all the way up to a 16.7 million-color display. People who design Web pages for a living are very familiar with the Web palette.

Paint Shop Pro makes reducing your GIF images to this *Web-safe* palette easy by loading what it calls the Jasc Safety Palette. Follow these steps:

1. **Choose File⇨Open to load your image.**

2. **Choose Image⇨Palette⇨Load Palette.**

3. **Click the Palette drop-down list box and choose the SAFETY.PAL file from the list.**

4. **Click Load.**

    Paint Shop Pro reduces things for you.

5. **Save your changes by choosing File⇨Save or File⇨Save As.**

Remember that Web palette optimization is for *only* 256-color GIF images. Applied to a 24-bit photograph, the Web palette destroys the quality by reducing 16.7 million possible colors to a whopping 216 colors. The result is barely recognizable!

What Size Is Best for the Web?

As you may already know, no single correct size exists for a Web image. If visitors to your site download an image that's bigger than their screen resolution, their browser still displays it. However, they have to scroll the image from top to bottom or side to side (or both) to view the entire thing, which is not the best solution.

Therefore, keep these guidelines in mind while you're deciding on the dimensions of your Web images:

✔ **Remember that most folks still use lower screen resolutions.** Although today's video cards and monitors allow ludicrous on-screen resolutions, how many people actually hang out at 1600 x 1200? Most site visitors are likely to use a resolution of 800 x 600 (with some a little higher, at 1024 x 768, and some still clinging stubbornly to 640 x 480). Therefore, if you want your images to be displayed without scrolling and downloaded in a bearable period of time, they should be significantly smaller than 800 x 600.

✔ **Use a common aspect ratio.** A typical computer monitor uses an aspect ratio of approximately 1.33 to 1. Therefore, most visitors have problems if you try to display an image that's 450 x 900. Instead, try cropping or resizing to bring such an image more in line with the standard aspect ratio.

✔ **Don't take thumbnails seriously.** Can you really expect anyone to appreciate an image that's only 100 x 75 (especially if it includes text)? Unfortunately, I've visited more than one Web site where the designer expects you to buy a product based on a thumbnail image! Thumbnails should be used only as part of a visual catalog. If your visitors deserve a better look (for instance, if you're offering high-resolution images for downloading on your site), give them a chance to see your image at 400 x 300 or 640 x 480 instead of as 100 x 75 thumbnails. There's one downside to using larger images. As you find out in the "Wait a Second: Is This Legal?" section, later in this chapter, if you offer a version of an original photograph that's too large, it can be stolen and used by others who don't care about copyrights.

If an image absolutely has to be larger than 800 x 600 or the aspect ratio must remain somewhat outrageous, consider using WinZip or the Mac OS X File⇨Create Archive command to archive that image to a Zip file, and allow your visitors to download the zip file rather than the image itself. They save time; plus, after they've unarchived the image, they can load it into their own image editor program and modify it to their liking. Everyone's happy this way!

Sending Your Scans through E-Mail

Sending a scanned image as an e-mail attachment is convenient and quick. All that's required on both ends is an Internet connection and an e-mail account that can send and receive binary attachments. To illustrate the process, I show you how to send an image to a friend using Microsoft Outlook 2003.

Follow these steps:

1. **Run Outlook by clicking the Outlook icon on your Windows desktop.**

   Outlook Express works fine as well.

2. **Choose File⇨New⇨Mail Message.**

   The new message window shown in Figure 10-7 appears.

3. **Click your cursor in the To field and type an e-mail address.**

   Or, if you're using the Address Book, click the To button and select an entry.

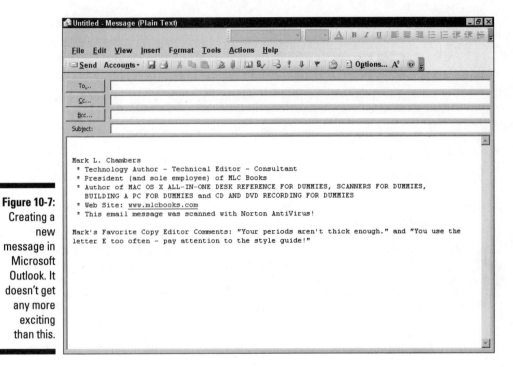

Figure 10-7:
Creating a
new
message in
Microsoft
Outlook. It
doesn't get
any more
exciting
than this.

4. Click in the editing pane and enter the text of your message.

5. Click Insert and choose File.

The Insert File dialog box appears, as shown in Figure 10-8.

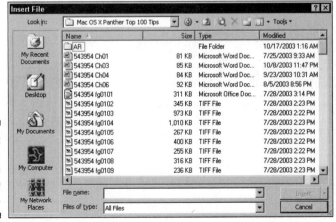

Figure 10-8:
Selecting a
file to attach
to the
message.

6. **Locate the image on your hard drive and then click its filename to select it.**

7. **Click the arrow next to the Insert button and choose Insert as Attachment from the pop-up menu.**

   An attachment pane is automatically added to the bottom of the window, showing you the attached file. See Figure 10-9.

8. **Click the Send button on the toolbar to send the message.**

After the recipients of your message receive your e-mail, they can easily save the attachment to disk. If they're using Outlook as well, they can right-click the attachment icon and choose Save As to display the Save As dialog box, choose a location, and save the file. Outlook preserves the filename (including the extension) on the receiving end.

Converting your images to JPEG format before you add them as attachments is always a good idea. Your Internet Service Provider is likely to have a maximum allowed size for attachments, and a 3MB bitmap or TIFF file may be rejected by your e-mail server when you try to send it. (Plus, you would be covered in cobwebs by the time your 56-Kbps modem finished sending it.)

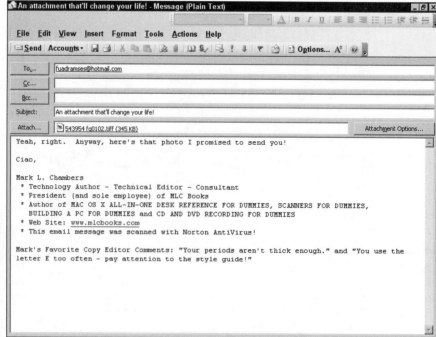

Figure 10-9:
The image is
ready to be
sent along
with the
e-mail
message.

If you're running Mac OS X and you use iPhoto to organize your scanned images, take advantage of that legendary Apple simplicity to accomplish this same task with a single button! Simply launch iPhoto, select the image you want to send, and click the Email button at the bottom of the window. iPhoto automatically converts the image to JPEG format and attaches it to a new e-mail message, ready for you to address and send. *Sassy.*

Wait a Second: Is This Legal?

Reproducing something by scanning it for your own, personal use is one thing. Often, the material is yours anyway, but communicating it to the outside world in any way could involve you in a legal wrestling match. The problem is one of copyrights, and the question of whether something can be legally reproduced is far more complex than most people think.

Let's get one thing straight: *I am not a lawyer.* I have friends and relatives who are lawyers, I've watched them on TV, and I know a half-dozen good lawyer jokes, but *do not* consider this section to be definitive legal advice! The guidelines I provide here are simply general warnings, so if you have copyright questions that need to be answered, you *must* employ a knowledgeable copyright lawyer!

Now that you're all cognizant that I'm not Perry Mason, I can furnish you with a few rules every scanner owner should know:

- ✔ **A work doesn't have to carry a copyright mark to be copyrighted.** In effect, a copyright is granted immediately when the author of a work completes it, and the work doesn't have to bear a copyright. (However, I show you at the end of this section how to add one to a scanned image.)

- ✔ **Movement from document to digital doesn't eliminate a copyright.** Just because the original is a paper document and you've scanned it as a digital image, it doesn't suddenly become your property. (If so, I would be the genius behind everything Mozart ever composed, everything Shakespeare ever wrote, and everything Escher ever drew!)

- ✔ **The source is immaterial.** Web sites, Internet newsgroups, your neighbor's trash, or the daily paper — no matter how you got it, if it's not your original work, you must receive permission from the author to use it.

- ✔ **Permissions must be obtained individually.** Even if the author of an original document has granted you permission for other, similar works in the past, no shortcut is allowed; you must receive permission for each work individually.

- ✔ **Changing an original doesn't change the copyright.** Substituting your face for the *Mona Lisa*'s kisser with your image editor doesn't change a thing. The rule is simple: If the work wasn't your creation, modifying it doesn't make it yours.

If you do decide to distribute a scanned image of your original work, I recommend that you add a visible copyright to it. Follow these steps in Paint Shop Pro:

1. **Choose File⇨Open.**

2. **Highlight the image you want to add a copyright to, and then click Open.**

3. **Click the Text icon (labeled in Figure 10-10), and then click the cursor where you want the line of text to begin (preferably where the text will be as visible as possible).**

   Paint Shop Pro displays the Text Entry dialog box, as shown in Figure 10-10.

4. **In the Font drop-down list box, choose a font. In the Size list box, choose a font size.**

   Both are located on the toolbar at the top of the window.

5. **Click in the Text box, and type the following line:**

   Copyright (c) [year] by [name], All Rights Reserved.

   where [year] is the year in which you created the work and [name] is your name or the name of your company.

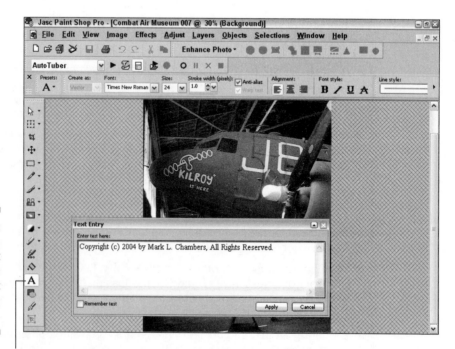

Figure 10-10:
Entering a copyright message in the Text Entry dialog box.

Text icon

6. **Click Apply to add the text to the image.**

7. **Save your changes by choose File⇨Save or File⇨Save As.**

Should 1 Keep This to Myself?

Let me be brutally frank here: Most travelers on the Web don't know (or don't care) about copyright law. If you're the creator and copyright owner of an image, *never offer it on your Web page or send it to another person if you want to keep exclusive rights!* As an author with a professional relationship with my publishers, I know that my rights are protected under contract. If you simply add an original high-resolution image to your Web page for anyone to download, however, don't be surprised if that work shows up on other Web sites and Internet newsgroups. Usually, you aren't credited, and to most people your image becomes part of the public domain (although, as I just discussed, it most certainly *isn't*).

"So how do I distribute an image without losing control?" Unfortunately, if you don't have a legal agreement or contract, about the only method you can depend on is to "brand" the image by adding a line of text over it (as shown in Figure 10-11).

Figure 10-11: Although this text doesn't prevent a patient person from restoring the image, it should prove troublesome.

You can also reduce its size to something that's worthless to redistribute, which means that your visitors get treated to something not much bigger than a thumbnail. Even these safeguards aren't guarantees. Other people have image editors too.

Chapter 11

Advanced Image Editing 101

Are you ready to try the deep end of the scanning pool? If so, you'll be testing the waters that many scanner owners never reach. Those folks are satisfied with a simple crop or a resizing, and they never wonder what an image would look like if the subject were swirling down a drain or pressed into aluminum — or even set on fire!

The moral of the story is a simple one. In fact, it's the Mark's Maxim that provides the foundation for this chapter. To wit:

You don't have to settle for the images your scanner produces.

Take my word for it: The artist inside you is just waiting for a chance to emerge. After you know how to modify your scanned images, the rest is simply finding the time you need to experiment.

I cover minor image surgery in Chapter 9. In this chapter, I introduce you to the procedures and tools you need to apply major changes and enhancements to your scanned images (as well as a number of additional software tools you may find valuable).

Making Magic with Scanned Images

All right, let me come clean: I never *really* sat for the portrait with President Abraham Lincoln you see in Figure 11-1. Figure 11-2 shows the original photograph of the Hero of the Republic, and the original scanned image of me is shown in Figure 11-3.

Figure 11-1:
Sitting with the President was such a thrill!

Figure 11-2:
Honest Abe,
before I
joined him.

So how did I do it? By using my image editor to "combine" the two portraits, using the same type of cut-and-paste commands you've grown to know and love with applications such as your word processor. Rather than cut paragraphs, though, I cut my image and pasted it into Lincoln's photograph. (I also converted my image to grayscale because brilliant color wasn't a feature of the cameras available back in those days.)

Such magic is easy, and you find out how to do it later in this chapter, in the "Copying and pasting (without glue) section." First, I want to introduce you to filters and special effects, which are probably the most powerful tools available in your image editor.

Figure 11-3:
An ordinary author, with no Presidential companion.

Introducing Filters and Effects

Whenever you feel creative, it's time to turn to the two big-name stars featured in most image editors: *filters* and *effects*. They both do the same thing: modify your image by applying mathematical formulas. Some filters and effects change only the pixels in a certain area of your image; others modify the entire image.

What's the difference between a filter and an effect? (Pay close attention — you can win your next trivia contest with this question.) An effect can typically be controlled, so you can specify just how much you want to change your image — and therefore it requires your input. A filter, on the other hand, is usually automatic. You simply apply it and forget it. Other than that, filters and effects are virtually indistinguishable from each other, so you can promptly forget this if you want.

What about text?

You may be wondering whether filters and effects can be applied to scanned images with text, such as a newsletter page you've scanned. The answer is yes (filters and effects can be used with any image), although in most cases you can't read the text! If you use a twist effect on that newsletter page, for example, the text appears to spiral into the center of the image. This trick can work, however, if you're using an effect that can be controlled; a slight twist may leave the text intact while imparting a, well, wacky feel! Trust me on this one.

I cover some of my favorite filters and effects elsewhere in this book. For now, just remember that they can change an ordinary snapshot into something that looks like it was taken in the Twilight Zone!

Going Wild with the Effect Browser

If you're reading this chapter from beginning to end, you should be on speaking terms with filters and effects. Let's visit our old friend Paint Shop Pro 8 and see how the program applies them.

Here I go, waxing enthusiastic about my favorite Windows image editor again. This program is so doggone cool, though, that I can't *help* it! Paint Shop Pro provides a browser that makes it easy to see the changes you can make to an image with any effect. (Note that the Effect Browser has nothing to do with Web pages or the Internet. Instead, it's a separate window displayed in the program. I've visited some mind-boggling Web pages, although not in Paint Shop Pro.)

To use the Effect Browser, follow these steps:

1. **Choose Effects⇨Effect Browser.**

2. **Click the plus sign next to the Effects folder in the tree display at the left of the Browser window, as shown in Figure 11-4.**

   The program expands the Effects to show the major categories of effects you can apply. (To collapse the folder and hide its contents, click the minus sign next to the folder icon.)

Figure 11-4:
Is it a bird?
Is it a plane?
Is it a Web
program?
No, it's the
Effect
Browser!

3. Click the Art Media Effects entry in the list to expand the category.

Paint Shop Pro displays a number of thumbnail preview images that demonstrate what types of changes are produced by the effects in this category. You also get a quick description of the effect on the status line at the bottom of the browser.

4. Click the Charcoal (Factory Defaults) preview to select it.

If you'd like to change the settings for the effect before you apply it, click the Modify button.

It's not necessary to use the Effect Browser if you already know what effect you'd like to apply to an image. Here's the shortcut: Click the Effects menu, and you'll see that the effects categories are mirrored on the menu. Move your mouse over a category menu item to display a hierarchical menu with the effects in that category. Click the desired effect, and it's automatically applied. *Sassy!*

5. After you've chosen the effect you want (and changed any settings, if necessary), click Apply to apply it or click Cancel to back out without making any changes.

Figure 11-5 shows the image from Figure 11-4 after Charcoal has been used. Wow! This effect looks great when applied to this image of a World War II airplane.

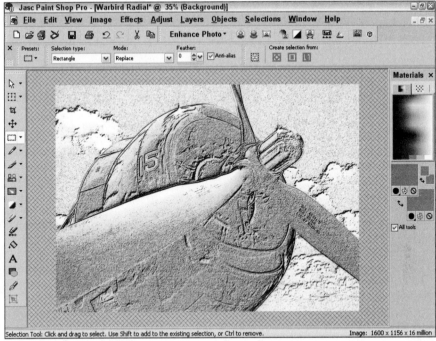

Figure 11-5:
The artistic
result
produced
by the
Charcoal
effect.

I know that the preview window provided by the Effect Browser may not give you an exact idea of what an effect does. A thumbnail can show only so much detail, so keep in mind that you can use Edit⇨Undo to reverse any effect you apply!

Let's Hear It for Plug-Ins!

I want to introduce you to a good friend of mine, the plug-in. A *plug-in* is an extension program that's not actually built into your image editor. It's a separate piece of software you buy or download. A plug-in is typically produced by a different developer than the folks who produced your image editor; in fact, some software companies are devoted to producing only plug-ins.

To give you some idea of how popular these beasties are, I have friends in the graphic arts who have installed literally hundreds of plug-ins! Extending the craziness available to you in your image editor can become addictive. It's much like those folks you probably know who are hooked on fonts.

Before I wax too enthusiastic about plug-ins, check your image editor's documentation. Although most well-known programs support them, exceptions exist. The most popular type of plug-in is designed to be used with Adobe Photoshop, Adobe Elements, and Paint Shop Pro. Other plug-ins you encounter may be designed for a specific image editor, so they may not work on your system. Check the system requirements in the documentation for the plug-in to make sure that it works with your editor.

If your image editor does indeed support plug-ins and you've bought or downloaded one or two compatible modules to experiment with, you're ready to install them and get down to business. (For a taste of what's available in the world of plug-ins, visit theplugnsite.com and www.extensis.com.)

In Paint Shop Pro 8, follow these steps to add a plug-in:

1. **Choose File⇨Preferences⇨File Locations.**

   The File Locations dialog box appears.

2. **In the File Types list, click the Plug-ins entry to display the settings shown in Figure 11-6.**

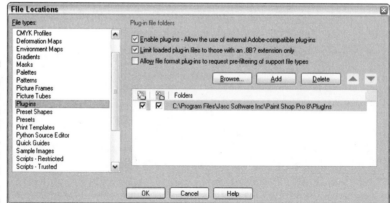

Figure 11-6:
Adding a plug-in is fun and educational. Well, at least it's not hard.

3. **Click the Enable plug-ins check box to enable external plug-ins in Paint Shop Pro.**

4. **If your plug-in comes with its own installation program, run the install program and smile quietly to yourself. Otherwise, copy the file to the \PlugIns folder under your Paint Shop Pro home folder.**

   Alternatively, click the Browse button and select the folder where you've installed your new plug-in files. Some people like to keep different sets of plug-ins from different developers in different folders so that they can add or remove them more easily. Personally, I prefer the easy route of keeping them all in the \PlugIns folder.

5. **Click OK to save your new settings and return to Paint Shop Pro.**

Photoshop users will find that things work much the same:

- ✔ If the plug-in comes with an installer, run the program.
- ✔ If the plug-in needs to be installed manually, copy it to the Plug-ins folder under the Photoshop home folder.

To set up an alternative folder in Photoshop for a plug-in, follow these steps:

1. **Choose Edit (Photoshop on a Mac), and then choose Preferences⇨ Plug-ins & Scratch Disks.**

   Photoshop displays the dialog box shown in Figure 11-7.

2. **Enable the Additional Plug-Ins Directory check box.**

3. **Click Choose, and highlight the folder where you installed the additional plug-ins.**

4. **Click OK (or click Choose, depending on the operating system) to save your changes.**

5. **Restart Photoshop so that the program can recognize the new plug-ins.**

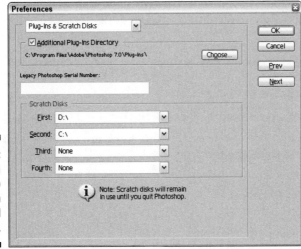

Figure 11-7:
Adding a
Photoshop
plug-in
folder. Feel
the power.

Editing Tiny Pieces of Your Images

Earlier in this chapter, I discussed all sorts of filters, effects, and plug-in fun. Now I want to turn your attention toward the manual joys of image editing. I show you how to change images by copying and pasting and by changing the colors of pixels.

Copying and pasting (without glue)

As I mention earlier in this chapter, I used the copy-and-paste trick to hang out with President Lincoln, but you can use it for more practical purposes, such as copying a piece of an image and pasting it in another place, either in the same image or another image. You can use it to replicate (by adding copies of people in the same scanned photograph, for example) or eliminate (by copying a blank area over an offending object).

To practice copying and pasting in Paint Shop Pro, follow these steps:

1. **Choose File⇨Open, and double-click the desired filename to load your image.**

2. **On the left side of the program's window, click the geometric selection tool.**

   The tool looks like a dotted rectangle.

3. **Click the top-left corner of the area to copy, and hold the mouse down while you drag the selection rectangle to the lower-right corner of the area you want to save. Release the mouse button to select the area.**

   The area remains surrounded by the animated rectangle, as shown in Figure 11-8.

4. **Choose Edit⇨Copy.**

   The image you selected is placed in the Windows Clipboard.

5. **Choose Edit⇨Paste as New Selection. Click the location where you want the selected area.**

   The piece you copied is pasted into the current image, as shown in Figure 11-9.

6. **Choose File⇨Close.**

7. **Click No when you're prompted to save changes, unless you made changes to the source image that you want to save.**

Figure 11-8:
Selecting
an area of
an image
to copy.

Figure 11-9:
Just call it
cloning for
the common
man (or
woman).

To paste the piece you just copied from the Clipboard into another image on your hard drive, follow these steps:

1. **Choose File⇨Open, and double-click the desired file to open the target image.**

2. **Choose Edit⇨Paste as New Selection.**

3. **Move your mouse to move the piece anywhere in the image, and click once to drop the piece where you want it.**

4. **Choose File⇨Save (or Save As) to save the new image with another filename, another format, or both.**

Changing colors (without crayons)

Face it: Pixels aren't always perfect, and most of the time the problem has to do with coloring. You can encounter a wide range of color problems in your scanned images, including

✔ Elements in the image that need to be changed or erased (but can't be cropped), such as a sign in the background of a photograph or a stray line of text in a document.

✔ Cosmetic imperfections in the original, such as flecks in a photograph or a thumbprint on a business card.

✔ Plain downright wrong colors. Aunt Harriet wore yellow and purple together again, didn't she?

Follow these steps to change the color of individual pixels (or a group of pixels) in an image using Paint Shop Pro:

1. **Choose File⇨Open, and double-click the desired file to load your image.**

2. **On the left side of the program's window, click the Pan tool.**

   The tool looks like a mouse pointer.

3. **To get a better look at your pixels, click the Zoom by 1 Step or Zoom by 5 Steps button in the toolbar.**

   Each click zooms in closer, so keep clicking until you can easily see the area of pixels you want to change. To move to a different spot in the image, just click and drag the image in the desired direction. Figure 11-10 illustrates a block of pixels that needs to be "painted" white.

4. **In the color selector (in the upper-right corner of the program window), click once to set the foreground color and right-click once to set the background color.**

   As you move the cursor, it changes to an eyedropper to indicate that Paint Shop Pro is ready to "pick up" that color.

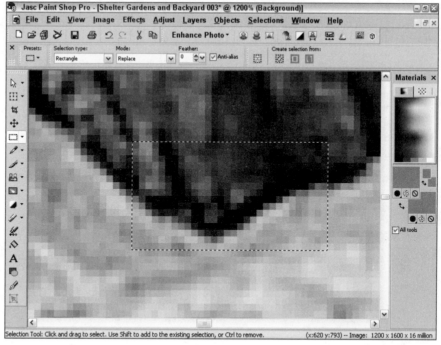

Figure 11-10:
Zooming
in close to
correct the
detail in an
image.

5. **Click the paintbrush tool on the left side of the program window.**

6. **Move the paintbrush cursor on top of the pixel (or pixels) you need to change and click to paint the pixel with the new colors. Repeat as necessary.**

7. **Choose File⇨Save or Save As to save the new image with another filename, another format, or both.**

Naturally, these basic techniques are nowhere near a complete catalog of everything you can do in a powerful image editor such as Paint Shop Pro or Photoshop. But then, covering everything you can do with such programs is far beyond the scope of this book, which is supposed to be about scanners (no matter how much I like image editing). Several books the size of this one — and many that are *much* bigger — are devoted to Photoshop and Paint Shop Pro.

For a complete guide to Photoshop (which is something akin to a complete guide to every grain of sand on Pismo Beach), I recommend all gazillion-plus pages of *Photoshop CS Bible,* by Deke McClelland (published by Wiley). For an in-depth guide to Paint Shop Pro (with a *For Dummies* attitude), turn to my comrades-in-arms, David C. Kay and William Steinmetz, the authors of *Paint Shop Pro 8 For Dummies* (also published by Wiley).

Talk about seamless!

What's that you say, Bunkie? You're having a hard time using the color selector to match the color surrounding a pixel? Well, I have good news: If you want, you can duplicate the exact colors in surrounding pixels! Paint Shop Pro provides an eyedropper you can use to match the colors of a single pixel in your image. Click the eyedropper tool (on the left side of the screen) and move the eyedropper cursor over the pixel with the color you want to use. Click once with the left mouse button to lock in the foreground color, and once with the right to lock in the background color.

Imaging Tools You Can't Resist

Before I close up shop for this chapter, expand your horizons and leave "pure" image-editing software behind! In this section, I familiarize you with other types of image applications you may want to use with your scanned images as well as cover a few of the best-known plug-ins on the market. These programs can add convenience and versatility to your digital toolbox!

Image manipulation

First on a wish list of image software is the *image manipulation* genre. This category covers a wide range of programs, all of which are designed to apply some sort of special appearance or perform a single type of editing procedure on an image. If you like, think of these programs as stand-alone plug-ins that run without an image editor.

Corel KnockOut 2

KnockOut 2 is a *masking* program: That term means you can use the program to isolate and remove just one element from an image and then copy that image the same way you paste a rectangular selection (as you do in the first part of this chapter). However, KnockOut provides much more precise selection tools than a plain image editor. For example, you can isolate and manipulate a scanned photograph of a tree, with every leaf intact, or even a subject with blurred or hazy edges. Imagine being able to "grab" an image of a Persian cat from one photo and seamlessly insert it into another image, without losing a single hair! The program has a street price of about $100, and it runs under both Mac OS X and Windows 98 or later.

Figure 11-11 shows you KnockOut at work. For more information on KnockOut, visit the Corel site, at www.corel.com.

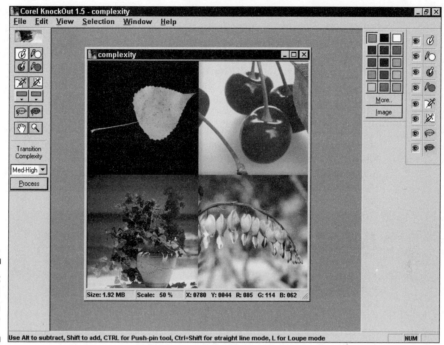

Figure 11-11:
What will I
mask from
this image?

Kai's SuperGoo

SuperGoo has been a favorite of my kids for years. This easy-to-use image manipulator has several built-in filters that allow you to see the effects of what you're doing in real time, while you're working. You can turn an innocent portrait into a wacky shot of an unearthly alien — all with no previous knowledge of image editing. Smudge a face this way or bash it that way or stretch a subject in a photograph like taffy! You can also animate your changes to an image and produce the resulting "goo" as an AVI or QuickTime movie.

SuperGoo is a steal at $20, and it can run on both Macs and PCs. Visit the SuperGoo home page, at `www.scansoft.com/supergoo`.

Image correction: Kai's PhotoSoap2

Another type of common image application is specially designed to correct specific errors in your images — a nasty case of red-eye, for example, or the scratches typically found on those old photographs kept in shoeboxes. These image-correction programs aren't used as often as your image editor, but when you do need them to rescue an image that's otherwise unusable, they're worth every penny you spend.

PhotoSoap2 shares many of the same ease-of-use features as its sister product SuperGoo. Scanner owners from 10 to 100 can easily use it, and no previous image-editing experience is needed. You can correct images scanned from wrinkled or scratched originals, brighten and sharpen, add or change colors, and even remove the speckles from a text document before you use an OCR program. All these tasks are performed with intuitive animated tools, such as brushes and pencils, in real time!

PhotoSoap2 includes more traditional editing chores that I cover in my discussion of Paint Shop Pro, such as cropping, rotating, and resizing. PhotoSoap2 also provides a basic image album feature so that you can store your images and retrieve them when you need them. For more information or to order PhotoSoap2 online for $20, visit www.scansoft.com/photosoap.

Image cataloging: Photo Album 4

The more you use your scanner, the more you may find yourself scratching your head and wondering "Exactly where did I put that image?" I show you in Chapter 9 how to use the Browse function in Paint Shop Pro, and it suffices for many folks who keep track of a hundred images at a time on their hard drive. But if you have to keep track of thousands of scanned images, you need a more powerful image-cataloging tool.

From the same folks who bring you my favorite image editor, Jasc Software, comes Photo Album 4, a program that can even keep images organized for someone like me. (I'm about as methodical and neat as Homer Simpson.) Figure 11-12 shows the main window in Photo Album 4.

To use an image-cataloging application, you display thumbnails (again, much like the Paint Shop Pro Browse screen) and double-click a thumbnail to load the file. An image-cataloging tool can also store much more, however, including audio (such as MP3 and WAV format files) and video (such as MPEG and Microsoft AVI movie files)! Even though you're concerned only with images in this book, you can think of this program as a Swiss Army knife for storing all your digital media.

You can acquire images from your scanner directly from Photo Album 4, display any image and print it directly from your catalog, or create a slideshow presentation (rather like the slideshow CD-ROM I show you how to create in Chapter 13) complete with background music. You can "attach" text keywords and descriptions to any media file so that you can search an entire catalog for a *Glorious Eagle Against Alaskan Sunset*. (I have that image somewhere.) To make life easier, MCP 3 can even convert images from one format to another, or apply simple effects — no need to fire up Paint Shop Pro!

Like Paint Shop Pro, Photo Album 4 is available directly from Jasc Software, at www.jasc.com. The program costs about $25 for the download-only version and about $30 for the boxed version. That's a bargain!

Figure 11-12:
Photo
Album 4 is
ready to
organize
your world.

Plug-in software: Eye Candy 4000

I have an easy way to demonstrate just exactly how many plug-ins are available
for image editors such as Photoshop (or Paint Shop Pro): Just drop by your
favorite online software store (or visit www.yahoo.com) and type **photoshop
plug-in** for your search criteria! Some plug-ins simply add effects, and others
add new commands and functionality.

Alien Skin Software has produced a number of fantastic plug-in suites over
the past several years, and Eye Candy 4000 is the company's latest work.
The package includes 23 Photoshop-standard filters, including Glass (adds a
realistic glass layer or fonts on top of an image, with accurate reflection and
refraction effects), Marble (which can create original marble patterns with
full control over coloring, veins, and shape), and Smoke (which can create
smoke, haze, and fog for those London shots that didn't turn out right).

Figure 11-13 illustrates what I did in just 30 seconds with the Glass filter,
and Figure 11-14 shows off the Marble effect!

You can buy Eye Candy directly from the developers for less than $200 by
visiting their site, at www.alienskin.com.

Figure 11-13:
The Eye
Candy
Glass filter
is a treat!

Figure 11-14:
Who would
guess that
this stone
master-
piece was
computer
generated?

Chapter 12

Maintaining the Scanner Beast

. . . .

In This Chapter

▶ Calibrating your scanner

▶ Cleaning your scanner

▶ Troubleshooting and solving hardware problems

▶ Troubleshooting and solving software problems

▶ Calling technical support

. . . .

Compared to other pieces of rather recalcitrant hardware you can attach to your computer, such as a printer or a digital camera, a scanner is, I'm happy to say, practically a walk in the park when it comes to maintenance. It has no bothersome batteries, ink cartridges, memory cards, or paper to change and no clogged inkjet nozzles or spilled toner dust. Jamming a sheet-fed scanner is possible (I tell you more about this topic in a bit), but a flatbed will never jam.

That doesn't mean, however, that you can simply ignore your scanner like it's a lawn gnome. You should follow basic steps that help keep your scanner (and the images it produces) in tiptop shape. Although most scanners these days sell for less than $200 or $300, that certainly doesn't make them disposable!

In this chapter, I provide all the information you need to keep your scanner clean, perfectly calibrated, and reasonably happy. I also cover the common problems that crop up most often with scanner hardware and software and provide possible solutions — and tell you what to do in case you need expert help from the manufacturer's technical support department.

Calibrate Your Way to Happiness

When you consider just exactly what a scanner does — digitizes thousands of pixels in a precise pattern from an original — you can easily understand why some scanner manufacturers recommend that you calibrate your scanner regularly. To be more specific, *calibrating* a scanner is somewhat akin to aligning the printer cartridges on your inkjet printer or even adjusting the timing for your car's engine: You're correcting the "drift" that occurs over time and returning the scanner's mechanism to its factory alignment.

Only sheet-fed scanners (including those that are built in and "all-in-one" multifunction printers) usually need to be calibrated. Check your scanner's manual to see whether it mentions this process. Some older flatbeds can be calibrated as well. If you don't need to calibrate your scanner, I invite you to skip this section and save yourself a section's worth of reading.

If you're still with me, your sheet-fed scanner likely requires calibration from time to time. Signs that you need to calibrate include

- ✔ Vertical black or white streaks in scanned images
- ✔ Images with pixels "lost" from the margin or margins, even from originals that were correctly aligned
- ✔ Empty areas in scanned images where text or graphics should be

Also, calibrating a scanner at least once a year is a good idea if it's used often, as in an office environment.

Although the exact steps you take vary according to your scanner's brand and model, here's the general procedure for calibrating a sheet-fed scanner:

1. **Run your scanner's control program and choose the Calibrate command.**

   (On an all-in-one multifunction device, you may need to choose Calibrate from the front panel menu.)

2. **Load a blank white sheet of standard 8½-x-11-inch printer paper into the all-in-one's document feeder.**

   If you're using a stand-alone sheet-fed scanner, the manufacturer typically provides a preprinted calibration page. If you use one of these pages, skip Step 3.

3. **The printer prints a calibration test page.**

4. **Take the calibration test page and load it into the scanner's document feeder.**

   The scanner loads the page and performs the calibration procedure using the pattern.

Would the real calibration please stand up?

You can perform another type of calibration, although it doesn't affect your scanner. Instead, you can calibrate your system's printer and monitor to more accurately reflect the colors in the scanned original. Under Windows 98, Me, 2000, and XP, and Mac OS 9 and OS X, colors are calibrated between different pieces of hardware using a *color-matching system.*

In the Macintosh world, the Mac OS features a system named ColorSync, which sets a definition for each color supported by each piece of hardware that matches the international color palette called the CIE XYZ standard. Most Macintosh hardware comes with its own, unique ColorSync profile.

On the Windows side, Microsoft supports a color-matching system called ICM/ICC. Again, the hardware you buy that can scan, print, and display images is likely to have an ICM/ICC profile that's copied to disk during the installation process.

For most people, worrying so much about color matching is basically "too much sugar for a nickel." Hot pink doesn't have to look exactly the same on the computer screen as it does when it's printed. For a graphics professional, however, the story is altogether different, and computer-savvy folks who work with print media rely heavily on color matching.

The Right Way to Clean Your Scanner

Want to find out how to clean the surfaces inside and outside your scanner? As I mention elsewhere, dust, smudges, and fingerprints can make an impression on your scanner — and therefore on your scanned images! It takes only a couple of minutes every few weeks to keep your scanner clean, and you benefit every time you produce a scanned image.

Never disassemble any piece of computer hardware without specific instructions from the owner's guide (or the company's technical support department)! Taking your scanner apart to clean it may expose you to a shock hazard. It can also damage your scanner and invalidate your warranty. (Besides, nothing deep inside your average flatbed or sheet-fed scanner is *meant* to be accessible for cleaning!)

I don't discuss how to wipe down the exterior of your scanner. It's a process called *dusting,* and most adults already have more than enough training to accomplish the task. However, I provide a number of guidelines in this section that can help prevent problems.

On the outside

I've met many, many computer owners who feel that both a computer's case and external peripherals are indestructible, which is why their systems usually look like a work of modern art. You may notice coffee cup rings, at least one Unknown Stain, and several dozen pieces of tape. As long as the fan and the CD-ROM drive aren't completely covered with sticky notes, it's all acceptable! (Personally, I use the Notes feature in Microsoft Outlook to keep things straight.)

Never use solvents!

When it comes to cleaning, you quickly find that your computer and your scanner are, well, all too human! Many types of household cleaners can discolor or damage your scanner's body (because it's most likely made of plastic).

A number of companies make antistatic cleaners especially for computer hardware; these cleaners are fine (they help repel dust, and they don't hurt your hardware). Take care, though, in using a spray or any uncontrolled aerosol around your scanner. I tell you more about this topic in the section after next, "On the inside."

Use the right tool

For the outside of your scanner, as well as the rest of your computer hardware, all you really need during spring-cleaning is a soft cloth. I recommend either a computer antistatic cloth or a clean, old T-shirt.

If, on the other hand, an accident occurs and something stains the outside of your scanner, you probably can remove it with a *slightly* moist paper towel. Again, don't spray anything directly on your scanner!

On the inside

I suppose that this section may not apply to all scanner owners because they don't open a hand scanner or an inexpensive sheet-fed model; their scanners are permanently sealed. However, it does concern owners of all flatbed scanners and more expensive sheet-fed scanners, where you can actually reach under the cover or inside the body of the scanner.

Abrasives are out!

Although this advice is self-explanatory, I want to mention it anyway: If you use the wrong type of cleaner, you can scratch the glass in your flatbed scanner. This problem is almost as bad as cracked or broken glass because (depending on the location and the size) a scratch can easily show up at a higher dpi setting! What's worse, a single scratch rarely occurs by itself, unless something sharp accidentally hits your scanner's glass.

Treat your scanner like the precision device it is, and take the same care with the glass as you do with those expensive sunglasses or that telephoto lens for your 35mm camera! As a matter of fact, a friend of mine uses a photographer's lens cloth to wipe down his scanner's glass.

Never spray liquids!

This piece of advice is a biggie! I have personally seen what happens when someone uses a glass cleaner delivered by an aerosol pump on a flatbed scanner: The liquid works its way between the edge of the scanner's glass and the body of the unit. In this case, the liquid that seeped through didn't cause problems with the scanner's electronics (although that *can* happen if enough liquid is applied). Instead, it resulted in enough condensation to produce a fogging effect whenever the temperature in the room changed by a few degrees! Anyone who drives a car on a cold morning has almost certainly encountered something similar on the inside of the windshield. Scanning through this mess proved impossible.

As you can imagine, a fogged scanner glass forces you to do either of the following:

✔ **Open your scanner yourself.** For those with technical knowledge and experience with electronic hardware, this task is no big deal. Most folks would consider it a tricky operation, though. Remember that opening your scanner is sure to void your warranty.

✔ **Take the unit to a repair shop.** (Insert sound of cash register ringing here.) If you spent around $100 for your flatbed scanner, is it worth spending $35 to have it fixed?

The moral of the story? Keep liquids — *including* water — away from the interior of your scanner. If you have to apply a liquid (for example, to eliminate streaks on your glass), apply a small amount to a cloth and *then* wipe down the glass.

While you're at it, wiping down the foam pad on the bottom of your flatbed scanner's cover is also a good idea.

Consider the monitor wipe

"Isn't there a simple way to take care of my scanner's glass?" You bet! Use what I use: an antistatic computer monitor wipe. Technonerds like myself get ridiculously hooked on these things. I guess it comes from spending so much time in front of a monitor.

Anyway, these wipes are nonabrasive and safe for your glass, and they carry just enough liquid to eliminate streaks and fingerprints (without risking the fogging problem I mention in the preceding section).

Cleaning a sheet-fed scanner

As I mention earlier in this chapter, most inexpensive sheet-fed scanners on the market are sealed; paper goes in, and paper comes out. End of story. However, more expensive sheet-fed units, and the scanning units in most multifunction devices, *can* be opened, and you should do so regularly to inspect and clean the interior clockwork.

How often? Usually your owner's manual gives you an idea of the time period between regular cleanings. If your manual is mute on this point, however, I recommend once every three months or so. As you may remember from Chapter 1, sheet-fed scanners move the original past a stationary scanning head, so they're more prone to ink smudges, dust, and dirt than a typical flatbed scanner.

Your manual provides the procedure for opening your sheet-fed scanner. Often, you tip forward a door on the front or back of the unit, or you may remove the top cover entirely. For example, Figure 12-1 illustrates a typical laser all-in-one device. In Figure 12-2, the access door on the front has been opened to expose the innards for cleaning.

Figure 12-1:
A multifunction device in its natural environment.

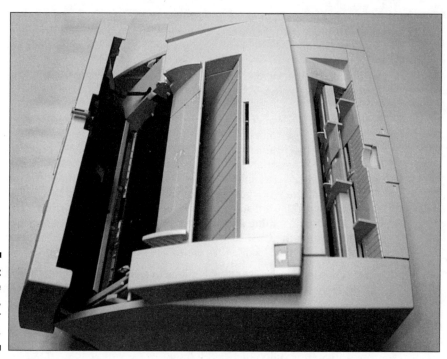

Figure 12-2:
The same device, ready for cleaning.

Exactly what you clean varies by model and manufacturer. If you're the proud owner of a multifunction device, what you encounter also depends on the type of printing engine that's used. For example, although laser all-in-one units are great, they get dirtier because of the toner that's used; devices based on inkjet printer engines are easier to maintain.

Don't blow in my ear!

When you're cleaning the inside of your sheet-fed scanner, I also highly recommend a can of compressed air. This stuff can blow dust out of the tiniest cracks and crevices inside your scanner as well as out of your other computer hardware (including troublesome parts of your system, like the fan and the keyboard) without damaging anything electronic or mechanical and without leaving any residue. If you can find the variety with the long, plastic nozzle for reaching the tiniest nooks and crannies, all the better!

While spraying, hold the can upright — spraying while holding the can upside down can result in a harmful temperature drop if the gas hits your skin or rubber components inside the machine. And in the same vein, keep that compressed air can away from the kids, because the urge to use it inappropriately is a strong one. (I've even seen grown men and women succumb to temptation.)

Some multifunction devices use a single *paper path* — that's the path the paper takes through the machine — for both scanning and printing. These units need to be cleaned more often than a device that has separate paper paths.

In just about every case, however, you end up cleaning the following parts in your sheet-fed scanner:

- ✔ **Rollers:** The rollers that move the paper in a sheet-fed scanner can get gunked over time by the residue on your documents, so the rollers are usually the primary cleaning targets. Make sure that you look closely for scraps of paper and other debris while cleaning. If necessary, you can use tweezers to remove pieces lodged at the bottom of the unit. As a general rule, you can use a cotton swab soaked with a *small* amount of isopropyl alcohol solution to clean the grime from your rollers; use a side-to-side wiping motion, and switch cotton swabs often. Figure 12-3 illustrates the CSSCP, short for *cotton swab scanner cleaning procedure*. (I can't help it. I work with weird acronyms all day long.)

- ✔ **Scanning lens:** The scanning lens in a sheet-fed scanner is a thin strip of glass or plastic set into one side of the paper path. Use the same caution as you would with a flatbed's scanning glass. Again, a monitor wipe is your best friend in this situation.

- ✔ **Pressure sensors:** These plastic sensors may look like speed bumps or wires; they tell your sheet-fed unit when you've loaded paper and when a sheet has passed through the scanner. Because they come in direct contact with your documents, they can receive the same grime and gunk as the rollers, so give them the cotton swab treatment as well.

Figure 12-3:
Doing the roller-cleaning thing.

Cotton swab

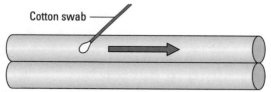

Hardware Nightmares and How to Fix Them

Suppose that the unthinkable happens and your scanner is suddenly silent or acts strangely. What do you do? Are you stuck with an expensive service call or a visit to your local computer repair shop?

In this section, I describe the common hardware problems that can occur with a scanner and how you can correct them. In many cases, you can fix a hardware problem without professional help by following my suggestions, and I can also identify those problems that *do* require you to call for technical assistance.

Do not panic!

Unless the scanner is smoking or on fire, *take your time in diagnosing the problem*. This is Rule Number One when it comes to any type of problem with your scanner. Most of the parts that make up your computer system are quite simple (especially when compared with your income tax forms), so if you work through things methodically, you're likely to hit on both the problem and the solution.

Check your manual first

Although I try to be as specific as possible with the problems and solutions in this section, I can't cover everything specific to your brand and model of scanner. Therefore, always check the troubleshooting section in your scanner's manual for more information before you try my suggestions!

Another good source of troubleshooting information is the support area on the company's Web site. Don't forget to check for FAQ (Frequently Asked Questions) files, which often contain problems and solutions reported by your fellow scanner owners.

Do jams happen often?

If you're continually fixing paper jams while you're using your sheet-fed scanner, something is wrong. In normal home use, you should encounter no more than one paper jam every month or so. First, make sure that the guides that adjust the paper path are correctly set; they should be snug against the paper in the document tray so that the paper is fed correctly into the machine. Also, it may be time for you to clean your scanner's roller system.

Finally, verify that the items you're scanning aren't too thick for your scanner. The owner's manual may tell you the maximum thickness of paper that your model can accept.

On to the fun stuff

With those two important rules in mind, let's get started with scanner hardware troubleshooting. If nothing works in this section, skip forward to the "Help!" section, at the end of this chapter, for critical information you need when you're contacting technical support.

Nothing works!

You've plugged everything in, turned on your scanner, and waited a minute or two (just to let things warm up and wake up). No lights, no sound, no signs of life from your scanner. Consider these possible causes:

- ✔ **The power cable is unplugged.** Sure, you've heard all the jokes, but let me tell you that even the most seasoned and experienced computer technician has wondered why a piece of hardware is acting as though it's not getting any power, only to discover that it's not plugged in!

- ✔ **The AC adapter is malfunctioning.** Many scanners use AC adapters, and they have been known to break. If you suspect the AC adapter and you bought your scanner locally, visit the store and ask a salesperson whether you can borrow an adapter to try. Alternatively, you can always buy a universal AC adapter, set it to match the scanner's adapter, and test the hardware.

- ✔ **The surge suppressor is malfunctioning or tripped.** If nothing that's plugged into a surge suppressor strip is working, the strip itself is the suspect! If your scanner is plugged into a surge suppressor strip, make sure that the strip is turned on. Also, check to make sure that the strip's built-in circuit breaker or fuse hasn't been tripped. If it has, your AC wiring was likely hit by a decent-size electrical surge during a storm. Reset the breaker and see whether the strip works correctly.

One-button copy/scan/fax doesn't work

Although malfunctioning buttons on your scanner may seem to be in the hardware, the glitch may be related to a software problem instead. Check these potential problem areas:

- ✔ **Background tasks are not loaded or are disabled.** When you press one of the buttons on your scanner, the scanner sends a signal to your computer to tell your computer, in effect, "Hey, someone just pressed the Copy button." To recognize the signal, your computer has to be running a special program that was installed with the scanner software. Under Windows 98, Me, 2000, and XP, you may be able to see this program running on the right side of the taskbar. If an icon for the program is there, right-click the icon to determine whether it's enabled. In the worst case, you have to reinstall your scanner software.

✔ **The scanner is not connected.** Although your scanner may be turned on, check to make sure that it's connected to your computer. Cables can work loose, especially if you've recently moved your computer to a new location.

✔ **Buttons are jammed or broken.** The problem could be with the button itself; for example, perhaps the button is jammed in the down position. If one or two of your buttons work on your scanner but another one doesn't, you may have a malfunctioning button on your hands. If you bought your scanner from a local store, take it by and let one of the salespeople check it for you.

✔ **The scanner has software or driver problems.** Check the following section for tips and tricks to fix a possible software problem.

Jammed sheet-fed scanner

Not much diagnosis is required when you have a jammed sheet-fed scanner, because that problem is obvious! However, you have two possible solutions:

✔ **The document is still visible.** If the document is still visible outside the machine, you're in luck. (It may not seem lucky, but take my word for it.) Grab the paper by both top corners and pull in the opposite direction from the paper path. Note that this direction is usually *not* straight up, but rather toward the back of the machine. Use a steady pull, and don't try to jerk the paper out of the machine.

✔ **The document is inside the scanner.** Remember how I said that things could be worse than a visible paper jam? Well, if the document is lost deep in the bowels of your sheet-fed scanner or multifunction device, it's worse. Follow the instructions in your owner's manual to open the unit's case, and locate the paper release lever. (If you're using a laser multifunction device, you may have to remove the toner cartridge.) The paper should then be free to move, and you should be able to pull it gently through the roller system and out into the open.

Flatbed scanning head doesn't move

Although flatbed scanners are less prone to problems than sheet-fed scanners, they're not perfect! If your unit is receiving power but the scanning head doesn't move when you attempt to scan something, here's a list of possible reasons:

✔ **The travel lock is engaged.** Most scanners come with a travel lock, which is a mechanical lever that holds the scanner head in place to avoid damage during shipment (and while you're carrying the scanner from apartment to apartment). If the lock has accidentally been engaged, you can damage your scanner's internal motor and drive system by repeated scanning attempts. Therefore, check this one first!

✔ **The drive belt is broken or misaligned.** Most scanners use a belt system to transfer motion from the motor to the scanning head. Shine a flashlight through the scanner's glass and check to make certain that the belt isn't broken or hasn't jumped the pulleys.

✔ **The screw drive has threading problems.** Some scanners use a screw drive, where the motor turns a screw shaft to move the scanning head. Again, use a flashlight to check the scanning head to make sure that it's still moving freely on the screw and that the screw is turning when the motor is working.

✔ **The rails are misaligned or damaged.** No matter what type of drive your flatbed scanner uses, the scanning head travels up and down the length of the machine on two rails. If the scanner was dropped or damaged during a move, these rails can become misaligned so that the scanning head "sticks" between them. Sometimes, the rails simply need a little lubrication with a few drops of light oil; you have to open your scanner's case to reach them.

✔ **Your system has software or driver problems.** Check the following section for tips and tricks to fix a possible software problem.

✔ **The motor is burned out.** A bad scene — and hard to test. Check to see whether your scanner motor works when you turn on the machine. Most models recalibrate themselves automatically when you turn on the scanner. If you're sure that the connection is working between your scanner and the computer (and your software is working properly), run your scanning-control software and try a quick preview.

Scanning light doesn't work

The scanning light on your flatbed should come on when you turn on the unit. (Some models also turn it off until your computer sends the command to start scanning.) If the scanning light doesn't turn on when the scanning head is moving, one of these problems may be the culprit:

✔ **The cable is loose.** Your scanning head receives power (and sends image data) through a cable. Use a flashlight and look through the scanner's glass to verify that the cable is still properly connected.

✔ **A bulb is burned out.** Depending on the manufacturer, you may be able to buy a replacement bulb; check the manufacturer's Web site or contact technical support. If the scanning head and bulb are combined into a single sealed unit, however, you're probably out of luck.

Parallel port problems

If you're using a parallel port scanner and your PC reports that it's having trouble connecting to your scanner, check the following possible problems. (These problems crop up only on PCs, because Macs don't have parallel ports.)

✓ **A cable is loose.** This check should be SOP (standard operating procedure) for any connection problem. Make sure that you check both ends of the cable, too.

✓ **Daisy-chaining isn't working.** If you're trying to plug your scanner into your parallel port Zip drive or other parallel port external device, you may encounter problems. The software and drivers for some scanner models require a direct connection to the computer. Try removing the other device and connecting your scanner directly to the computer. (If the scanner works then, try connecting the Zip disk to the scanner's second parallel port.)

✓ **The port mode is wrong.** Your computer's parallel port must be set to ECP/EPP mode before a scanner can use it to communicate with your computer. Your computer's manual should tell you how to display the BIOS settings that control your port mode. Usually, you press F1 or Delete when you're prompted right after you turn on your PC.

✓ **The parallel port is faulty.** If a standard parallel port printer also has problems on this port, it may be malfunctioning. In Windows XP, right-click My Computer, choose Properties, and click the Hardware tab. Click the Device Manager button to display the Device Manager dialog box (as shown in Figure 12-4), and make sure that Windows properly identifies your port. If the port has a yellow question mark or a red X through it, Windows is having trouble accessing the port, so bring your PC to your local computer shop for a checkup.

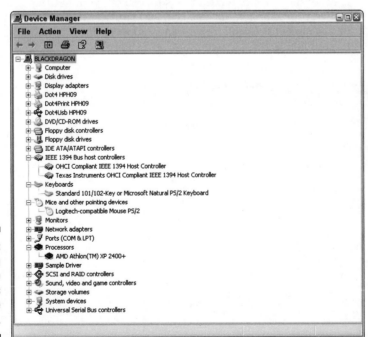

Figure 12-4:
Investigating
with the
Windows
XP Device
Manager.

Always reboot after a potential parallel port fix because Windows checks for parallel port operation during the boot sequence.

Send out a probe!

Your scanner probably shipped with a program designed to test the connection between it and your computer. For example, Figure 12-5 illustrates the program that came with my Microtek scanner. If you suspect a problem with your scanner's connection, run your probe program first, and let it test your system and offer advice on what's wrong.

USB or FireWire isn't working

Because both USB and FireWire are similar in operation, they share the same potential trouble areas and solutions:

- ✔ **The cable is loose.** Check both ends of your cable, just in case.

- ✔ **Your system has device driver problems.** Both USB and FireWire devices require specific drivers, and these drivers can be accidentally overwritten or deleted from your system. Reinstalling your scanner's software (which includes the drivers) should fix the problem.

- ✔ **Your system has bus problems.** No, I'm not talking mass transit here. If your USB or FireWire scanner is connected to your computer through another device and that device is turned off, your computer may not recognize your scanner. Turn all USB and FireWire devices on and reboot, or disconnect the other device and connect your scanner's cable directly to your computer.

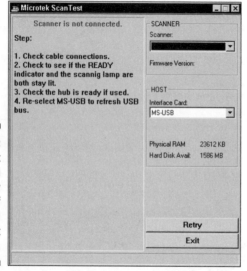

Figure 12-5:
My test program can't find my scanner. Of course, I did disconnect it on purpose.

SCSI isn't working

Unfortunately, if SCSI isn't working, this major problem is likely to affect not just your scanner but also every other SCSI device inside and outside your computer. Thus, the entire system may grind to a permanent halt until you've tracked down the configuration problem and fixed it.

Therefore, run — do not walk — to Chapter 4, where I harp on and on about what needs to be set correctly for your SCSI device chain to hum like a well-tuned Cadillac.

Software Nightmares and How to Fix Them

I have good news and bad news. Because I always ask for the bad news first, here it is: Software nightmares are harder to diagnose than hardware nightmares, and in my experience they tend to happen more often.

Here's the good news: You have more to work with because software problems usually generate at least some sort of error message you can use to point you in the right direction. With that in mind, in this section I cover a number of common software errors and what they mean and give you tips and tricks you can use to solve them.

Reboot — just reboot!

First and foremost, if you experience a software error while using your scanner, follow the hardware technician's first solution to absolutely everything: *Reboot!* (I spent a number of years as a hardware technician for a major hospital, and I wish I had a dime for every time I've heard someone say "Oh, okay, it's working now!" after simply rebooting the computer.)

Why does this work so well? For a number of reasons:

- Software you're running can occasionally lock up, and it may not necessarily be your scanning software, so you may not immediately be aware of it. For example, if you're running Microsoft Outlook in the background and you lose your Internet connection, your system may freeze.

- Some external devices, particularly those on a parallel port connection, can get "confused" when your computer communicates with several pieces of hardware at a time. The classic example is a parallel port Zip drive and a parallel port scanner daisy-chained together. They may work perfectly when they're accessed separately but may lose track of their own existence when you try to write to a Zip disk and scan a document at the same time.

✔ Both Windows and Mac OS can sometimes crash. (Yes, I *know* that you don't believe me, but I've heard stories from the victims.)

A reboot can solve these problems by resetting everything to its normal state, so try it first, before you think "Nightmare."

Keep that software current!

Here's another tip that applies to every one of your computer's peripherals, including your scanner: Keep your drivers up-to-date. Check the manufacturer's Web site regularly (once a month is usually about right) for software and driver updates, and apply them immediately when they appear.

This advice is especially important for people who are continually upgrading their operating system or hardware. Often, a driver that was installed when you bought your scanner isn't completely compatible with a new operating system, so what worked under Windows 98 may not work under Windows 2000 or Windows XP.

Manufacturers try to get their drivers updated as soon as possible because compatibility means a decrease in customer support requests. Minimize your software problems by keeping your system current.

Okay, it is a software nightmare

Arrgh! Rebooting didn't help, and you're using the latest drivers. The manual doesn't say anything about your current predicament, and the manufacturer's Web site is clueless. You have a software nightmare, so you should examine the problems and solutions.

Scanner software doesn't load

If nothing happens when you run your scanner software, check these possible problems:

✔ **The scanner is offline.** Make sure that your scanner is powered on and connected. You can't control something that's not working.

✔ **Your system is missing program files or drivers.** This problem can rear its ugly head in one of two ways: Either a program you ran "cleaned up" your hard drive (in fact, cleaned it *too* well) or you've erased important files by accident. Reinstalling your scanner software should correct the problem, although (depending on the extent of the damage to your system) you may find that other programs or hardware devices aren't working either.

✔ **Your system has software incompatibilities.** Have you just installed another program or even upgraded your operating system since the last time you used your scanner? First, try reinstalling your scanner software. If that doesn't work, call the manufacturer's technical support department for help because the incompatibility is likely buried deep in the lower levels of the operating system.

Scanner software doesn't recognize the scanner

Your scanner software appears but then promptly informs you that you need to purchase a scanner. Your scanner, however, lies dormant. You may be experiencing difficulty with the following:

✔ **The scanner is offline.** Again, check your scanner and its connections to make sure that all is well.

✔ **Changes in USB, FireWire, or SCSI configuration.** If you've recently swapped devices around in your USB, FireWire, or SCSI configuration (and you haven't rebooted), I can practically guarantee that your software thinks that the scanner is still operating in its old location. Although the persnickety nature of SCSI makes this diagnosis easy, this problem is not *supposed* to happen with USB and FireWire. Unfortunately, my experiences have shown that these connections are not quite as automatic as they say, especially if your USB hub is supplying additional USB devices. (By the way, check that hub to make sure that it's plugged in, too.)

✔ **Your system has software incompatibilities (again).** If you've just finished installing a new piece of software, you may end up having to reinstall your scanner software to overwrite the changes made by the new installation and restore things to normal.

Scanner freezes in midjob

When a scanner freezes in midjob, you have a nasty software problem. If your scanner is halfway through a scanning job and everything grinds to a halt, potential causes include the following:

✔ **Your system has a hardware conflict.** If your scanner has been working well and you've just installed a new piece of hardware or changed your old hardware configuration, the culprit is likely to be an "argument" between the two components for the same system resources. You can either remove the new component and restore the old system configuration, which is generally not the option you want, or call the technical support department for your scanner and have someone there help you isolate which Interrupt Request (IRQ) is causing the problem.

"What system resources can cause problems?" In Windows, a beastie called an IRQ is the likely culprit. Windows needs a separate IRQ to communicate with a device, and if two devices are trying to use the same IRQ, the scanner or the entire system may lock up. IRQ problems can also occur with modems, sound cards, and SCSI adapters.

✔ **The scanner is low on memory or hard drive space.** Remember that your scanner can create a whopping-big image file, and it can take quite a bit of processing power, hard drive space, and system RAM to make a high-resolution, 1200 dpi image a reality. If your computer runs out of either hard drive space or system RAM, Windows or your scanner program (or both) are likely to lock up and your scanner can stop dead in its pixels. Check your scanner's manual for the recommended amount of system RAM and hard drive space. If this problem occurs only when you're scanning the largest originals at the highest resolutions, you may need to upgrade your computer system.

✔ **Your system has software incompatibilities (again).** You know the drill: Reinstall your scanner software, and make sure that you're using the latest drivers for your hardware.

Help!

You've checked, rechecked, and covered all your bases. You've tried every possible solution that I list in this chapter, plus a few you thought up on your own, and still nothing helps.

You have reason for hope, though, because no matter what piece of hardware or software falls ill — scanner, software, operating system, or even your entire computer system — help is available! In this case, though, you're likely to need technical support from only one source: your scanner manufacturer.

So what do you need (besides a telephone and a dialing finger)? Just in case you do need to call for help, let me give you a pointer or two on what those fighting men and women need from you! (Remember, I've been in their shoes.)

You're likely to be asked for this information:

✔ The model number of your scanner

✔ The interface that connects the scanner to your system

✔ The version of operating system you're using

✔ The version of the scanner software you're using

✔ The brand of computer you're using and any peripherals you've added

✔ The serial number of your scanner and software

✔ Any error messages you've received

✔ Precisely what you were doing when the error occurred (and any steps you took afterward)

You should find the technical support number for your scanner in the manual. The number is probably listed on the company's Web site as well.

Chapter 13

Scanner Projects for Crafty People

・・・

In This Chapter

▶ Printing a custom wine label

▶ Creating a custom T-shirt

▶ Creating a slide show

▶ Using optical character recognition

▶ Faxing a scanned image

・・・

*W*hen you think of your scanner, *handicrafts* may not be the first word that leaps to mind. That's because most people add a scanner to their system for something practical, such as business or schoolwork. (If you're a parent, try convincing the kids exactly *why* you bought a scanner.)

Therefore, you may be surprised when you take a walk through your local shopping mall. If you keep your eyes open, you see just how versatile a tool your scanner really is. You may see stores (and even kiosks) creating custom T-shirts from your photographs, recording computer CD-ROMs with your photographs, or printing custom calendars and greeting cards. Heck, one store owner I know uses a basic computer system with a good inkjet printer, a scanner, and a digital camera to fashion custom wine labels for parties and special occasions!

To be truthful, those entrepreneurs may be pretty angry with me because in this chapter I expose their secrets. You find out how to create some of those same items by using the same techniques (but without the expense). I even make an effort to stay friendly with the "practical" business crowd by showing you how to send a scanned image as a fax and how to use an OCR program.

Creating a Custom Wine Label

If your computer system includes an inkjet printer, you're ready to create the perfect gift for any wine connoisseur — and the lucky recipient won't even know that you bought that "bargain-priced" $6 bottle! (At least, not until the tasting — after all, I can't help you change the vintage.) You also need a length of double-sided tape, a pair of scissors or a paper cutter, and one or two sheets of glossy photo paper.

Again, I'll use Paint Shop Pro to illustrate the process — but you should be able to keep up by using similar commands in just about any image editor (on either a PC or a Mac). Run your image editor and follow these steps:

1. **Open the scanned image you want to use for the label.**

2. **Resize the image to about 5 x 4 inches.**

   To be sure that your custom label will completely cover the existing label, measure the existing label and allow for at least half an inch of overlap on all sides.

   a. **Choose Image⇨Resize.**

   b. **In the Width field of the Print Size section, enter 5 inches, as shown in Figure 13-1.**

   c. **If the existing aspect ratio doesn't work, you can crop the image to change the ratio or disable the Lock aspect ratio check box and allow Paint Shop Pro to alter the image to fit.**

   d. **Click OK to resize the photo.**

Figure 13-1: Resizing a scanned image to 5 x 4 inches.

3. **Next, add the text for your new label.**

    a. **Click the Text icon on the toolbar on the left side of the screen.**

       The icon looks like the letter *A*.

    b. **Click the cursor where you want the line of text to begin.**

       Paint Shop Pro displays the Text Entry dialog box, as shown in Figure 13-2.

    c. **Select a font from the Font drop-down list box and a font size from the Size list box.**

       Both list boxes appear on the toolbar at the top of the window.

    d. **Click in the Text box, type your message, and click Apply to create the text.**

4. **Set your printer for Photo paper and the best possible print quality.**

5. **Load a sheet of glossy photo paper in your printer.**

6. **Choose File⇨Print to print the label.**

7. **Using a paper cutter or scissors, trim around the edges of the label.**

8. **Turn the label facedown and add double-sided tape around all four edges.**

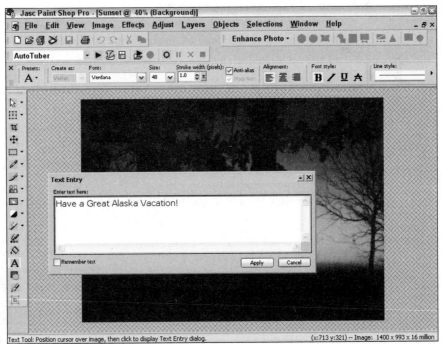

Figure 13-2:
Adding a bit
of bon
voyage to a
wine label.

9. **Center the label so that it completely covers the existing label on the wine bottle, and press down to apply.**

10. **Smooth the new label with a cloth, moving from the center of the label to the outside edges.**

The double-sided tape makes the label easy to remove later and save.

A T-Shirt with a Personal Touch

Adding a scanned image to a T-shirt (or another fabric item, such as a canvas book bag) is great fun, and you end up with a unique gift that pleases kids and adults alike. And (unlike what some people may have told you) this is not rocket science. Because I'm a big fan of NASA, however, I treat things in stages.

I recommend a T-shirt or other fabric item made of pure cotton, a mixture of cotton and polyester, or canvas. You also need an iron, a pair of scissors, an inkjet printer, some T-shirt transfer paper, and a sheet or pillowcase.

Kids and a hot iron don't mix. Adult supervision is needed for this project!

Stage 1: Preparations

First, follow these general steps to prepare the item for the transfer:

1. **Wash the item in cold water.**

   Applying a transfer to a brand-new T-shirt, for example, usually causes problems when the shirt is washed for the first time.

2. **Machine-dry the item at a normal temperature (*without* using any fabric softener or other additives during the drying cycle).**

3. **Iron the item (without starch or steam) to remove wrinkles in the fabric.**

   Allow the item to cool to room temperature before applying the transfer.

Stage 2: Printing

To print your transfer on your inkjet printer, follow these general steps:

1. **Import your scanned image, design your transfer, and save it to disk.**

   You can use any program that prints in color to prepare your design, including a word processor, such as Microsoft Word. If you're using a

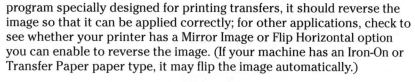
program specially designed for printing transfers, it should reverse the image so that it can be applied correctly; for other applications, check to see whether your printer has a Mirror Image or Flip Horizontal option you can enable to reverse the image. (If your machine has an Iron-On or Transfer Paper paper type, it may flip the image automatically.)

Never print a T-shirt transfer on a laser printer. T-shirt transfer paper isn't designed for laser printers, and you may damage that expensive toy. (Plus, if it's your *company's* expensive toy, you could be in deep trouble.)

2. **Print a test page using regular paper, to make sure that your design fits on the item.**

   Leaving two or three inches of border all around the design is a good idea. If you're creating a T-shirt, this "test fit" also allows you to ensure that the design doesn't wrap around, effectively appearing on the other side of the shirt! Use your design program to resize things if necessary, and then print another sample page to check the fit.

3. **Place a single sheet of transfer paper on top of a few sheets of regular paper and load them into the printer.**

   Typically, each sheet should have some sort of markings that indicate which side is the front and which is the back. (To make sure, though, don't forget to read the instructions that accompany the transfer paper. You may have to take specific steps to prepare a transfer sheet for print-ing, or you may have to follow some loading instructions.)

4. **Depending on the program you use to print the design, you may have to enable a printer setting to reverse the image. Choose the Transfer Paper or Iron-On paper type, if it is present.**

5. **Select the best possible print quality.**

6. **Choose the Print command from the program's File menu to send the design to the printer.**

7. **Trim around the edges of the design with scissors.**

   For a professional look, maintain a consistent distance from the border of your design. Be sure to leave a "flap" of border that's a little wider to allow easy removal of the transfer after you've applied it.

Stage 3: Liftoff!

First (don't you just hate these pauses in the countdown?), an important word about ironing! Depending on the brand of T-shirt transfer you're using, you may need different iron settings or a different amount of time to apply your transfer. Check the instructions that came with your transfer, and follow those instructions whenever they differ from my steps.

Follow these general steps to apply the transfer:

1. **Choose a smooth, hard table or countertop wide enough for the entire item. Cover this surface with a sheet or pillowcase, and smooth all wrinkles from the backing.**

   A kitchen countertop is a good candidate. *Do not* use an ironing board, which can cause wrinkles.

2. **Fire up your iron on the highest setting it provides, and let it preheat for at least ten minutes.**

   Remember: No steam or starch!

3. **Arrange the item in the middle of the backing, with the side that receives the transfer facing up.**

4. **Align the transfer on top of the item, printed side down.**

   Because the design is reversed, it should now be facing in the correct direction, as shown in Figure 13-3.

5. **Move the iron slowly from the top of the design toward the bottom along one edge of the transfer, applying constant pressure. The iron should be in contact with the transfer for at least 30 seconds.**

   Make sure that the iron overlaps the transfer so that the edge of the transfer bonds to the fabric. If you're applying the transfer to a cloth with a heavy weave (such as canvas or rough cotton), you should press harder to ensure proper bonding between the cloth and the transfer.

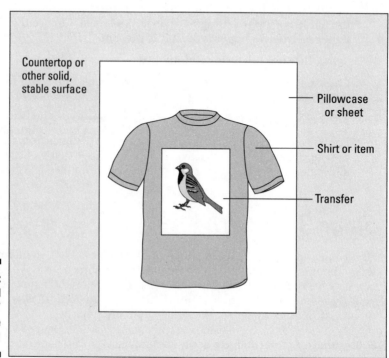

Countertop or other solid, stable surface

Pillowcase or sheet

Shirt or item

Transfer

Figure 13-3: Houston, all looks "go" for image transfer!

To avoid scorching, *never* allow the iron to rest in one place for more than a second or two!

6. **Repeat Step 5 with the other three edges of the design.**

   Completely sealing the edges of the transfer is important so that the item can survive a trip to the washing machine.

7. **Move the iron slowly in a circular motion around the middle of the transfer, again applying constant pressure and keeping the iron in motion.**

8. **Time to remove the transfer! Turn your iron off and set it down safely. Pull the transfer backing from the fabric immediately with a slow, steady motion, beginning at the wider edge.**

   Do not allow the transfer to cool before you remove the paper backing. Otherwise, you can ruin the design when you try to peel it off!

9. **That's it! Hang the completed item on a hanger and set it aside to cool.**

Creating a Slide Show CD

As I mention in Chapter 5, I recommend archiving your scanned images by recording them on a CD-ROM. (If you really need the space, a DVD-ROM can provide over 4GB of elbow room, but most of us simply don't need that much acreage.) A CD-ROM is also the perfect method of distributing an entire album of images or documents, ready to be loaded into any computer with a CD-ROM drive.

What if you're sending to a computer novice (you know — someone who's not the technowizard you've become) some scanned photos on a CD-ROM you've recorded and he or she can't view those images? Perhaps the person doesn't have an image editor or doesn't know how to run the built-in image viewers in Windows or Mac. That's no problem for a compuguru like yourself. Simply create a custom slide show disc!

For this demonstration, I use Broderbund's popular Print Shop Photo Organizer, although you can use any photograph-management program that includes a slide show feature, where your images are displayed in sequence, much like a screen saver. Naturally, the steps aren't exactly the same, although this example helps you understand the procedure.

Follow these steps under Windows XP:

1. **Choose Start⇨All Programs⇨Print Shop Photo Organizer⇨Photo Organizer.**

   The program's main window appears, as shown in Figure 13-4. The next step is the creation of a collection of pictures, or a photo album, as this program calls it.

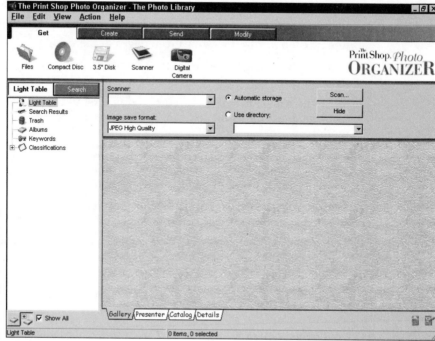

Figure 13-4:
Ready to
create a
slide show
with Print
Shop Photo
Organizer.

2. **Click the Create tab at the top of the screen, and then click the Album toolbar button.**

   The Create Album dialog box appears, as shown in Figure 13-5.

Figure 13-5:
You have to
name that
album,
pardner.

3. **Enter a name for your album, and then click OK.**

   The album icon appears at the left side of the screen.

4. **Click the album icon you just created to select it as the destination for the images. Click the Get tab, and then click the Files toolbar button.**

Although the program can acquire directly from the scanner, I think that a better method is to use the program after all the scanned images are saved to disk (and edited to perfection). That's why I'm having you click Files. The Import Photographs dialog box appears, as shown in Figure 13-6.

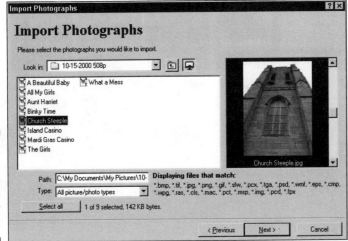

Figure 13-6: Selecting images for a Photo Organizer album.

5. **Click the Look in drop-down list box and specify the folder containing your pictures.**

You can click individual images to select them or hold down the Ctrl key to choose multiple images. If you want all the pictures in this folder, click the Select All button.

6. **Click Next.**

Photo Organizer displays the Specify Photograph Attributes dialog box, where you can enter a photographer's name and search keywords, the scan date, and other comments. Because the slide show doesn't display this information, however, you can simply leave these optional fields blank.

7. **Click Next.**

8. **Specify the current album as the destination for the images.**

9. **Click Finish to add the pictures.**

The album window displays thumbnails of all the images you've added, as shown in Figure 13-7.

10. **Click the Create tab, and then click the Slideshow toolbar button.**

The Publish Slideshow wizard appears.

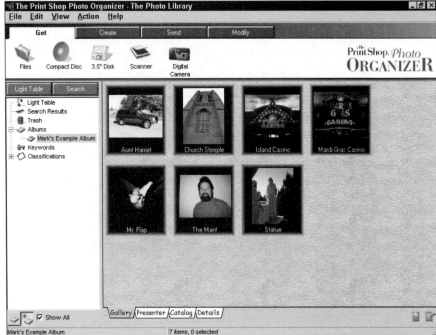

Figure 13-7:
The album is filled. On to the slide show!

11. **Click Next to continue.**

    The Select Photographs dialog box appears.

12. **Click Select all, as shown in Figure 13-8, and then click Next.**

    Because the new album was still selected, it's automatically the source for your slide show images. You've filled your album with only images you want to add to the slide show, so that's why you click Select All.

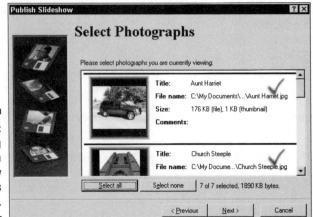

Figure 13-8:
Selecting images for a slide show is child's play.

13. **Click Folder, select a directory where the presentation should be stored, and click Next.**

    By storing your images temporarily in a folder, you can add other documents or files to your slide show CD before you record it.

14. **Click Yes to confirm the creation of the new folder.**

15. **Choose the operating system the recipient will use, as shown in Figure 13-9, and then click Next.**

    Note that the program supports Mac OS 9.2, but not Mac OS X; launching Presenter in Mac OS X will open the application in Classic mode.

Figure 13-9:
Would you like Windows or Macintosh with that?

16. **Click Finish to create the slide show. If you want to see the slide show before recording it, click Yes; otherwise, click No.**

17. **Choose File⇨Exit to close the program.**

Now you can save your slide show to a CD-R, CD-RW, or even a portable USB flash drive. If you're sending only a handful of images, you can probably fit everything on a standard 1.44MB floppy! (But don't store your only copy of a show on a floppy disk . . . they're far too unreliable.)

Using an OCR Program

Earlier in this chapter, I mentioned the wonders of OCR (optical character recognition). Now it's time to see for yourself how much time and trouble this technology can save you! In this example, I use the Mac OS 9 version of OmniPage Pro to show you how to re-create a text document within Microsoft

Word. (OmniPage Pro works much the same under both Windows and Macintosh, which is another reason why I recommend it to everyone.) After all the dust has settled, you have a Word document with the same text as your scanned original!

Follow these steps:

1. Click the OmniPage icon on your desktop.

OmniPage Pro displays the main dialog box, as shown in Figure 13-10. I could simply tell you to click the Auto button (which automatically takes care of the next several steps for you), but instead I'll follow the manual route so that you can see what steps the program takes.

Figure 13-10:
The OmniPage main dialog box may look simple, but plenty of power is on tap.

2. Choose Process⇨Scan Image to display the control program you installed with your scanner.

3. Scan the original.

For more information on scanning, see Chapter 6.

4. Choose Process⇨Zone Image.

As you can see in Figure 13-11, the program draws borders around the major boundaries of text and graphics in the image (hence, the word *zones*), and assigns each zone a number. You can use these numbers to change the order in which the text and graphics are placed in the document, but you rarely have to do this. Typically, you want things read in the traditional order of up to down, left to right, so the default zone order is usually the best.

5. Now for the amazing part: Choose Process⇨OCR & Check.

Sit back and watch OmniPage Pro zip through your document, paste the recognized text into the editing window, and then automatically check for recognition errors with its built-in proofreader! (Moments like these make me proud to be a first-generation computer nerd from the late 1970s and early 1980s, back when it wasn't cool.) Figure 13-12 shows you the completed text document.

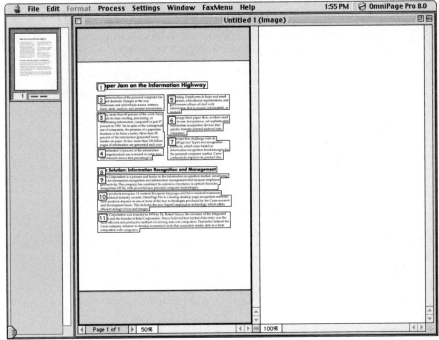

Figure 13-11:
You're in
the zone!
(Sorry —
I couldn't
help that.)

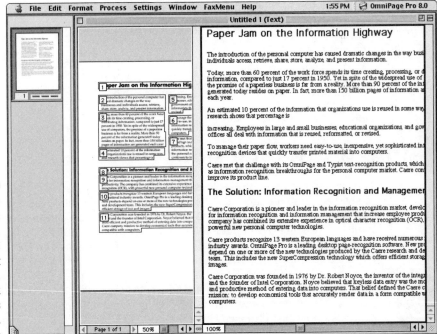

Figure 13-12:
The text is
recognized,
the
document
created.
Your work
here is
done.

Wait! I promised you a Word document, didn't I? No problem. If the formatting weren't important, I could simply have you select all the text and copy it into an empty Word document, but you want things to look exactly like the scanned image.

6. Choose File⇨Save As.

The Save dialog box appears, as shown in Figure 13-13.

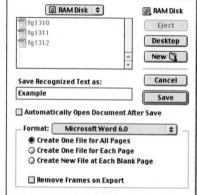

Figure 13-13:
Saving a
document in
Word
format.

7. Click the Format drop-down list box and choose Microsoft Word 6.0.

8. In the Save Recognized Text as box, type a filename.

9. Click Save.

There's your file!

10. Choose File⇨Quit to close OmniPage Pro.

Faxing a Scanned Image

The project in this section teams your scanner and your computer's modem to send a scanned image as a fax. This feature is a favorite with telecommuters and small businesses around the world. In the Windows world, WinFax PRO can do as good a job as any traditional stand-alone fax. In fact, because the program can use a flatbed scanner, you can send things you couldn't send with the sheet-fed scanner that's built in to most fax machines.

Oh, and lest I forget, Mac OS X 10.3 (popularly named Panther) allows you to send a fax from any application by using the telephone numbers in your Address Book. Just choose File⇨Print and click the Fax button at the bottom of the Mac OS X Print panel. Mac owners running older versions of Mac OS 9 and Mac OS X are not left out in the cold; if you're looking for a commercial faxing solution, I recommend FAXstf X Pro for Mac OS X and FAXstf 6 for Mac OS 9 (both from Smith Micro software at www.smithmicro.com).

To fax a scanned image, using WinFax PRO, follow these steps:

1. **Run WinFax PRO by clicking the WinFax PRO Message Manager icon on your desktop.**

   The Message Manager appears, as shown in Figure 13-14.

2. **Prepare the original as you normally would for your scanner.**

   For a flatbed, lay the original facedown on the glass and close the cover. For a sheet-fed scanner, load the document into the machine.

3. **Choose Send⇨Send New Fax.**

   The Send dialog box appears, as shown in Figure 13-15.

4. **Choose Insert⇨From Scanner to display the scanner-control program you installed, and scan the original as you usually would.**

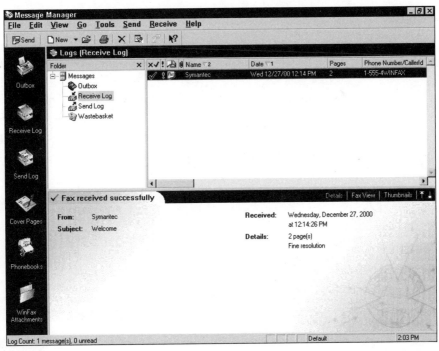

Figure 13-14:
The WinFax Message Manager is your "virtual" fax control center.

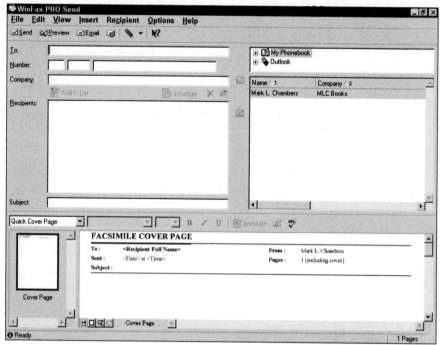

Figure 13-15:
Setting up
a new fax.

5. **Close the scanner-control program to redisplay the WinFax Send dialog box.**

6. **Enter the recipient's fax number and information, or select one from your WinFax phonebook or Microsoft Outlook address book.**

7. **Use the Cover Page drop-down list box to choose a cover page.**

8. **Click Send to start the dialing process.**

Part V
The Part of Tens

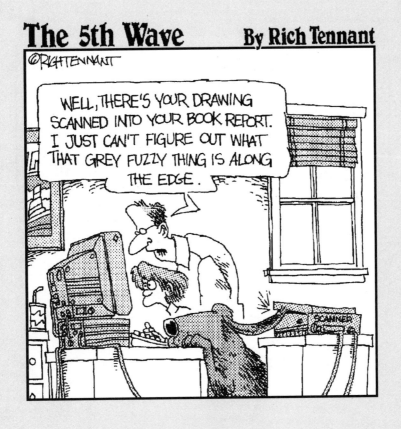

In this part . . .

You'll find tips and advice that will help you use your scanner more effectively and creatively, including things to avoid, signs of a good scan, and a showcase of image-editing effects.

Chapter 14

Ten Tips and Tricks for Better Scanning and Editing

*A*lmost all the tips and tricks I cover elsewhere in this book revolve around your scanner, its software, and your image editor — no big surprise there. Without a good working knowledge of your scanning hardware and the software you need to acquire and edit images, why go any further?

However, if you've read the rest of this book, you are now a seasoned scanning veteran and are familiar with both your scanning hardware and software. In this chapter, I cover your entire system, listing tips and tricks to optimize not only your scanner and image software but also your hard drive, system RAM, and monitor. Even your rodent gets coverage.

Investigate New Software

I don't watch daytime drama (soap operas, to most of us), but I'm told by my friends who do that it's essential to watch every day or at least to stay current with the story line. Otherwise, how would you know who's doing what to whom and why?

The same is true in the software world. Well, not necessarily "who's doing what to whom," but rather the need to stay up-to-date with new scanning software. Scanners are a hot peripheral these days. With more and more computer owners investing in scanners, an explosion of both commercial and shareware image editors, scanning applications, and plug-ins has occurred. Although your scanning hardware may not change over the next few years, what you can *do* with that flatbed changes and expands!

How can you stay on top of new trends in software? Here's how I stay connected:

- ✔ **Online and print magazines:** Whether you choose the old-fashioned paper version or the Web, computer magazines are now your best bet for software reviews, product announcements, opinions, and rumors. My favorites are *Desktop Publisher's Journal* (www.dtpjournal.com), *PC Magazine* (www.pcmag.com), *PC World* (www.pcworld.com), *MacAddict* (www.macaddict.com) and *Macworld* (www.macworld.com).

- ✔ **Web sites:** A number of great Web sites are well known for their coverage of hardware and software, including Tom's Hardware Guide (www.tomshardware.com) and Ace's Hardware (www.aceshardware.com). You can also browse online shareware sites such as CNET Shareware, at shareware.cnet.com, for scanning software. I can also highly recommend VersionTracker (www.versiontracker.com), which can help you stay up-to-date on a wide range of Windows and Mac applications.

- ✔ **Internet newsgroups:** Talk about opinions! Fire up your newsgroup reader and visit the following hotbeds of scanning and imaging discussion: comp.periphs.scanners, alt.comp.periphs.scanners, alt.graphics.photoshop, comp.graphics.misc, comp.graphics.apps.photoshop, and comp.graphics.apps.paint-shop-pro.

Experiment!

Your scanner is a fantastic piece of equipment. Throughout this book, I do my best to give you an overview of what it can do, what's available, and how you can use it.

However, no book can take the place of your own eyes — so use them! Take your image editor, OCR program, plug-ins, and image-manipulation software out for a drive and try a new filter, new effect, or new command every day. Unless you're looking for a specific appearance in your image, take your shoes off and experiment.

For example, whenever I'm trying to create an original piece of artwork for publication (either in a book like this one or as part of one of my Web sites), I generally try several different filters on the same scanned image. You see some of the results of this kind of work in Chapter 17, where I demonstrate the appearance of ten of my favorite filters and effects on the same image. Dark and frightening, light and fanciful, hi-tech or natural, antique or gleaming chrome — you can project all those moods and many more from the same image!

Before you utterly throw caution to the wind, however, keep three important tips in mind:

- ✔ **Never, *never* overwrite the original.** I make it a rule never to overwrite an original with an edited copy — no matter how happy I am with the results of my work — unless I'm sure that I will never need that image for another purpose. You would be surprised how often you turn to a favorite image for new inspiration. (This is yet another argument for archiving your image collection on a rewriteable CD or DVD disc; it has plenty of room for all your experiments as well as all the originals.)

- ✔ **Don't forget the Undo command.** Oh, man! That was *not* the effect you were looking for. Luckily, virtually every image editor on the face of the planet has an Undo command. Some allow you multiple Undo steps, so you can back off of the last two (or ten) commands rather than just one.

- ✔ **Don't degrade the image.** Applying an artistic filter or effect works fine; just don't obliterate the image in the process! Keep your subject recognizable (even if that subject is suddenly embossed, rendered in pastels, changed into glass, or covered with flames). Change the image too much and you lose the message you were trying to convey. Avoid enjoying too much of a good thing — if necessary, don't forget to use your image editor's Undo command to yank your image back from the last change you made.

Thanks for the Memory

Memory. Your computer needs it to function; it stores data while your CPU performs calculations and then holds the results for you to examine or save to disk. You probably know how much memory your computer has, but did you also know that your computer's operating system creates more on-the-fly?

This pseudomemory, called *virtual memory,* is well hidden in both Windows and Mac OS. However, virtual memory is vitally important — without it, a computer with only 128MB of system RAM would find it very hard indeed to open a 60MB image file with a huge, memory-hungry application such as Photoshop.

Why? When your computer runs out of physical RAM (for example, when all 128MB has been filled by the operating system, the application you're running, and the image itself), it uses space on your hard drive to temporarily store the excess data. Although this process is much less efficient and much slower than storing data in actual RAM, it gets the job done.

To enhance the memory usage (and therefore the performance) of your computer while editing images or using your OCR software, follow these guidelines:

- ✔ **Buy at least 512MB of system RAM.** The more physical memory you can afford, the less your computer has to rely on virtual memory, and the faster your entire system runs. This is the reason that power users demand at least 512MB of RAM when they're buying a computer; 1GB or more, of course, is even better.

- ✔ **Free up as much hard drive space as possible.** If you're running Windows, the virtual memory file (also called a *swap file*) is set to dynamically increase and decrease as your program requests and frees up more memory. To make sure that you have sufficient space for the swap file, I recommend that you try to keep at least 2GB of free space available on the hard drive that holds your Windows directory or serves as your Mac startup disk.

- ✔ **Defragment your hard drive.** I talk about this issue in more detail later in this chapter, in the section "Defragment Your Hard Drive." Defragmenting your drive helps the performance of virtual memory.

- ✔ **Configure more virtual memory.** If you're running Mac OS 9 with less than 256MB of RAM, you can benefit from configuring additional virtual memory for programs such as Photoshop and Super Goo. (If you have more than 256MB of system RAM, it's really a trade-off, and I recommend that you disable virtual memory; see the next set of steps.) Mac OS X controls virtual memory automatically, so there's no need to set anything and you can ignore the following steps.

To disable virtual memory, follow these steps:

1. **Click the Apple menu and choose Control Panels.**

2. **Click the Memory menu item to run the Memory Control Panel, which is shown in Figure 14-1.**

3. **If Virtual Memory is turned off, click the On button in the Virtual Memory portion of the dialog box.**

4. **Click in the Virtual Memory field and enter a higher value.**

   I recommend around 128MB more than the amount of system RAM you have.

5. **Click the Close box to close the dialog box and save your changes.**

6. **Restart your Mac.**

Figure 14-1:
Configuring
memory
on a Mac.

Update Everything

Although I've mentioned that it makes sense to monitor new commercial and shareware scanning applications, staying current on your scanner's drivers and scanner-control software is even more important. After all, these programs are responsible for keeping your scanner happily humming.

I recommend that you check your scanner manufacturer's Web site at least once a month to check for updates, and apply them as soon as you've downloaded them. New updates can

- Add functionality to your scanning-control program
- Fix bugs in your scanner's driver
- Add compatibility with the latest operating system and applications

If you have to reinstall your scanner software because of a hard drive crash, don't forget to apply past updates. This is often the cause behind the oft-heard remark "This was working like a charm before I had to rebuild my system!"

Avoid the Edge

It's sad, but true: Because of age and normal wear, calibration problems, or rough handling, some flatbed scanners don't produce an even image quality across the entire area of the glass. If you notice that your scans are dark around the edges when you place an original flush against your scanner's home corner, try scanning the same original when it's placed smack-dab in the center of the scanner glass. After you have saved both images, open both of them side by side in your image editor and compare them. If the image produced from the centered original is better, it's time to avoid the edges of your scanner's glass.

"How can I fix this problem?" That depends on the manufacturer, the age of the unit, whether it's a single-pass or triple-pass model, and what type of handling the scanner has received. If your scanner-control program allows you to perform a calibration, that may take care of the problem. If not, just continue to center your originals.

Toss Your Mouse

I jettisoned my mouse many years ago, and now I use a Logitech Trackman Marble. It's a *trackball,* which is something like an upside-down mouse, as shown in Figure 14-2. Unlike a traditional mouse, the body of this pointing device stays stationary on your desk, and you move the ball with your thumb or forefinger.

A mouse came standard with your computer, so why choose another type of pointing device? After all, the mouse has been around since the early days of graphical user interfaces: Even before Windows 3.0, the Macintosh, Atari ST, and Commodore Amiga all used mice.

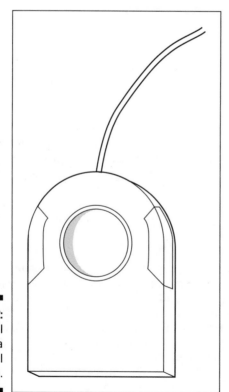

Figure 14-2:
A trackball is a beautiful thing.

Here's the inside story on your typical standard equipment mouse:

- ✔ **It's less precise.** Most mice lack the precise control necessary for proper image editing. If you're serious about image applications, you need a high-resolution pointing device.

- ✔ **It places strain on your wrist.** With a trackball, your wrist and forearm barely move at all, reducing the strain.

- ✔ **It's harder to maintain.** Most standard equipment mice still use an anti-quated ball and roller system. The rollers get covered with gunk and have to be cleaned regularly, and you probably need a mouse pad to get consistent tracking response. I strongly recommend an *optical* system, which eliminates the rollers (no maintenance) and doesn't need a mouse pad.

- ✔ **It takes up more of your desktop.** With a traditional mouse, you end up readjusting its position from time to time when you reach the edge of your desktop. A trackball doesn't move on your desktop, so it doesn't need position adjustments — and it takes up much less room than a mouse and mouse pad, which constantly drags that cord around behind itself.

A USB trackball typically costs anywhere from $20 to $80, depending on the features you get. However, if you want to stay with the basic design of a mouse but you want to eliminate some of these problems, consider a wireless mouse (which has no cord) or an optical mouse (which doesn't use a ball, so maintaining it is much easier) or a model that's a combination of both.

Hard Drive Tips and Tricks

Let me give you a quick prediction here. In Chapter 15, I talk about how quickly you use up drive space by trying to squeeze an entire family's worth of software and Windows XP and your scanned images onto a single 4GB drive; therefore, I don't go into these things now.

After buying a scanner, though, you may not have enough spare pocket change to afford a new 80GB or 120GB drive. What then? How can you help make sure that you have the space you need for 100MB of scanned images when elbowroom is tight on your system?

First, consider cleaning house! Delete as much unnecessary data as possible from your hard drive. Remember to *use caution!* I strongly recommend that you delete only those data files you *know* are scrap, such as MP3 files you no longer want. If you decide to delete those game demos and forgotten shareware applications, use the application's uninstall program (or use the Add/Remove Programs option in the Control Panel, which you can reach by choosing Start➪Settings➪Control Panel).

You can usually also delete a number of files without fear of causing problems in Windows. They include

- ✔ **Trash/Recycle Bin files:** To regain the space from your deleted files, empty the Trash (in Mac OS) or the Recycle Bin (in Windows). Under Windows, right-click the Recycle Bin icon and choose Empty Recycle Bin. Under Mac OS 9, click the Special menu and choose Empty Trash. Under Mac OS X, click Finder and then click Empty Trash.

- ✔ **Temporary Internet and Web browser files:** You can often reclaim an amazing amount of space by deleting the images and HTML pages stored in your Web browser's cache. In Internet Explorer, for example, click Tools and choose Internet Options to display the dialog box shown in Figure 14-3 and click Delete Files to purge the cache directories. Click OK to return to Internet Explorer.

- ✔ **Windows temporary files:** Shut down any applications running on your PC, run Windows Explorer, and delete the contents of your \WINDOWS\TEMP directory. This action eliminates all the temporary files created by programs in Windows (at least those that aren't locked by a background application).

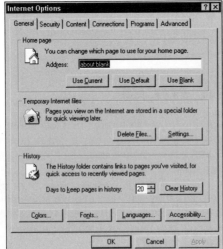

Figure 14-3:
Time to nix
all that
temporary
Web clutter.

If you're running Windows 98, SE, Me, 2000, or XP, you can also use the Disk Cleanup Wizard (shown in Figure 14-4) to automate the entire cleaning process. For Windows XP, choose Start➪All Programs➪Accessories➪System Tools➪Disk Cleanup to run the Wizard.

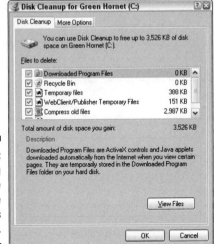

Figure 14-4:
Cleaning
your drive
the
Windows
wizard way.

Another good idea is to reserve a drive for your scanned images. This idea is a great one if you happen to have an old, scavenged 8GB drive lying around and gathering dust. By dedicating a drive just for your scanner, you gain a number of advantages:

✔ Locating your image files for editing is easier than searching all over your system.

✔ You know that the reserved space is always available.

✔ Using the Windows Find Files or Folders feature takes less time.

✔ Backing up an entire drive to CD, DVD, Zip disk, or tape with a backup application is easier. You're assured that all your images are located in one place.

If you don't have a spare drive, you can still create one by using a program such as Partition Magic from PowerQuest. Figure 14-5 shows the main menu from this great utility. Even if you only have one physical drive, you can subdivide that drive into more than one logical drive, so your drive C can become both a drive C and a drive D! (Partition Magic also allows you to choose a smaller cluster size, which yields more efficient use of your existing drive.) With a dedicated partition, you have the advantages of a separate drive reserved for your images, which I mention in Chapter 5.

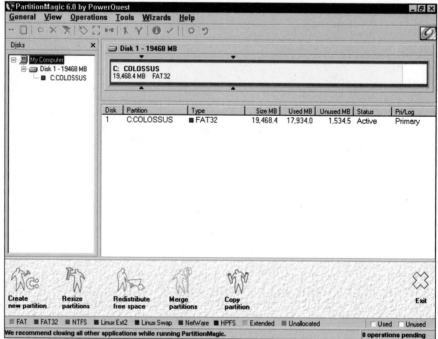

Know Thy Scanning Software

I know that it's not a particularly popular thing to say, but as a technical writer who has written many product manuals, I can honestly say that it pays to read the documentation! Sure, most programs for Windows and Mac OS that are now on the market are designed with ease of use in mind, and you can probably figure out — eventually — 60 percent of the commands in that new whiz-bang editor you bought without cracking open the manual. Any graphics professional can tell you, however, that the other 40 percent of the commands save you time and significantly improve your work.

Even if you have a phobia about reading software manuals, image applications now include a host of other methods you can use to train yourself in more than just the basics, including

✔ **Tutorials:** I think that tutorials are the cat's meow. Nothing can help you master concepts like hands-on training. I highly recommend that you try out the tutorials that accompany all your applications.

✔ **Online Help files:** Why try to puzzle things out by yourself? Unless you like frustration and would rather spend your time scratching your head, use the online help system! Both Windows and Mac OS allow you to search for keywords, so it's usually even more convenient than checking the index in the manual.

✔ **Web site tips and tricks:** Take advantage of the extra content provided on the manufacturer's Web site. I've seen everything from program walk-throughs to additional filters and effects, free for the downloading!

✔ **Frequently Asked Question (FAQ) files:** FAQ files are pure gold in my book. Why? Because they address the most common questions about a program, with a minimum of fuss and formatting. Also, most FAQ files are written by customers for customers, so I get more of the information I'm likely to need.

✔ **Customer mailing lists and newsgroups:** Think of a customer mailing list and a topical newsgroup as ongoing FAQ discussions. Because you can join in, however, you can ask the specific questions you want, and other folks provide the answers.

Defragment Your Hard Drive

If you're not familiar with disk fragmentation, it's high time I introduced you! A fragmented hard drive can slow down your entire system.

As you delete files and copy new files into the free space on your hard drive, the files on the drive become *fragmented*. They're separated into dozens of smaller pieces, and your drive and computer have to work together to keep track of them and "reassemble" the smaller pieces into the original file when-ever it's needed. This reassembly step takes time — only a few milliseconds or so — but those delays add up when your computer has more than one application open or when you're editing images while checking your mail and working on your word processor. The older the CPU and the slower the hard drive, the more noticeable this slowdown becomes. Figure 14-6 illustrates the effects of fragmentation.

Luckily, you can reverse the effects of fragmentation with a defragmenter, which rewrites the files on your drive in contiguous form, as shown in Figure 14-7. This file now takes much less time to read, improving the performance of your hard drive and your computer. When you're working with larger scanned image files, you definitely can tell the difference.

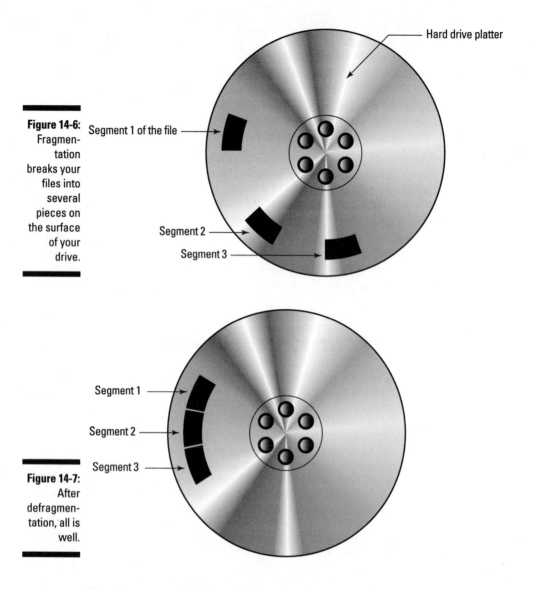

Hard drive platter

Figure 14-6:
Fragmentation breaks your files into several pieces on the surface of your drive.

Segment 1 of the file

Segment 2

Segment 3

Segment 1

Segment 2

Segment 3

Figure 14-7:
After defragmentation, all is well.

If you're running Windows 98, Me, 2000, or XP, I recommend running the Disk Defragmenter program at least once a month. Follow these steps in Windows XP:

1. Choose Start ⇨All Programs⇨Accessories⇨System Tools⇨Disk Defragmenter.

The screen shown in Figure 14-8 appears.

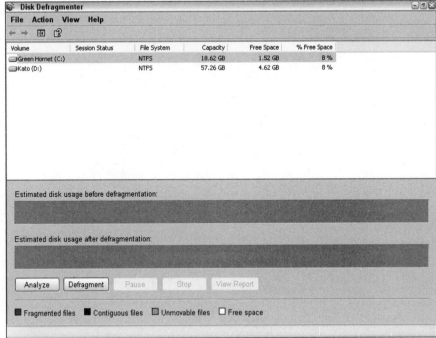

Figure 14-8:
Microsoft
thoughtfully
provides a
defrag-
menter with
Windows
XP.

2. **Click the hard drive you want to scan. If you have more than one drive, choose the drive that holds the files you're recording.**

3. **Click Defragment.**

4. **When the defragmenting process has finished and the completion dialog box appears, click OK.**

5. **Click the Close button to return to Windows XP.**

Although neither Mac OS 9 nor Mac OS X comes with a defragmenter, you can choose from a number of utility programs to do the job. For Mac OS 9 users, I recommend Norton Utilities for the Macintosh, which comes with the Speed Disk program (www.symantec.com), as shown in Figure 14-9. If you're running Mac OS X, my choice is DiskWarrior, from Alsoft, Inc. (www.alsoft.com).

Splurge on Your Monitor

Ever end up tired after an hour or two of image editing, with red eyes and a headache? Perhaps it's that 15-inch monitor you're using. You know that this is the problem if you spend most of your time at your computer with your nose six inches away from the screen. (Watch out for the famous techno-suntan.)

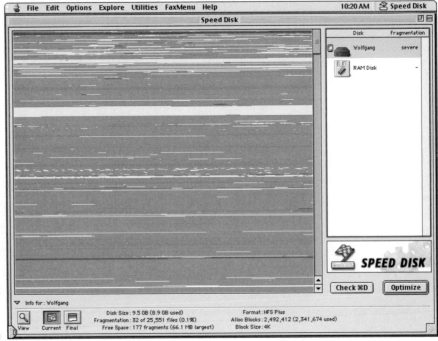

Figure 14-9:
You're
ready to
defragment
a Macintosh
hard drive.

You may be saying, "Hey, Mark, I work with image files only once or twice a week. Do I really need a new monitor?" Here's my reply: Even if you use your scanner just twice a week, what about all those other computer activities? Do you play your fair share of computer games, use a word processor several times a week, or maintain a checkbook on your computer? If you're still using a 15-inch monitor, shouldn't you spend a little to improve your computing experience and ease the strain on at least one set of eyeballs?

Part of the reason I stress this concept so much is the rapid drop in prices for monitors over the past few years. Sure, a 17-inch traditional CRT monitor used to cost $400, although now you can pick a good one up for $120 at any Web store. That same $400 now buys you an excellent 21-inch CRT screen (like the one I use). If you want to save energy and lower the radiation level of your system even further, you can invest in a crystal-clear LCD display. However, be prepared to pay $500 for a 17-inch LCD monitor.

You have to consider more than just your ocular health — as though that weren't enough. With a larger viewing surface (and, typically, a higher resolution), you can see more of an image on a 17-inch, 19-inch, or 21-inch monitor, which means less scrolling. (I'm all for less scrolling!)

That covers ten tips to help optimize your system and enhance your scanning and image editing. After applying these tricks, I think that you'll be well on your way to becoming a true power user (without the bleary eyes and the strained wrist, too).

Chapter 15

Ten Things to Avoid Like the Plague

1 love this chapter. I have a chapter with the same title and general direction in another of my *For Dummies* books, too. Why? Well, it's not every day that you can pull up a soapbox and launch word missiles at the things that have earned your wrath!

Naturally, I don't tear into things just to amuse myself. (Not in a book, anyway.) The idea behind this Part of Tens chapter is to save *you* the frustration and wasted time that these things represent. Consider these words as "distilled experience." In my consulting practice and my years as a hardware technician, I've been forced to put up with a number of the items in this chapter personally, and I wouldn't wish things such as printer cartridge scanners on my worst enemy.

Evade these ten things as you pass them in life, and I can guarantee that you'll be a happier person.

The Pentium II and the PowerPC 60x

I'm the first to admit that the Intel Pentium II and the Motorola PowerPC 603/604 were great CPUs (short for central processing unit) in their time. Heck, I can remember when PCs and Macs based on these chips were cutting edge, and technowizards would fall asleep at night dreaming of them. You would spend $2,500 or more for one of these machines a mere seven years ago.

My friends, those days are over. Boy, howdy, are they over. If you've just spent $200 to $500 on a new scanner, why connect it to a computer that most experienced computer owners would ignore if they saw it at a garage sale? Yes, I admit that — technically, anyway — a Pentium II-based computer can power a scanner. However, keep the following concepts in mind:

✔ **You have less.** Unless someone has spent a fortune upgrading that old computer, you'll have a smaller hard drive — probably much less than a couple of gigabytes (1,000 megabytes) — that can't hold more than a handful of high-resolution images after you've installed Windows. A machine that old also has an older video card that may not even be able to display the 24-bit color displayed by your scanner. And don't even mention the amount of RAM you have: Back then, 64MB or 128MB was all you needed!

✔ **Ports? What ports?** Older PCs and Macs don't support USB and FireWire (unless you spend more money than the computer's worth to upgrade them). On the PC side, you end up with a parallel port scanner, which is not my first choice. On the Macintosh side, you end up with SCSI, which is fast but significantly more expensive. You miss out on more peripherals than just a scanner, especially because more and more hardware will rely on USB and FireWire in the future.

✔ **Performance is futile.** Running Windows XP on a Pentium II PC is the equivalent of trying to pull a double-wide mobile home with a lawn tractor. Every application you run (not just your scanning software) acts like the silicon equivalent of a Galapagos turtle. How much is your time worth? Most people can't spend all day sitting in front of their computers, so a slow computer converts directly into lost productivity.

Upgrading a computer that's more than five years old isn't a cheap proposition, especially when you compare the amount you have to spend to the cost of a new machine. If $800 buys you a brand-new PC with an Athlon XP or Pentium 4 processor or a 1.25 GHz eMac, why break yourself with technology used by the Pharaohs?

Here's my recommendation: If you're using a PC or Macintosh that has already reached its fifth or sixth birthday and you're serious about producing the best scans for home or business use, it's time to put that computer out to pasture. If someone tries to give you or sell you such a machine, smile quietly to yourself and pass on that "bargain."

Printer Cartridge Scanners

Every time I see a printer being used as a scanner, I start chuckling. I can't help it! The idea made sense back in the days when a typical flatbed cost well over $500: You bought an inkjet printer, and then you snapped in a scanning head that masqueraded as a printer cartridge. Because an inkjet printer's ink cartridge takes the same path across a sheet of paper as a scanning head — voilà — you had an instant inexpensive scanner.

Not quite. Oh, printer cartridge scanners do indeed work (after a fashion), although the caveats are ridiculous:

- ✔ They deliver a lower dpi than even the cheapest modern flatbed. (The maximum I've ever seen for this technology is 360 dpi.)
- ✔ They scan significantly slower than a dedicated flatbed scanner.
- ✔ You can't use your printer at the same time as your pseudoscanner.
- ✔ You have to snap in the scanning cartridge every time you want to use it, and then replace it with the ink cartridge again to print.
- ✔ As with a sheet-fed scanner, you're restricted to a standard-size paper document. Unlike with a sheet-fed scanner, however, you can't use a sleeve to scan smaller items.
- ✔ Your pseudoscanner uses a parallel port interface.

A printer cartridge scanner is basically half of a multifunction device — it prints and scans — but with none of the convenience of a genuine all-in-one unit. Leave your printer to do the job for which it was designed, and for $30 or $40 more invest in the convenience and versatility of a flatbed scanner.

Serial Scanners

Serial scanners are another variety of scanner technology that should have faded into obscurity years ago. An older serial scanner may look similar to a typical modern flatbed that uses a USB connection. So why do I dislike them? The issue is speed!

Let me explain: The data bytes in a serial connection travel in a series, one after the other (hence the name *serial*), and the data bytes in a parallel connection travel simultaneously on separate wires (hence the name *parallel*).

A serial connection is therefore much slower than any type of connection in use with modern scanners. As you may recall, I'm not particularly a fan of parallel port scanners either, but even a parallel port model is a speed demon when compared to a clunky serial scanner.

Speed becomes more of an issue as the size and dpi of a scanned image increases. You may be able to wait while a 200 dpi JPEG image (with a file size of 256K) crawls across a serial connection, but what about a 600 dpi Windows bitmap image that may take up 30 or 40 megabytes? You can play a game of Monopoly while you're waiting!

Compared to a sweet and simple USB connection, serial ports are also finicky beasts to configure. If you're using an older PC with a serial mouse, adding a serial scanner could interfere with the mouse, causing it to lock up your computer.

Like the human appendix (and, in the world of computers, the antique Turbo button), the serial port itself is becoming more of an anachronism. Traditionally the port of choice for modems and digital cameras, the once lofty position held by the serial port has been superseded by USB and FireWire ports, which are much faster, much easier to use, and much more versatile. With a serial port, you can attach only one device. With a USB port, you can attach more than a hundred devices!

Steer clear of a serial scanner. You'll be much happier.

Old Printer Cables

A 10-year-old printer cable can cause you more headaches than you would think possible: It can prevent your parallel port scanner from working, a problem that's practically impossible to track down!

Suppose that I pick up a used printer cable at a garage sale. Figuring that all printer cables are created equal (and I would *almost* be right), I decide to use it to connect my parallel port scanner to my computer. (The same problem also crops up for parallel port Zip drives and external tape backup units.)

The problem lies in the cable's design. It doesn't conform to the IEEE-1284 standard, which is an international cable specification that's required for bidirectional devices. Whoa, sorry about that. The technonerd in me took over. In terms that a normal human being can understand, your scanner needs to be able to communicate with your computer through the cable (hence the term *bidirectional*). However, that antique cable was made back in the Dark Ages of computing, when printers only received data from a computer and didn't talk back.

Therefore, even if you have everything set correctly on your scanner and your computer (including your parallel port mode, which I cover in Chapter 12), the connection still doesn't work. Essentially, your scanner can understand your computer, but your computer can't receive data from your scanner.

Fixing this problem is refreshingly simple: Check the cable you intend to use with your scanner and see whether the words *IEEE-1284 Compatible* are stamped on it. If so (or if your cable came with your scanner), you should have no problem with bidirectional communications between your scanner and your computer.

Refurbished Hardware

I know I'll catch some flak from some readers when I list refurbished scanners as something to avoid. If you're not familiar with the refurbishing process, here's the tale:

1. A scanner returns to the manufacturer from the original owner. Typically, the reason is that because the scanner was broken "out of the box" or broke soon after it was opened.

2. The manufacturer takes the scanner back to the factory, repairs it, and then tests it — or tests at least the part that broke. (This step is also called "remanufacturing," which I find amusing.)

3. The newer, even-fresher-smelling scanner is sold for pennies on the dollar to an eager discount chain (or, increasingly, to an online Web clearinghouse).

4. The scanner is sold again to another person.

By law, a refurbished scanner must be clearly marked as refurbished or remanufactured, although you usually have no other way to tell other than the bargain-basement price.

Some of my friends point out that refurbished hardware is repaired and tested by the manufacturer. You definitely can't beat the price. For example, I recently saw a $120 flatbed scanner selling in refurbished form for $50. You may even receive a short warranty from the manufacturer.

So why do I dislike refurbished stuff so intensely? Here's an *abbreviated* list of my grievances:

- ✔ **I'll bet you that all sales are final.** Most of these companies cut you off from returning that refurbished scanner. If it breaks again, you're stuck.

- ✔ **It's a traveling thing.** When that refurbished scanner finally arrives at your door, it has likely been shipped to Timbuktu and back, and it may have picked up scratches, dings, and nicks to prove it. Call me picky, but I take good care of my equipment, and cosmetic damage isn't pretty.

- ✔ **You're in the dark.** *Something* was wrong. You don't know what, but this scanner was already broken once. If you're a Vegas gambler, consider the odds: Would you rather pay full price for something brand new from the factory or save money buying a secondhand piece of repair work.

✔ **How well do you trust the manufacturer?** Did the entire scanner get tested or just the broken components? How thorough was the examination?

✔ **You call that a warranty?** Personally, a 90-day warranty from the manufacturer just isn't enough for me (especially when all sales are final). Buy a brand-new scanner, and you're protected by a full year of warranty coverage. In fact, some stores even have the shameless urge to sell you an extended warranty on a refurbished scanner. What a deal! You get a used piece of hardware (previously *broken*, mind you) with an expensive extended warranty for about the cost of a new scanner and an equivalent standard warranty!

If you do decide to take the plunge and save money up front on a refurbished scanner, promise me that you'll read the fine print before you click the Buy Now button. As that sharp Mr. Barnum once said . . . well, you know that one. (Another adage that works: "If it seems too good to be true, then it probably is.")

Scanning Copyrighted Work

Choosing not to scan copyrighted work is just common sense. Why risk it? I can understand if you're scanning a photograph from a book or some text from a magazine article for your own personal use. But scanning copyrighted work and *distributing* it? Entire Internet newsgroups and Web sites are devoted to the "anonymous" posting of scanned images, but I avoid them.

What's even worse, however, is representing someone else's copyrighted work as your own and trying to profit from it. I'm told that lawyers are tenacious. Luckily, I don't know from personal experience, and I'm going to try my hardest to keep things that way.

Call me old-fashioned and narrow-minded, but *copyright infringement is against the law.* Chalk it up to my profession: As an author, I'm very sensitive to copyrighted work.

Windows 95 and System 7

You may remember my tirade on tired processors at the beginning of this chapter. Well, the same argument also holds true for antique operating systems — and, believe it or not, that includes the venerable Windows 95 (and, on the Mac side, the august System 7).

Why upgrade your operating system just for your scanner? Good question, and I have plenty of reasons:

- ✓ **That acronym again:** I know that I keep harping about USB and FireWire, but they really are that easy to use and that simple to set up. Both the original version of Windows 95 and System 7 were released in the halcyon days before USB, and neither supports it. (Later versions of Windows 95 do support USB, although not nearly as well as Windows 98, Me, and XP.)

- ✓ **Support for more image formats:** More info about this topic is coming up soon in this chapter. Let me just say that the more support in your operating system for built-in image formats, the better! Although you can install image-display or image-editing software, Windows 95 by itself typically recognizes only the Windows bitmap format.

- ✓ **Better performance:** Windows 98, Me, 2000, and XP and Mac OS 8, OS 9, and OS X provide significant improvements in disk access and virtual memory usage, which translates into faster scanning times and faster image editing.

- ✓ **Updated software requirements:** Naturally, you want to run your scanner for several years to come. Unfortunately, however, both Windows 95 and System 7 have reached the end of their operational careers. Software developers know this, and they're writing image software (and updated scanning-control software) that requires a later version of Windows. I'm a procrastinator by nature — except when it comes to drivers, application software, games, and operating systems, which I like to keep updated whenever possible.

- ✓ **Cutting-edge operating systems are the cat's meow:** Am I right? Or am I just a big-time technonerd? (Don't answer that.)

You have to upgrade your operating system sooner or later. Why wait if upgrading helps improve your efficiency and productivity with your scanner (as well as all your other programs and devices)?

Obscure Image Formats

"Oh, I've got just the document you need. I'll send it as a WIF file. You *can* read WIF images, right?"

What exactly is a WIF file? That's a scanned image that's saved in what I call weird image format. No one else on earth *ever* uses WIF files, but for some unknown reason, you're sure to run into some poor soul who sends a WIF file to you as an e-mail attachment. Of course, *everyone* has an image editor that can display it. Right?

Don't get me wrong here: I use several obscure image formats myself, and I know that proprietary formats are a way of life for professions such as computer-aided drafting (CAD). I use images in Targa (TGA) when I'm rendering three-dimensional graphics, and Mac OS 9 still produces PICT images (PCT) whenever you snap a screenshot.

What I don't understand, however, is why some otherwise wonderful folks insist on using murky formats to send images to their innocent friends, family, and fellow employees! For example, in just this past year, I've received images in the following well-known formats on disk or through e-mail:

- ✔ **MAC:** MacPaint, the program that reads this file type, uses a Macintosh format so antiquated that it creaks when you use it.

- ✔ **FPX:** FlashPix is a recent format developed for digital camera owners and used by virtually no one else on the planet.

- ✔ **IFF:** This format was used on the Amiga, which until recently, when the brand was revived, no longer even existed!

Luckily, I have an entire shelf full of different image editors, and I had no problem converting these things — but what about Aunt Harriet? She's running her original copy of Windows 95, and she knows as much about displaying a digital image as she does about nuclear physics. Send her a WIF file and you're wasting both your time and hers, especially when you end up sending two or three e-mails to lead her through the process of downloading and installing the trial version of Paint Shop Pro.

Follow my recommendations in Chapter 10 by sticking with JPEG and TIFF formats, and you'll never be accused of wasting someone's time with an incomprehensible image on a Web page or in an e-mail message.

Small-Capacity Hard Drives and Floppy Disks

I enjoy scale modeling. Creating a detailed miniature of something in a smaller scale gives you some idea of how the real McCoy works and how it was constructed.

On the other hand, I do *not* enjoy working with a "miniature" hard drive, especially when I'm trying to prepare high-resolution scanned images. A 4GB hard drive just doesn't do the trick, unless you've dedicated the entire drive to scanning and you run Windows from another drive. As listed in Table 15-1, suppose that your family's computer system has a single 4GB drive (which used to be the norm just six or seven short years ago).

Table 15-1	Where All Your Disk Space Goes	
Software	*Typical Size*	*Remaining*
Windows XP Home	1.2GB	2.8GB
Four of the latest 3-D games	400MB each	1.2GB
Microsoft Office XP	400MB	800MB
A collection of 100 MP3 songs	4MB each	400MB

That hard drive territory vanishes pretty quickly, doesn't it? And note that I haven't added any other applications, either. Now factor in the space you need to store your scanned images, edit them, and store a few experimental images before you print them. Do you remember saying to yourself just a few years ago, "Who could ever fill up all that space?"

Let me be blunt: *Don't shortchange yourself on hard drive space!* At the time this book was written, an 80GB drive cost only about $60 on the Web. Don't forget that you can add a second or even a third hard drive to today's PCs. If you would rather not crack open your computer's case, both PC and Macintosh owners can choose an external hard drive that uses a USB 2.0 or FireWire connection.

Now that I've held forth with my opinions on small-capacity hard drives, I want to turn my scathing attention to an icon of PC computing: floppy disks. You may be wondering why. After all, I just finished talking about the need for a high-capacity drive on a system with a scanner. JPEG and GIF images are small enough, however, to store on floppies, and many computer owners store their only copies of their priceless scanned images on a floppy rather than on a CD-R or a USB flash drive. I can understand this logic: Floppies are cheap and plentiful, and virtually every PC has a floppy drive. Not a bad solution, right?

Wrong. I mean *dead wrong.* In fact, floppies are about the most unreliable storage media on the face of the planet! Here are the facts that every PC owner should know — unless, of course, you've already fallen victim to floppy disaster, in which case you already know this stuff:

- ✔ **They're unreliable.** Floppy disks have the shortest shelf life of any common media. In English, that means that you can't use them for long and be 100 percent sure that your computer can reliably read that data, primarily because of wear and tear on the disk's spindle mechanism and magnetic fields. (If you must use floppies, *never* store them near a magnetic source, like a set of stereo speakers. Magnetic media and Jimi Hendrix do not mix.)

- ✔ **They're not error free.** Floppies from one computer may not be readable on another, even *immediately* after you've copied files, because of the minute discrepancy between the magnetic read-write heads on the two drives. (You should still be able to read that disk on the source drive, but for how long?)

✔ **They can carry viruses.** Floppies are a prime transmission method for viruses. Keep your antivirus program running in the background, and check any floppy you receive from someone else. Also, write-protect a floppy as soon as you've copied files to it to prevent catching a nasty digital something.

So what *are* floppies good for? Temporary storage, that's what — carrying an image home from school or work or sending it through the mail, but definitely not for storing your only copy of an important document. They're simply not the right choice for permanent storage.

As you probably have guessed, I recommend a CD-R or CD-RW for storing those images permanently and without worry about data loss, errors, or compatibility between drives! Chapter 5 tells you more.

Materials That Should Never Be Scanned

In Chapter 12, I caution you about cleaning your flatbed scanner's glass with solvents or abrasive cleansers. Remember that even the smallest shallow scratch can interfere with a high-resolution, high-dpi scan.

A host of other damaging items can make contact with your glass, and many folks don't think about them until they end up with a scratch or stain. Some of these materials are

✔ Fabrics with a coarse, heavy weave, such as canvas or leather

✔ Metallic items, such as coins, jewelry, rings, or keys

✔ CD-ROM or DVD-ROM discs

✔ Originals that carry oil, fresh ink, paint, or other liquids that can stain your scanner's glass

✔ Items that carry adhesives

✔ Exceptionally heavy items that can break your scanner's glass

My point? *Think before you scan!* Before you place an original on your scanner's glass, consider whether it fits into the category of Materials That Should Never Be Scanned. And no matter what materials you scan, take care in placing and removing them.

Consider this chapter as a series of ten signposts to help you out of ten potential minefields. It's my sincere wish that you never encounter any of these. If you do, however, remember that Chapter 12 has troubleshooting information and that you can always obtain technical support from your scanner manufacturer.

Chapter 16

Ten Signs of a Good Scan

*I*n other chapters in this book, I trundle on and on about specifics: what to do in certain situations, when to edit your images, what steps you need to take to accomplish something. Don't get me wrong: I'm not saying that that's a bad thing! Specific instruction is the bread-and-butter of any title in the *For Dummies* series, and it's what I would want to read if I had bought this book.

However, I want to take a chapter from "the other direction" and examine the scanning process by presenting the top ten general characteristics of a good scanned image. I don't go into any great detail here, although I list the hallmarks that every image should have — no matter what the subject and no matter what application uses the image.

(By the way, thanks for buying this book! I like to say that at least once in every dusty tome I write.)

Keeping Things Straight

Naturally, a scanned image doesn't look its best when tilted. Believe me: Your eye can tell when things aren't straight! As I mention in Chapter 6, aligning the original correctly with the sides of your scanner's glass is essential to a good scan. You can also save yourself a session of image editing by marking which edge of the scanner glass is "up" (according to your scanning software's preview display) or by changing the orientation before you scan. Your scanning software or your image editor may include features that make straightening easy (or even automatic).

Even if the original is aligned and facing in the right direction, you may still have an alignment problem if you're capturing just a portion of the image. For example, suppose I scanned just the title text from the book cover shown in Figure 16-1. I would still have to use the Rotate feature in Paint Shop Pro (which I show you in Chapter 8) to make those words level, as shown in Figure 16-2.

Figure 16-1:
A *For Dummies* book cover I chose *completely* at random from the hundreds of titles in the series.

Figure 16-2:
By rotating
and
cropping the
scanned
image, I can
bring the
title in line.

Because the edges of the image were tilted after the rotation, I further cropped the scanned cover, which both straightened the edges of the image and focused the viewer's interest on the words. Always be prepared to crop after rotating an image.

Crop 'Til You Drop

Speaking of cropping, you can't consider your scan complete if it contains extraneous details or text. That extra area not only detracts from the image but also adds to the file size. Even if you caught only an elbow at the corner of the sofa or an unnecessary paragraph heading at the bottom of a document, taking a moment to crop an image to improve it is worthwhile.

For example, Figure 16-3 may look fine as it is — after all, this photo is centered, the subject fills most of the frame, and nothing appears particularly out of place. To my photographer's eye, however, too much free space is surrounding the baby, and she's "floating" in the open expanse of white that fills the foreground.

Figure 16-3:
An innocent
piece of
chocolate
cake is
consumed.

Figure 16-4 illustrates one possible crop that maintains the centered approach, but loses a portion of the baby's arm. The second crop in Figure 16-5 keeps the baby's arm in view, although she's somewhat off center in the frame. Which is the "right" choice? It's up to you and your tastes when you're cropping scanned images.

Figure 16-4:
One
possible
crop,
keeping
everything
centered.

Figure 16-5:
This
cropped
image
keeps the
baby intact.

You're Looking Sharp

I'm a dyed-in-the-wool fan of the Sharpening filter available in image editors and many scanner-control programs. A certain amount of sharpening is suitable for just about every photograph — even text documents can benefit from sharpening. It enhances details and helps your subjects stand out, particularly when little contrast exists between the light and dark areas in the original.

In Figure 16-6, for example, the features in the stone statue are less distinctive than they should be because of its distance from the camera and the shadow cast by the sun.

Figure 16-6:
The face of this statue needs a good sharpening.

By applying the Sharpen More filter in Paint Shop Pro, the curves of the face are now cleaner and easier to see, as shown in Figure 16-7.

As I point out in Chapter 8, however, you can easily get carried away with sharpening! I strongly recommend that you never apply more than one level of Sharpen or Sharpen More to a scanned image. Remember that this technique can't add detail that doesn't exist. For example, Figure 16-8 illustrates the results when I apply the Sharpen More filter again to the statue.

That second level of Sharpen More has turned the fine marble into what looks like coarse concrete. The program has enhanced the already enhanced pixels a second time, so they end up looking like something drawn on bubble wrap with a felt-tip permanent marker.

Figure 16-7:
A level of
Sharpen
More adds
stronger
lines and
improves
the image.

Figure 16-8:
Whoa! Too much sharpening is not a good thing!

Flat Is Nice

In Chapter 6, I recommend that you always close the cover on your scanner because many types of originals can be completely scanned only if they're perfectly flat (or as flat as possible). Of course, if you're using a sheet-fed scanner, you can scan only flat originals.

For example, Figure 16-9 illustrates a scanned image I made of a hardbound book — with my scanner's cover raised. Figure 16-10 shows the same material with the cover adjusted and down.

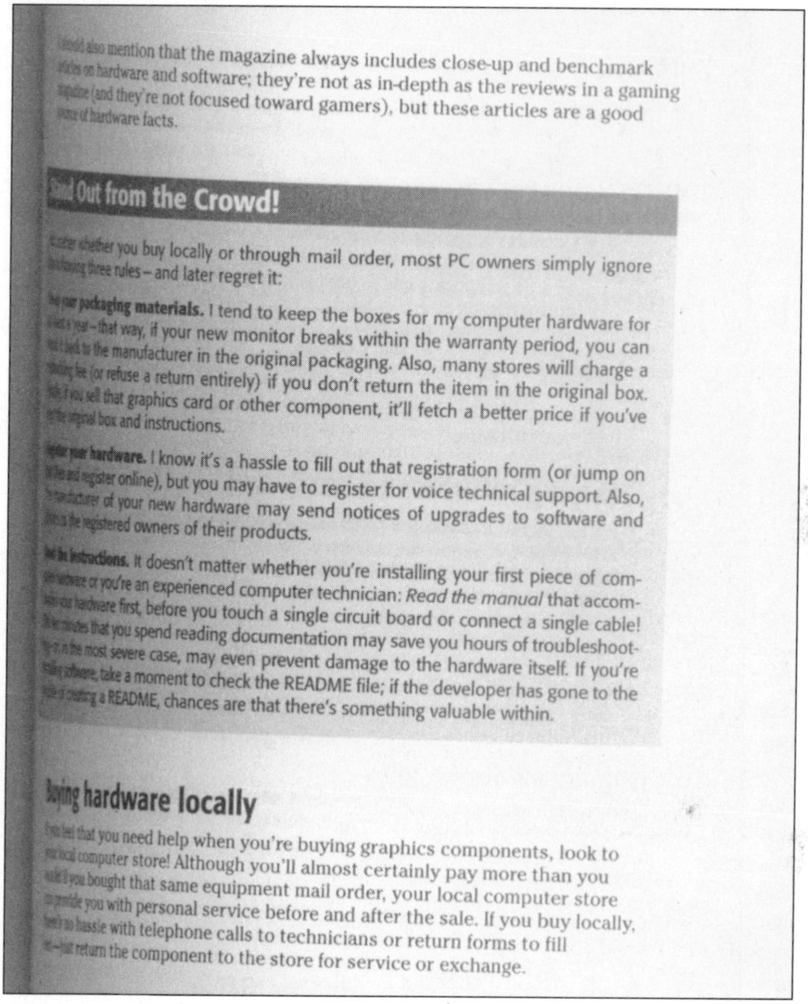

I should also mention that the magazine always includes close-up and benchmark articles on hardware and software; they're not as in-depth as the reviews in a gaming magazine (and they're not focused toward gamers), but these articles are a good source of hardware facts.

Stand Out from the Crowd!

No matter whether you buy locally or through mail order, most PC owners simply ignore these three rules — and later regret it:

Keep your packaging materials. I tend to keep the boxes for my computer hardware for at least a year — that way, if your new monitor breaks within the warranty period, you can send it back to the manufacturer in the original packaging. Also, many stores will charge a restocking fee (or refuse a return entirely) if you don't return the item in the original box. Plus, if you sell that graphics card or other component, it'll fetch a better price if you've got the original box and instructions.

Register your hardware. I know it's a hassle to fill out that registration form (or jump on the Web and register online), but you may have to register for voice technical support. Also, the manufacturer of your new hardware may send notices of upgrades to software and drivers to the registered owners of their products.

Read the instructions. It doesn't matter whether you're installing your first piece of computer hardware or you're an experienced computer technician: *Read the manual* that accompanies your hardware first, before you touch a single circuit board or connect a single cable! The minutes that you spend reading documentation may save you hours of troubleshooting — or, in the most severe case, may even prevent damage to the hardware itself. If you're installing software, take a moment to check the README file; if the developer has gone to the trouble of creating a README, chances are that there's something valuable within.

Buying hardware locally

If you feel that you need help when you're buying graphics components, look to your local computer store! Although you'll almost certainly pay more than you would if you bought that same equipment mail order, your local computer store is able to provide you with personal service before and after the sale. If you buy locally, there's no hassle with telephone calls to technicians or return forms to fill out — just return the component to the store for service or exchange.

Figure 16-9:
With the cover up (or not properly adjusted), a book's spine is likely to give you trouble.

As you can see, a dramatic difference exists in the amount of text you can see, as well as the quality of the image overall. If you were planning to use the scanned image shown in Figure 16-9 with your OCR software, I would have to confiscate your mouse — you would be wasting your time because many characters are unreadable.

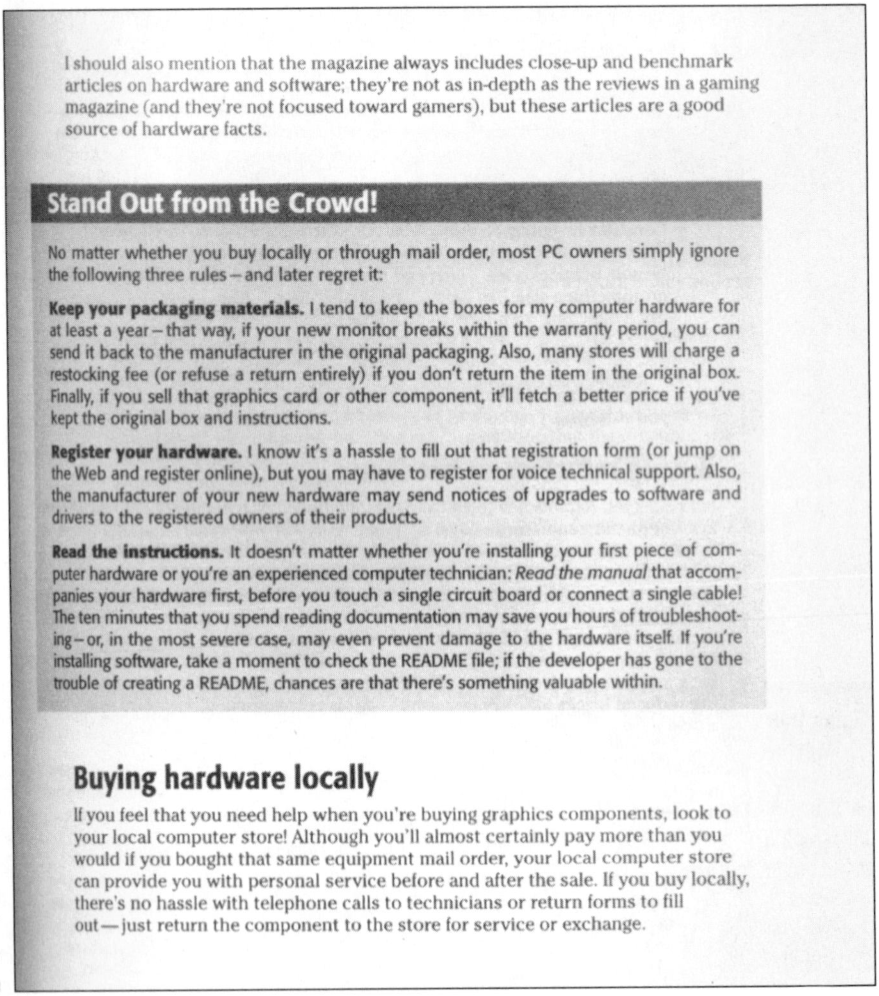

I should also mention that the magazine always includes close-up and benchmark articles on hardware and software; they're not as in-depth as the reviews in a gaming magazine (and they're not focused toward gamers), but these articles are a good source of hardware facts.

Stand Out from the Crowd!

No matter whether you buy locally or through mail order, most PC owners simply ignore the following three rules—and later regret it:

Keep your packaging materials. I tend to keep the boxes for my computer hardware for at least a year—that way, if your new monitor breaks within the warranty period, you can send it back to the manufacturer in the original packaging. Also, many stores will charge a restocking fee (or refuse a return entirely) if you don't return the item in the original box. Finally, if you sell that graphics card or other component, it'll fetch a better price if you've kept the original box and instructions.

Register your hardware. I know it's a hassle to fill out that registration form (or jump on the Web and register online), but you may have to register for voice technical support. Also, the manufacturer of your new hardware may send notices of upgrades to software and drivers to the registered owners of their products.

Read the instructions. It doesn't matter whether you're installing your first piece of computer hardware or you're an experienced computer technician: *Read the manual* that accompanies your hardware first, before you touch a single circuit board or connect a single cable! The ten minutes that you spend reading documentation may save you hours of troubleshooting—or, in the most severe case, may even prevent damage to the hardware itself. If you're installing software, take a moment to check the README file; if the developer has gone to the trouble of creating a README, chances are that there's something valuable within.

Figure 16-10:
By adjusting the book and lowering the cover, you get better results.

Buying hardware locally

If you feel that you need help when you're buying graphics components, look to your local computer store! Although you'll almost certainly pay more than you would if you bought that same equipment mail order, your local computer store can provide you with personal service before and after the sale. If you buy locally, there's no hassle with telephone calls to technicians or return forms to fill out—just return the component to the store for service or exchange.

That's, Like, So . . . Transparent

Creating a good scan from a transparent original may seem like holding a wriggling fish in your bare hands: It takes practice to get a handle on things. Why?

✔ Many scanners use a black foam backing on the underside of the cover. This is great when your original has an opaque background, such as a white piece of paper (it helps differentiate the edges of your original). However, if the original has a transparent background, such as an overhead transparency or an animation cell, the text or images on the original are surrounded in a sea of black.

✔ A transparent original often reflects the light from the scanner head, which can produce "hot spots" in your scanned image.

✔ Inkjet printers and colored markers can both create semitransparent colors themselves, which just don't have the necessary contrast to show up well in the scanned image.

Check out Figure 16-11 (scanned with a black background), and you can see what I mean — the original is a transparent overhead line drawing printed by a laser printer. As you can see, the text is virtually impossible to distinguish; in effect, it's a solid black page.

Figure 16-11:
Don't expect to see much detail here — the original is transparent.

On the other hand, Figure 16-12 looks fine! That's because I added a simple, blank white piece of paper between the transparency and my scanner's cover. The white background helps to add depth and clarity to the transparency.

CAN YOU SEE THIS?

This transparency can be very hard to scan without either:

- A transparency adapter

- A white backing sheet

Don't scan a transparency without them!

Figure 16-12: With a white piece of paper added as backing, the scanned image is an award winner!

As I mention in Chapter 2, the manufacturer of your scanner may also offer a transparency adapter for your scanner, which eliminates the need for a background (and also allows you to easily scan photographic negatives). Visit the company's Web site and check out your scanner's description to see whether you can buy an optional transparency adapter.

Your Original Is Your Friend

In the end, the quality of your scan depends on the quality of your original, and the next three signs of a good scan all concern the condition and quality of your original.

I realize that not every scanned document is in pristine condition. Old family photographs, for example, present more of a scanning challenge than a document that has just arrived from your laser printer. However, you can take action to ensure the best possible scan from an original that has seen better days:

- **Remove staples and paper clips before you scan.** These items are double trouble. They show up in your scanned image, so you have to remove them by using your image editor, and they can scratch your scanner's glass.

- **Fix creases whenever possible.** In most cases, you can bend a crease back to straighten it. If the original is brittle or the crease is a different color, however, you have to load the image into your editor and do your best to remove the crease by matching pixel colors with the surrounding area. (If you're using Photoshop, this situation calls for the Healing Brush; under iPhoto, you can use the Retouch brush.)

- **Roll crumpled documents.** If your original is a paper document that has been crumpled up, roll it into a tube (if possible) and then roll it in reverse. This trick helps flatten the original, producing a better scan. (Don't forget to close the cover on your scanner, which also helps to even out those wrinkles.)

Favor the First Generation

When you're shooting for The Perfect Scan, avoid the following types of originals whenever you can:

✔ **Photocopies:** The copy machine is a modern miracle — just ask any hardworking medieval monk or Egyptian scribe. Using a photocopy as an original, however, is likely to produce a scanned image of much lower quality than scanning the original document itself. If you're sending that image with a fax/modem to a fax machine, on the other hand, the quality of the image is less important, so feel free to give away the original document in that case.

✔ **Photographs printed on older inkjet printers:** If your printer provides less than 600 x 600 dpi in either black-and-white or color, consider finding a laser printer or a newer inkjet that can produce higher resolutions. A high-resolution scan of a photograph printed on an inkjet at 300 x 300 dpi probably doesn't provide the results you're looking for. That photograph is likely to look like a halftone even to the naked eye, which is always a bad sign!

✔ **Faxes sent in Standard mode:** Whenever possible, ask those who send you faxes to send them in Fine or Superfine mode; the former delivers 203 x196 dpi, and the latter provides 300 x 300 dpi. (Unlike the color photograph produced on an inkjet printer that I mention in the preceding paragraph, 300 x 300 dpi is pretty doggone good for a fax transmission.) A fax sent in Standard mode may be okay for the human eye, but at 203 x 98, it's dismal for scanning, especially when you want to use the image with your OCR software.

Size Does Matter

When it comes to an original you want to scan, less is *not* more. Although you can certainly resize your scanned image with an image editor, you can stretch pixels only so far. Here's a Mark's Maxim that seems to grow more true every day:

Resizing doesn't add detail — it simply expands the image by "inflating" the elements in the image.

Speaking of inflating, that's a good analogy. Think of a balloon with a printed logo on the side: If you blow up the balloon, the logo grows in size; when the balloon is full of air, however, the logo doesn't look as good as it did before the surface was stretched.

If you need to use an original at its actual size in another document, you don't have this problem because you don't have to resize the image. Simply scale the image at 100 percent and forget it.

Translated to scanners, the rule is simple: Always try to use an original that's at least the size of a typical 35mm print. For example, Figure 16-13 illustrates an image the size of a postage stamp blown up to 1024 x 768. Not the best quality, is it? The image just didn't have enough pixels to allow that kind of expansion without introducing jagged edges and a loss of focus.

Figure 16-14, though, was scanned from a standard-size 35mm photograph print. Notice that resizing the image to 1024 x 768 had no adverse effect. In fact, I could have probably jacked this image up to a whopping 5000 pixels horizontally before you would see any significant problem.

"What if I *have* to use a small original?" Well, I can give you one tip: When an original is particularly small, increase the dpi rating by 100 to 600 dpi. This increase allows your image editor to do a better job of resizing (but results in a much larger file size).

Figure 16-13:
Resizing a scanned image from a tiny original usually leaves much to be desired.

Figure 16-14:
With a larger original, the scan works much better.

Colors That Balance

I discuss color balance and how you can take care of it through your scanner software or your favorite image editor in other chapters, so I won't go into great detail here. However, I want to remind you to take a moment before scanning any original to check for the symptoms of a color-balance problem.

(Professional printing shops do the same thing as soon as copies of a color publication begin to emerge from an offset press.) You can look for

✔ Washed-out or oversaturated flesh tones

✔ Sections of your image that should be a pure color (such as a red stop sign) but are a diluted hue

✔ An overall tinge to the lighted areas of the original, usually caused by harsh fluorescent lighting or colored lights

By the way, an exception to those colored lights exists: I would never (and I mean *never*) correct the color balance for photographs taken at a concert or play! Such "mood lighting" is there for a reason, and unless you want to diminish the impact of *Romeo and Juliet* (or Mozart or Devo or the Violent Femmes), I suggest that you leave them as is.

A Finely Tuned Format

Here's one other sign of a superb scan that's destined to become royalty (or the head of a democracy, if you will): It *must* be saved in the proper format for the application you're using! I don't care whether your scanned image proves the existence of a dinosaur that looked like Elvis — an image stored in the wrong format causes problems for owners of other computers, as well as most of your e-mail recipients and Web site visitors. (To be honest, I would want to see that particular image no matter *what* format it was in, but I would see it faster if it were a JPEG! You get my point.)

I cover this subject in greater detail elsewhere in this book, but here are the highlights:

✔ **Word processing and importing:** If you're going to import your scanned image into a word processing document, spreadsheet, or presentation, I recommend saving the image in the TIFF or Windows bitmap formats.

✔ **Printing or displaying:** For scanned images that are destined to be printed or displayed on a computer monitor, choose TIFF (for all computers) or Windows bitmap (for computers running any breed of Windows). Although they take up more space, quality is the name of the game.

✔ **OCR or faxing:** Scanning for OCR or faxing use? A JPEG works well for these applications. However, the documentation for the program may recommend a specific format, so check the manual too.

✔ **Web or e-mail use:** Choose GIF or JPEG for Web image scans (depending on the color depth and file size you need). Using JPEG format for scanned images you're sending through e-mail is always a good idea.

✔ **Archival storage:** I typically use the Windows bitmap format for images I'm saving on CD-R or DVD disks. If you're using a Mac or a Linux machine, though, TIFF is likely a better choice.

As a general rule, use a format that offers compression whenever you're sending images through any medium on the Internet, and avoid lossy compression where space is not a problem or image quality must be the best.

Chapter 17

Ten Favorite Effects

*T*his last chapter is pure, unadulterated fun. (Or, I should say, it's even more fun than the other chapters in this book.) Because I talk about filters and effects everywhere after Chapter 11, now you can take the time to see how ten of my favorite Paint Shop Pro effects look when they're applied to a sample image. No, I do *not* ask you to apply all ten at one time. Remember that you want the subject to resemble something more coherent than a random pattern of colored pixels.

I've also selected the ten effects in this chapter because of their universal nature. You find similar filters in Photoshop, Elements, and PhotoImpact, for example, and in most of the other Windows and Mac OS image editors on the market. Therefore, no matter what editing program you're using, you should be able to achieve results like these at home. I can't go into every control in every dialog box — at least, not if I want to keep this book at less than 600 pages. I can, however, point out the settings I use most often to control these effects and tell you what they do to your image.

So, go ahead: Fire up your image editor, select a favorite scanned photograph or drawing, and exercise the artist in you!

Introducing the Sample Scan

I've chosen the scanned image shown in Figure 17-1 as a sample image. It shows the business end of a WWII Curtiss P-40 Warhawk fighter plane I shot with my trusty 35mm film camera at a local air show. The image has plenty of detail and bold contrast as well as a number of recognizable elements that should show up after you apply any effect to it, including the signature shark's mouth used by the Flying Tigers. The image was scanned at 300 dpi, using 24-bit color.

Without further ado, start applying yourself!

The effects in this chapter can be applied only to 24-bit color and grayscale images. If you have to increase the number of colors in your image, choose Image⇨Increase Color Depth.

Figure 17-1:
That,
ladies and
gentlemen,
is a distinc-
tive grin.

Fur

The first effect, Fur, may not produce exactly the effect you may have thought. It does produce feathered or spiky borders along the edges of strong contrast lines in your image, as shown in Figure 17-2. The default settings, though, create an effect that I would liken to a bristle brush or a hedgehog.

Most effects in this chapter can be configured before you apply them — usually with a preview dialog box like the one shown in Figure 17-3. I encourage you, therefore, to tweak settings and see the result on the thumbnail on the right before applying the filter. Remember that experimentation is the key to discovering the perfect effect.

Important settings to try with Fur are

- ✔ **Density:** Controls the thickness of your fur
- ✔ **Length:** Determines the length of the fur

Figure 17-2:
Spiky! The effects of the Fur effect.

Figure 17-3:
The Fur
effect dialog
box is a
typical
preview
dialog box
from Paint
Shop Pro.

Texture

The Texture effect is a Pandora's box of nifty fun; you may find yourself lost in this one for some time. In general, the effect makes your scanned image appear as though it had been painted on top of a specific surface. You can choose from 66 grayscale textures to be used as the surface, and you can control the lighting. In Figure 17-4, I've used one of the presets to give the illusion of a plaster surface.

Following are some settings to experiment with in the Texture dialog box:

- **Texture drop-down list box:** Lets you choose a texture on your own
- **Presets drop-down list box:** Provides a number of common settings combinations
- **Light Elevation:** Can cast dramatic shadows on your textures
- **Image Depth:** Determines the height of the texture

Figure 17-4:
Now how
did I paint
that image
on a plaster
wall?

Buttonize

Web developers are familiar with the Buttonize effect, used to create those cool thumbnail buttons with the three-dimensional edges. Figure 17-5 illustrates the sample image made into a huge button.

Figure 17-5:
After
buttonizing,
you're ready
to click the
image.

Important settings to try with Buttonize are

✔ **Solid/Transparent edge:** Specifies whether you want a colored edge or a semitransparent edge to your button

✔ **Width:** Determines the width of the edge in pixels

Page Curl

Another great effect that's popular among both graphic artists and Web developers is the Page Curl effect, which makes it look like a corner of your image is curling up. I've also seen this effect used often on the first page of an interactive demo or tutorial. Figure 17-6 shows a modest curl on the image.

With the Page Curl effect, you can move the two "handles" at the corners of the edge to determine how deep the curl should extend. Other settings you should try are

✔ **Corner:** Determines which corner of the image is curled

✔ **Curl color and Edge color:** Specifies the background and foreground color for the curled section

Figure 17-6:
Now the image is curling at the corner.

Ripple

Rippling an image turns its surface into water, and then drops a pebble directly in the center! This dramatic effect looks great in grayscale as well. Figure 17-7 shows the fighter plane underwater.

Figure 17-7:
With a
Ripple
effect,
anything
can be put
in a pond.

When you use the Ripple effect, try adjusting these settings:

✓ **Amplitude:** Controls the width of each ripple

✓ **Wavelength:** Controls the distance between ripples

Sunburst

Because the sample scanned image was originally taken outside on a sunny day, why not add an artificial sunburst? This great effect simulates the glare from the sun on a camera lens, as you can see in Figure 17-8. Note how realistically the sunburst "emerges" from the propeller of the plane. If I hadn't taken this picture myself, I would certainly be fooled. I like to use this effect to add a dramatic quality to shots of towers and churches as well as scenic photographs.

Note that you can move the handle within the left preview thumbnail to specify the origin of the light source. The presets for the Sunburst effect can place the glare spot wherever you like, although I recommend that you try experimenting with these settings as well:

- **Rays:** Determines how many rays of light radiate from the lighted spot
- **Circle Brightness:** Determines the brightness of the "halos" cast by the spot

Figure 17-8:
With the application of the Sunburst effect, a glare spot is added to the image.

Glowing Edges

Boy, do I love the Glowing Edges effect! Essentially, Glowing Edges creates a negative of your image and then applies a neon look to all the edges. As you can see in Figure 17-9, the effect is beautiful and the subject remains recognizable. No wonder you see this effect used in magazines all the time. That shark's mouth looks really good here.

Glowing Edges has only two settings you can change:

- **Sharpness:** Specifies the number of strokes (and hence the amount of detail) used to apply the effect
- **Intensity:** Specifies the strength of the glow

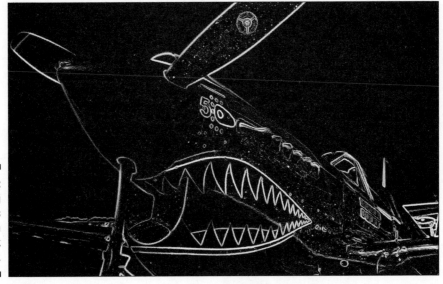

Figure 17-9:
Glowing
Edges
creates a
surreal look
to an image.

Rotating Mirror

The Rotating Mirror effect is self-explanatory, as shown by the results in
Figure 17-10! This great fun house effect projects a somewhat crazy feel.
Now the entire shark's mouth is in one image!

Figure 17-10:
Mirror,
mirror on
the plane . . .

Try changing the Rotation control, which sets the angle of the rotation around the center of the image.

Punch

Here's another effect I group in the funhouse category. Punch "pushes" the center of your image out toward the edges of the image, resulting in the neat distortion you see in Figure 17-11.

Punch has only one control: You can use the Strength control to determine how much of the image is pushed outward.

Figure 17-11:
This effect
packs a lot
of punch.

Brush Strokes

The final favorite effect I describe in this chapter of tens is a true classic: Brush Strokes, shown applied to the image shown in Figure 17-12. I wish that I had a dime for every time I've seen this great effect used in all sorts of print media (including business cards and menus). I've even seen it used on stills in video presentations! Brush Strokes is an easy way of turning an image into an instant oil painting or watercolor.

Figure 17-12:
Rembrandt himself would have been proud of these brush strokes.

This effect comes with a number of presets, such as Impasto, Large Drybrush, and Watercolor. You can also create your own look by changing these settings:

- **Strokes:** Controls the length of the brush strokes
- **Density:** Determines how many strokes appear in the image
- **Bristles:** Specifies how many bristles are used in your brush
- **Width:** Controls the width of the brush

To end this chapter, I leave you with a Mark's Maxim that's sure to keep the artist in you happy and busy for hours:

When it comes to image effects, experiment!

(Oh, and don't forget that Undo command for those experiments that go awry.)

Part VI
Appendixes

The 5th Wave   By Rich Tennant

"Hey- let's put scanned photos of ourselves through a ripple filter and see if we can make ourselves look weird."

In this part . . .

The appendixes feature a wealth of information. You'll find a scanner hardware and software manufacturers list, a glossary to familiarize you with those pesky terms and acronyms, and all the details on the programs you'll find on this book's companion CD-ROM.

Appendix A

Scanner Hardware and Software Manufacturers

· ·

In This Appendix

▶ Contact information for manufacturers of scanner hardware

▶ Contact information for developers of scanner software

· ·

*I*n this appendix, you find contact information for manufacturers of scanner hardware and developers of scanner software of all kinds. Whenever possible, I list both the Web site and fax number for each entry.

Please note that many companies listed in the first section, "Hardware Manufacturers," also produce their own scanning software. On the other hand, the software in the "Software Developers" section is produced by independent companies, and these programs usually run on any scanner under one or more specific operating systems.

Hardware Manufacturers

Agfa USA
Phone: 201-440-2500
Fax: 201-440-5733
www.agfaus.com

Brother USA
Phone: 908-704-1700
Fax: 908-704-8235
www.brother.com

Canon Computer Systems, Inc.
Phone: 800-OK-CANON
www.canon.com

Corex Technologies
Phone: 800-942-6739
Fax: 617-492-6659
www.corex.com

Epson America
Phone: 800-GO-EPSON
www.epson.com

Fujitsu
Phone: 800-626-4686
us.fujitsu.com

Hewlett-Packard Company
Phone: 650-857-1501
Fax: 650-857-5518
www.hp.com

Howtek
Phone: 603-882-5200
Fax: 603-880-3843
www.howtek.com

I.R.I.S. Inc.
Phone: 561-921-0847
Fax: 561-921-0854
www.irislink.com

Intelli Innovations Inc.
Phone: 919-468-0340
Fax: 775-201-2036
www.intellisw.com

Lexmark International, Inc.
Phone: 800-358-5835
www.lexmark.com

Microtek
Phone: 800-654-4160
www.microtekusa.com

Mustek
Phone: 949-788-3600
Fax: 949-788-3670
www.mustek.com

Nikon USA
Phone: 800-645-6689
www.nikonusa.com

Ricoh Corporation
Phone: 800-FAST FIX
www.ricoh-usa.com

Umax
Phone: 214-342-9799
Fax: 214-342-9046
www.umax.com

Visioneer US
Phone: 925-251-6398
Fax: 925-416-8615
www.visioneer.com

Xerox Corporation
Phone: 800-ASK-XEROX
www.xerox.com

Software Developers

Adobe Systems Incorporated
Phone: 800-833-6687
Fax: 408-537-6000
www.adobe.com

Captiva Software Corporation
Phone: 858-320-1000
Fax: 858-320-1010
www.captivasoftware.com

Corex Technologies
Phone: 800-942-6739
Fax: 617-492-6659
www.corex.com

Hamrick Software
www.hamrick.com

Intelli Innovations Inc.
Phone: 919-468-0340
Fax: 775-201-2036
www.intellisw.com

Jasc Software
Phone: 800-622-2793
Fax: 952-930-9172
www.jasc.com

Jetsoft Development
Company
www.jetsoftdev.com

ScanSoft
Phone: 800-654-1187
Fax: 978-977-2434
www.scansoft.com

Westtek
Phone: 425-861-8271
Fax: 425-861-7926
www.westtek.com

Appendix B

Glossary

· ·

adapter card: An expansion board that plugs into your computer's motherboard and adds functionality, such as a FireWire card to provide support for devices such as FireWire scanners and DV camcorders.

application: A program that allows you to complete a task. Your scanning application, for example, controls your scanner and allows you to digitize images and save them to disk.

aspect ratio: The ratio of height to width in an image. If the aspect ratio isn't maintained when resizing an image, it becomes distorted.

binary: The common language used by computers to store information and communicate with each other, composed of just two values: 0 and 1.

BIOS: Short for *Basic Input Output System*, used to change the low-level functionality of a PC, such as configuring your parallel port.

bit: The smallest unit of data that can be stored or used by a computer, with a value of either 1 or 0.

bitmap: An uncompressed image format used in the Windows operating system. Although bitmaps deliver great image quality, they're uncompressed and use a large amount of space.

bps: Short for *bits per second*. Dial-up modem speeds are measured in Kbps, or kilobytes per second.

bus: A slot on your motherboard that holds adapter cards. Most slots are now 32-bit PCI or 16-bit ISA slots. Video cards also have a special slot, called an AGP slot, reserved for them.

byte: A group of 8 bits that represents a single character of text — and a sure-fire hit as a subject of conversation with strangers. Your computer's programs store and read data as bytes in your computer's RAM.

calibration: The process of correcting the misalignment of a scanner's moving parts and scanning head. Most modern flatbed scanners don't require calibration, although sheet-fed scanners should be calibrated regularly.

case: The metal enclosure that surrounds your computer, usually fastened with screws or thumbwheels.

CD-R: Also called a *CD recorder*, a drive that acts as both a CD recorder and a regular CD-ROM drive. Recorded discs can store computer data, and you can record standard audio CDs. Although CD-R discs can be read on any CD-ROM drive, they can be recorded only once.

CD-ROM drive: A drive that reads both CD-ROM discs and standard audio CDs.

CD-RW: A drive that can record and re-record CDs. Older CD-ROM drives and audio CD players cannot read discs made with a CD-RW drive.

CECSAUB: Short for *confusing everything with a collection of silly acronyms used as buzzwords.* (I don't like acronyms dreamed up by engineers just to muddle things up.)

color depth: The measurement used to indicate the number of colors in a scanned image. Popular color depths are 16 colors, 256 colors, 64,000 colors, and 16.7 million colors (commonly referred to as 24-bit color).

color-matching system: A software standard designed to ensure correct colors on all output and display devices in a computer system. With a monitor and printer that are color matched, for example, you can be sure that the colors you see on your display are as close as possible to the colors produced by your printer.

component: A piece of computer hardware; usually used to indicate an internal piece of hardware, such as a hard drive or a SCSI card.

compression: The use of a mathematical formula to reduce the amount of disk space taken up by a file. In the case of scanned images, the most popular compressed formats are JPEG and GIF. A lossless compression scheme loses no detail; a lossy compression scheme loses detail as the degree of compression is increased.

cropping: Removing a portion of the background from a digital image, usually to remove unneeded objects or extra white space.

CPU: Short for *central processing unit,* the "brain" in your computer that performs the commands in the programs you run. Popular CPUs on personal computers are manufactured by Intel, AMD, IBM, and Motorola.

digital camera: A type of camera that saves images as digital data (for uploading directly to a computer). Unlike with a traditional camera, no film and no development are necessary.

DIP switch: One of a bank of tiny switches that allows you to configure hardware devices and your computer's motherboard. You use the tip of a pen to set the switches in the proper sequence.

dpi: Short for *dots per inch*, a measurement of the number of dots per linear inch of an image. This measurement is commonly used with scanners, although technically a scanner uses spi (samples per inch). No matter the terminology squabble, they're basically the same thing.

driver: One or more programs written by a hardware manufacturer that allow your operating system to recognize and use a device.

effect: A mathematical formula applied to a digital image to modify either individual pixel colors or the entire image. Most image editors include a number of effects that can change the appearance of an image.

external: A peripheral that's connected outside your computer's case, such as a scanner.

FAQ: Short for *Frequently Asked Questions,* a document containing the answers to the most common questions asked in a group. A scanner manufacturer's technical support department usually creates a FAQ file for downloading by customers who are encountering problems.

FireWire: The common name for the Apple IEEE 1394 High Performance Serial Bus connection standard. Sony uses a different name, i.Link, but the technology is the same. Like a USB connection, a FireWire device can be added or removed without rebooting. As many as 63 FireWire devices can be connected to a single port. Today's FireWire scanners are very fast because of the connection's high data-transfer rate of 400 Mbps. The new FireWire standard recently introduced on Macintosh computers doubles that throughput to 800Mbps.

flatbed scanner: A scanner that resembles a copy machine, featuring a long sheet of glass and a cover. Originals remain motionless while the scanning head moves across the scanner bed. A flatbed scanner is now the preferred scanner type because you can scan items such as books and other objects that can't be scanned with a sheet-fed scanner.

flat-panel monitor: A monitor that uses liquid crystal display (or LCD) technology rather than a traditional tube. Most folks think of these monitors as displays for laptop computers. However, flat panels are much thinner than traditional tube monitors and use less electricity. Now that prices have dropped dramatically on LCD monitors, they're only slightly more expensive than tube monitors.

floppy disk drive: A single 3½-inch floppy disk can store as much as 1.44MB of files and data. Although a floppy disk drive is cheap and practically every computer has one, it isn't reliable and shouldn't be used for long-term storage.

format: A standard file layout used to store the data that makes up an image. Popular image formats now in use are GIF, JPEG, and TIFF.

GIF: Short for *Graphics Interchange Format,* a compressed image format that's popular on the Web. GIF, which supports only 256 colors, was the first major cross-platform image format.

gigabyte: A measurement of data equal to 1,024MB (megabytes).

grayscale: Images with continuous tones in 256 shades of gray rather than color.

halftone: An image that represents tones with patterns of dots rather than continuous shades. Most illustrations in books and newspapers are halftones.

handheld scanner: An external scanner you pass across the surface of an original. Handheld scanners can read anywhere from a single line to about a 4-inch strip of an original. This type of scanner is generally useful for people traveling with laptop computers.

hard drive: Also called *hard disk.* A hard drive stores your data while the computer is turned off. All standard laptop and desktop computers use hard drives. Most hard drives available these days store anywhere from 20 to 300 gigabytes of files and data.

home corner: The corner of a flatbed scanner's glass that is marked. Your document normally should be positioned close to this corner.

image editor: A program that allows you to edit and modify digital images. Popular image editors such as Photoshop and Paint Shop Pro are standard tools for people who scan photographs.

inkjet: An inexpensive printer that injects ink from a cartridge to paper.

interface: A method of connecting a peripheral to a computer. For example, a scanner can use a parallel port interface, a FireWire interface, or a USB interface (which needs only the proper port and a cable); others use a SCSI interface (which typically requires an adapter card and a cable).

internal: A component installed inside your computer's case.

JPEG: Short for *Joint Photographic Experts Group,* the most common image format used on the Web and the default format produced by most scanning-control programs. JPEGs, because of their compression and small size, are often used as Web images and e-mail attachments.

jumper: A set of two or more pins that can be used to configure devices and adapter cards. You select a setting by moving a plastic-and-metal crossover on or off certain pins.

kilobyte: A measurement of data equal to 1,024 bytes.

laser printer: A printer that bonds toner powder to paper. Laser printers are fast and produce excellent print quality. They're somewhat more expensive than typical inkjet printers.

line art: A drawing produced in black and white (or two other colors) with no shading or tones.

Mac OS X: The UNIX-based graphical operating system created by Apple, used on today's Macintosh computer systems.

megabyte: A measurement of data equal to 1,024 kilobytes.

modem: A computer device that converts digital data to and from an analog signal so that computers can communicate over standard telephone lines. Modems are used to access the Internet, online services, and computer bulletin-board systems.

monitor: An external component that looks like a TV screen and displays all the graphics produced by your programs.

motherboard: The main circuit board inside your computer that holds the CPU and RAM chips and any adapter cards you've installed.

mouse: A standard computer pointing device used in Windows and Mac OS. You control programs by moving the mouse and pressing buttons to select items.

multifunction device: Also called an *all-in-one unit,* an external computer peripheral that can scan, print, fax, and copy documents. Multifunction devices are popular in home offices, where space is at a premium.

negative scanner: A scanner specially designed to scan photograph negatives, yielding a much higher quality scan than a typical flatbed scanner can. A negative scanner is much more expensive than a typical home flatbed scanner.

newsgroup: An Internet message area dedicated to a special interest. Anyone can read or post messages in a newsgroup.

OCR: Short for *optical character recognition,* a type of software that can, using your scanner, "read" images and text from physical documents and place the material into a word-processing program.

one-button scanning: A feature offered by many scanners that allows you to push a button on the scanner to copy, scan, or fax automatically, without having to run any programs manually on the computer.

original: The document, object, or material you're scanning.

parallel port: A standard connector on every PC. Although initially used only to connect printers, other devices, such as scanners and Zip drives, now also use this connection.

PC card: Also called a *PCMCIA* card; a thin device that plugs directly into most laptops and provides most of the functions of a full-size adapter card, including SCSI adapters and network connections.

photo feeder: An attachment that automatically feeds standard-size photographs to your scanner. Originally an optional feature, many home and small-office scanners now include a photo feeder as standard equipment.

photo paper: A heavy inkjet printer paper with a glossy or matte finish that's specifically made for producing high-resolution color prints.

photo scanner: An internal scanner specially designed to read film prints, business cards, and smaller paper documents.

pixel: A single dot in an image. Text and graphics displayed by a computer monitor (or created by a scanner) are made up of pixels.

Plug and Play: A type of hardware that can automatically be configured by computers that support the Plug and Play standard, possibly eliminating the need for you to configure the hardware manually.

plug-in: An extension program that can be installed in your image editor to provide additional effects.

PNG: Short for *Portable Network Graphics,* a compressed image format developed primarily to replace the older GIF format used on Web pages. Some versions of the PNG format can store 24-bit color images with lossless compression.

port: A connector on your computer or an external device you plug something into. A scanner, for example, may plug into your USB, FireWire, or parallel port.

printer: An external device that can produce documents on paper with text and graphics from your computer.

RAM: Short for *Random Access Memory;* memory modules that hold programs and data until you turn off your computer.

red-eye: A reflective red shine produced by human and animal eyes that are illuminated by a camera's flash.

refurbished: A piece of broken computer hardware that has been "remanufactured" (read that as "fixed") by the manufacturer and typically sold again at a greatly reduced price. I generally recommend that you give refurbished hardware a wide berth.

resizing: Changing the dimensions of an image to make it larger or smaller.

resolution (dimensions): A common method of measuring the number of pixels displayed on a screen or in an image, expressed as horizontal by vertical. For example, a resolution of 640 x 480 means that you see rows of 640 pixels across your screen and columns of 480 pixels down your screen.

resolution (image): The number of pixels in an inch within an image. Scanner resolution is usually referred to as dpi, although this reference is technically incorrect.

rotation: The turning of an image to the left or right.

scanner: A device that digitizes (or converts) text or graphics from a printed page or object into a digital image stored on your hard drive. Scanners are often used to create images for documents, for display on your computer monitor, or for use on a Web page.

scanner sensor: An array of photosensitive cells that return variable electrical currents, depending on the amount of reflected light each cell receives. Every scanner has a sensor array.

SCSI: Short for *Small Computer Systems Interface,* an older interface technology that supports the connection of anywhere from 8 to 15 devices, including hard drives, CD-ROM drives, and scanners.

SCSI ID: A unique numeric identifier assigned to each device in a SCSI chain.

SCSI port: A connector included with a SCSI adapter card to connect an external device, such as a scanner, to your SCSI device chain.

secure connection: A Web server that creates an encrypted session between itself and your computer, allowing you to send your personal information and credit card information to Web sites without fear of being monitored. Whenever you order hardware or software from a Web store, make sure that you have a secure connection before sending any information.

selection box: An area of an image you choose with your mouse when you're using a scanning-control program or image editor. The selection box is the target of your next command, like scanning a particular area of an original or cropping an image to just the selected area.

serial port: A standard connector on every PC and older Macs. Serial ports are typically used to connect mice, joysticks, and external modems to PCs, and to connect printers and external modems to older Macs.

sharpening: An image editor effect that's often used to enhance a scanned image. Sharpening increases the contrast at all the edges of an image.

sheet-fed scanner: A scanner that resembles a fax machine, where documents are loaded through a slot. In a sheet-fed scanner, the scanning head remains motionless and the original moves past it. Although sheet-fed scanners take up much less room than flatbeds (making them popular in all-in-one and multi-function devices), they're limited in the type of materials that can be scanned, and they're sometimes subject to alignment and distortion problems.

single-pass scanner: A scanner that requires only one pass with the scanning head to capture an image. Most scanners now available are single-pass models.

terminator: A switch or jumper found on nearly every SCSI device. Each end of a device chain must be terminated properly.

thumbnail: A small version of a full-size digital image. Because many thumbnails can fit on a single screen, selecting an image from a group of thumbnails is much faster than loading the full-size images — making thumbnails a typical feature in image catalogs and Web pages that offer images for downloading.

TIFF: Short for *Tagged Image File Format*, an image format favored by Macintosh owners, graphic artists, and the publishing industry.

trackball: A pointing device that looks like an upside-down mouse. You control the device by rolling the ball with your finger or thumb and clicking buttons with your other fingers.

transparency adapter: A device used with a standard flatbed scanner that allows you to scan transparent originals, such as photographic negatives and overhead transparencies. Many manufacturers of flatbed scanners now offer transparency adapters as standard equipment.

triple-pass scanner: A scanner that requires three passes with the scanning head to capture an image. Most older scanners are triple-pass models.

TWAIN: Short for *technology without an interesting name,* a standard that ensures that TWAIN-compatible image hardware (such as scanners) and software (such as image editors and scanning-control programs) understand each other and work together properly.

USB: Short for *Universal Serial Bus,* a standard connector that enables you to connect as many as 127 devices at data transfer rates of as much as 12 megabits per second. The latest version of USB — commonly named USB 2.0 or high-speed USB — offers transfer speeds slightly better than first-generation FireWire connections. USB connectors are common for all sorts of computer peripherals, including digital cameras, scanners, speakers, joysticks, external CD/DVD-ROMs, and hard drives. You get the picture.

USB flash drive: A removable solid-state storage drive that acts as an external hard drive. Flash drives have no moving parts. Instead, they store up to 1GB of data in a special type of memory chip, making them extremely small and lightweight. A flash drive can be connected to any USB port, and the drive is automatically recognized in Windows XP, Windows 2000, and Mac OS X.

USB hub: An external switch that allows you to plug additional USB devices into a single USB port.

Windows 2000: The business and professional version of the Windows operating system, designed as a network or Internet server. It's much more expensive than Windows XP.

Windows XP: The most popular 32-bit graphical operating system for the PC.

wireless mouse: A battery-powered mouse that doesn't require a cord to connect it to the computer.

Zip drive: A removable cartridge drive that stores anywhere from 100MB to 750MB of data. Zip drives are available with parallel port, SCSI, and USB connections.

Appendix C

About the CD

System Requirements

Make sure that your computer meets the minimum system requirements shown in the following list. If your computer doesn't match up to most of these requirements, you may have problems using the software and files on the CD. For the latest and greatest information, please refer to the ReadMe file located at the root of the CD-ROM.

✔ A PC with a Pentium II or faster processor; or a Mac OS computer with a 68040 or faster processor

✔ Microsoft Windows 98 or later; or Mac OS system software 8.0 or later

✔ At least 32MB of total RAM installed on your computer; for best performance, we recommend at least 64MB

✔ At least 600MB of hard drive space available to install all the software from this CD. (You need less space if you don't install every program.)

✔ A scanner

✔ A CD-ROM drive

✔ A sound card or built-in sound support

✔ A mouse or other pointing thing

✔ A monitor capable of displaying 24-bit color or grayscale

✔ A modem with a speed of at least 14,400 bps

If you need more information on the basics, check out these books published by Wiley: *PCs All-in-One Desk Reference For Dummies,* by Mark L. Chambers; *Macs For Dummies,* by David Pogue; *Building a PC For Dummies,* by Mark L. Chambers; *Mac OS X Panther All-in-One Desk Reference For Dummies* by Mark L. Chambers; *Windows 95 For Dummies, Windows 98 For Dummies, Windows 2000 Professional For Dummies, Microsoft Windows ME Millennium Edition For Dummies,* all by Andy Rathbone.

Using the CD with Microsoft Windows

To install the items from the CD to your hard drive, follow these steps.

1. **Insert the CD into your computer's CD-ROM drive.**

2. **Click Start⇨Run.**

3. **In the dialog box that appears, type** D:\Start.EXE.

   Replace *D* with the proper drive letter if your CD-ROM drive uses a different letter. (If you don't know the letter, see how your CD-ROM drive is listed under My Computer.)

4. **Click OK.**

   A license agreement window appears.

5. **Read through the license agreement, nod your head, and then click the Accept button if you want to use the CD — after you click Accept, you'll never be bothered by the License Agreement window again.**

   The CD interface Welcome screen appears. The interface is a little program that shows you what's on the CD and coordinates installing the programs and running the demos. The interface basically enables you to click a button or two to make things happen.

6. **Click anywhere on the Welcome screen to enter the interface.**

   Now you are getting to the action. This next screen lists categories for the software on the CD.

7. **To view the items within a category, just click the category's name.**

   A list of programs in the category appears.

8. **For more information about a program, click the program's name.**

   Be sure to read the information that appears. Sometimes a program has its own system requirements or requires you to do a few tricks on your computer before you can install or run the program, and this screen tells you what you may need to do.

9. **If you don't want to install the program, click the Back button to return to the previous screen.**

   You can always return to the previous screen by clicking the Back button. This feature allows you to browse the different categories and products and decide what you want to install.

10. **To install a program, click the appropriate Install button.**

    The CD interface drops to the background while the CD installs the program you chose.

11. **To install other items, repeat Steps 7–10.**

12. **When you've finished installing programs, click the Quit button to close the interface.**

    You can eject the CD now. Carefully place it back in the plastic jacket of the book for safekeeping.

To run some of the programs on the CD, you may need to keep the disc inside your CD-ROM drive. This is a "Good Thing." Otherwise, a very large chunk of the program would be installed to your hard drive, consuming valuable hard drive space and possibly keeping you from installing other software.

Using the CD with Mac OS

To install the items from the CD to your hard drive, follow these steps.

1. **Insert the CD into your computer's CD-ROM drive.**

   In a moment, an icon representing the CD you just inserted appears on your Mac desktop. Chances are, the icon looks like a CD-ROM.

   If you're running Mac OS X Panther, the CD-ROM icon may not automatically appear on your desktop — instead, you may have to open a Finder window, where the CD-ROM icon will appear in the sidebar to the left of the window.

2. **Double-click the CD icon to show the CD's contents.**

3. **Double-click the License Agreement icon.**

   This is the license that you are agreeing to by using the CD. You can close this window after you've looked over the agreement.

4. **Double-click the Read Me First icon.**

   The Read Me First text file contains information about the CD's programs and any last-minute instructions you may need in order to correctly install them.

5. **To install most programs, open the program folder and double-click the icon called "Install" or "Installer."**

Sometimes the installers are actually self-extracting archives, which just means that the program files have been bundled up into an archive, and this self-extractor unbundles the files and places them on your hard drive. This kind of program is often called an .sea. Double click anything with .sea in the title, and it will run just like an installer.

6. **Some programs don't come with installers. For those, just drag the program's folder from the CD window and drop it on your hard drive icon.**

What You'll Find on the CD

The following sections are arranged by category and provide a summary of the software and other goodies you'll find on the CD. If you need help with installing the items provided on the CD, refer to the installation instructions in the preceding section.

Shareware programs are usually fully functional, free, trial versions of copyrighted programs. If you like particular programs, register with their authors for a nominal fee and receive licenses, enhanced versions, and technical support. *Freeware programs* are free, copyrighted games, applications, and utilities. You can copy them to as many PCs as you like — for free — but they offer no technical support. *GNU software* is governed by its own license, which is included inside the folder of the GNU software. There are no restrictions on distribution of GNU software. See the GNU license at the root of the CD for more details. *Trial, demo,* or *evaluation* versions of software are usually limited either by time or functionality (such as not letting you save a project after you create it).

Adobe Acrobat Professional, from Adobe Systems

30-day trial version. For Windows NT, Windows 2000, and Windows XP.

Create electronic documents in the popular PDF format that can be viewed and printed on several different operating systems and computer platforms using Adobe's free Acrobat Reader application.

You can find more details at Adobe's site at www.adobe.com.

Adobe Reader, from Adobe Systems

Commercial version. For Windows 98, Windows NT, Windows 2000, Windows XP, and Mac OS X.

Use Acrobat Reader to view and print electronic PDF documents created with Acrobat or other applications.

Check out the complete line of Reader applications at Adobe's site at www.adobe.com.

GraphicConverter, from Lemke Software GmbH

Shareware version. For Mac OS 8, Mac OS 9, and Mac OS X.

Although it's best known for importing 175 graphic formats and exporting 75 different formats, GraphicConverter takes care of a number of other image-related chores as well, including browsing, slide show creation, and basic image editing. GraphicConverter is an indispensable tool for getting your scanned images in the form you need.

For all the details, visit the Lemke Software GmbH site at www.lemkesoft.com.

Paint Shop Pro, from Jasc Software

30-day trial version. For Windows 98, Windows Me, Windows NT, Windows 2000, and Windows XP.

Paint Shop Pro provides the same features found on image-editing packages that cost several hundred dollars more. I use it extensively throughout this book. *Nice!*

For additional information on the latest version of this great program, visit the Jasc site at www.jasc.com.

Paint Shop Photo Album 4, from Jasc Software

30-day trial version. For Windows 98, Windows Me, Windows NT, Windows 2000, and Windows XP.

Paint Shop Photo Album 4 is a great "Swiss Army knife" for scanner owners. It can acquire images directly from your TWAIN scanner, display images, browse, and print. Paint Shop Photo Album even has a handy set of basic image-editing functions!

You can read more about this program at the Jasc site at www.jasc.com.

PhotoImpact XL, from Ulead Systems

Trial version. For Windows 98, Windows Me, Windows NT, Windows 2000, and Windows XP.

Another great inexpensive image editor that delivers the power of the big boys, PhotoImpact XL includes features that you'll find appealing if you're editing images that you've scanned for use on the Web.

For the whole story, visit the Ulead Systems site at: www.ulead.com.

Photoshop Elements, from Adobe Systems

Trial version. For Windows 98, Windows NT, Windows 2000, Windows XP, Mac OS 9, and Mac OS X.

A powerful, easy-to-use cross-platform image editor that includes most of the functionality of Adobe Photoshop — but at less than $100, Photoshop Elements is a true bargain!

For the latest information on Photoshop Elements, visit Adobe's site at www.adobe.com.

snapCopier, from snapApps.com

15-day trial version. For Windows 98, Windows NT, Windows 2000, and Windows XP.

Turn your scanner and printer into a basic copy machine! snapCopier can produce multiple copies, and it's only $20.

For the rest of the story, visit the snapApps.com site at www.snapapps.com.

ViewIt, from HexCat Software

Shareware version. For Mac OS X.

The ViewIt image viewer is a major improvement over the built-in image viewing in Mac OS X, providing full-screen display, support for PNG and PSD formats, preview printing, and the capability to import images from your digital camera.

For all the details, visit the HexCat Software site at www.hexcat.com.

VueScan, from Hamrick Software

Trial version. For Windows 98, Windows NT, Windows 2000, Windows XP, Mac OS 9, and Mac OS X.

If you're looking for a better scanning-control program, give VueScan a try. It works on dozens of different scanner models and provides options for batch scanning and image correction. (It's also great if you're using a scavenged scanner that didn't come with any software.)

You can find out more about this program at the Hamrick Software site at www.hamrick.com.

WinRAR, from RARLAB

Evaluation version. For Windows 98, Windows NT, Windows 2000, and Windows XP.

WinRAR is a favorite with scanner owners who need to compress and archive all sorts of data so that files take up less space and are easier to manage. If you need to store a huge directory of images in Windows bitmap format, for example, you can save 50 to 75 percent of the space they would normally take up by "zipping" them. Use this great tool — you won't be sorry!

For support and more information, visit the WinRAR site at www.rarlab.com.

Troubleshooting

I tried my best to compile programs that work on most computers with the minimum system requirements. Alas, your computer may differ, and some programs may not work properly for some reason.

The two likeliest problems are that you don't have enough memory (RAM) for the programs you want to use, or you have other programs running that are affecting installation or running of a program. If you get an error message such as `Not enough memory` or `Setup cannot continue`, try one or more of the following suggestions and then try using the software again:

- ✔ **Turn off any antivirus software running on your computer.** Installation programs sometimes mimic virus activity and may make your computer incorrectly believe that a virus is infecting it.

- ✔ **Close all running programs.** The more programs you have running, the less memory is available to other programs. Installation programs typically update files and programs; so if you keep other programs running, installation may not work properly.

- ✔ **Have your local computer store add more RAM to your computer.** This is, admittedly, a drastic and somewhat expensive step. However, if you have a Windows 95 PC or a Mac OS computer with a PowerPC chip, adding more memory can really help the speed of your computer and allow more programs to run at the same time.

If you still have trouble with the CD, please call the Customer Care phone number: 800-762-2974. Outside the United States, call 1-317-572-3994. You can also contact Customer Service on the Web at `http://www.wiley.com/ techsupport` Wiley Publishing Inc. will provide technical support only for installation and other general quality control items; for technical support on the applications themselves, consult the program's vendor or author.

Index

• *C* •

● *K* ●